MACK
AND THE
BOYS

A look deep inside the secret world
of gay male escorts in the nation's
capital and inside ourselves

By Malcolm Stallons

---

*Well, the years go by and my voice gets lower and all things
can change so fast. Still, nothing can set off your heartbeat
as when you return yourself to your past.*
– HARRY CHAPIN
Singer/songwriter/humanitarian

Mack And The Boys
Published by:
The Mack And The Boys Project, LLC
P.O. Box 54856
Lexington, Kentucky 40555-4856

www.MackAndTheBoys.com

ISBN: 978-0-615-26204-8

Printed version: November 2008
Online version: November 2008

Printed in the United States of America

Overview

In a town where it's generally accepted that it's better
for a politician to be found in bed with a dead girl
than a live boy, secrets are essential to one's survival.

I was the keeper of such secrets.

I created, owned and operated what became Washington, D.C.'s,
most-successful gay male escort referral service at the time.
I also bought and ran what many consider to be the District's
best gay male service ever.

I answered telephones. I took down names and addresses
and phone numbers.

I sent escorts to spend time with clients who gladly paid them
to do things behind locked doors, in rooms where shades
had been drawn and lights turned down low or off entirely.

I did all of that and more.

I am a journalist. Investigating a story, taking notes,
recording conversations, interviewing people, documenting
meetings, and then writing about what he has learned
is what a journalist does.

I did all of that and more in Washington.

I also did it without anyone there knowing it, until now.

Forward

Some stories need to be told ...

By all accounts, the escort call Chris was assigned to take on that particular night was ordinary.

The repeat client had called Marvin at Tops Referrals and arranged to meet a cute young man in his hotel room at 10 that night. Having been pleased booking escorts through Marvin in the past and being short on time this particular day, the client left it to Marvin to decide whom to send.

Marvin chose Chris, a cute guy who had done several calls in the past and who had always received good reports.

Arriving at the hotel on time, Chris made his way through the lobby, into the elevator, up a few floors, then down the hallway.

Arriving at the client's room, Chris knocked on the door. Normally, on such a call, the client would open the door and invite the escort in, eagerly anticipating the time – most likely intimate – they would spend together.

But this was no ordinary call. When the door opened both the escort and the client were shocked by what they saw.

On one side of the doorway stood Chris, the gay male escort, on the other side, stood the client, Chris' father.

"Needless to say, the call never went through," Marvin says. "It was an awkward situation for both of them. Neither could say anything about the other's role: The kid was working, the dad was hiring."

The world of gay male escorts is full of unusual stories. It is that way, in part, because society forces those who escort and those who hire escorts to do so in the shadows.

Meeting secretly and conducting hush-hush encounters is especially true in Washington, the nation's capital. You cannot have this many powerful men – elected and non-elected – all in one town and not have some of them itching to unzip their pants or to pull someone else's down.

Take former Rep. Mark Foley, who went into rehab after it was made public he had a passion for teenage boys serving as congressional pages. Take toe-tapping Sen. Larry Craig, who pleaded guilty after being arrested in an airport bathroom by an undercover police officer on suspicion of lewd conduct.

Washington's fascination with escorts and sexual escapades is not limited to the gay community. Straight politicians have had their embarrassing situations too.

Remember Monica Lewinsky and her blue dress? Remember Rep. Wilbur Mills and the Argentine stripper?

One cannot be linked sexually with a high-ranking government official and not become media fodder if the encounter becomes public knowledge.

The same is true about those who own and/or manage escort referral services, gay or straight.

The world came to know Deborah Jeane Palfrey as the notorious "D.C. Madam" after the government charged her with crimes relating to running her Washington escort service.

Palfrey

Preston Burton, one of Washington's leading criminal defense attorneys, handled Palfrey's defense in *The United States of America v. Deborah Jeane Palfrey.*

Palfrey's case was a tough one for a defense lawyer. The government had investigated her company – Pamela Martin & Associates – for five years and likely had spent hundreds of thousands of dollars gathering evidence and building a case against her.

The government claimed Palfrey was guilty of racketeering, money laundering and of using the mail for illegal purposes while running a "high-end prostitution ring." Tawdry stuff for many, the kind of activity society has been conditioned to curl its nose at as if a bad odor is wafting by.

Some consider escorting as evil and those associated with it as evil-doers. Overcoming such prejudices would be difficult for any defense attorney.

The Palfrey case was also difficult because of the facts: Assistant U.S. Attorney Catherine Connolly read from a newsletter she claimed Palfrey sent to her escorts, which said: "The client is paying for the 'activity,' not the 90 minutes itself." Tough words for anyone to explain away.

The Washington Post reported that many of the 13 former escorts who testified said Palfrey was careful not to talk about prostitution explicitly with them. The women said, however, that they discussed the subject many times with Palfrey in veiled terms and that they understood she would not employ them unless they engaged in paid sex acts with clients.

Then there was logic: Assistant U.S. Attorney Daniel Butler told jurors that "men don't normally pay $250 for 90 minutes of casual conversation." Such a statement is easy to believe. Palfrey had claimed clients were paying for a "fantasy, role-playing session" with her escorts, not sex.

"It was a pretty clever system," Butler said. "She gave herself plausible deniability." Radio station WTOP reported Butler then turned, looked at the jurors and said: "But ladies and gentlemen, you (know) that she knew."

Burton told jurors that escorts and clients were the ones who decided whether or not to engage in sex acts – without Palfrey's knowledge.

Burton argued what went on during appointments was between the client and the escort. He compared Palfrey to a taxi dispatcher, who should not be penalized for "the route the cab driver took."

Yes, the Palfrey case was a tough one for a defense attorney, even a great one like Burton.

While the prosecution had social conditioning, damning evidence and logic on its side, Burton had something that should have trumped all of those – truth. While defying reasonable logic, the premise of Burton's defense was factually correct.

What Burton needed but did not have was someone with insider knowledge about Washington's escort world, someone to take the stand and tell the jury that – at some services – sex was never promised to any client nor expected from any escort.

I could have been that witness. I could have sat in the witness box and told how it is possible for someone to run a successful escort service in the nation's capital where sex – if it happened – was strictly between two consenting adults.

I could have placed my hand on the court's Bible and told the jury about the people I met while running my escort referral service. Everything I would have said would have been the gospel truth.

I do not know a lot about the Palfrey case – how she ran her service, what she expected or demanded from escorts she represented, why the case was brought to trial or why the prosecution felt the need to humiliate the women who used to work with Palfrey while they were testifying.

I do, however, know the truth about escorts and escort services in the nation's capital. I could have gone to Washington and told the truth about what I learned. I could have gone and told them about Mack and the boys.

I could have, but instead I kept quiet, afraid of paying the price coming forward would surely exact from me.

The jury convicted Palfrey on all four charges on April 15, 2008, the day after I e-mailed Burton with an offer to come forward, a willingness to tell what I knew.

Sixteen days later, Palfrey was found hanged in a shed near her mother's home. Police say she committed suicide.

Though we only met once, I know a lot about Palfrey. I know how alone and isolated she felt; how trapped she was by her past – trapped by having once run an escort service and not being able to leave that world and move on with her life.

I know what it is like to be damned for having such a past and yet have the same people turn their backs on you when you try to live a "better life." People, who have sins of their own.

Palfrey had tried to have a "better life" but found such a thing impossible after having served 18 months in a California prison. Palfrey had been convicted of operating a prostitution business.

"She viewed herself as a convicted felon who couldn't do anything else," journalist Dan Moldea told *The Washington Post*. With no other options, "she came to Washington and got back into the (escort) business." Moldea had interviewed Palfrey for a possible book.

It is too late tell Palfrey I know how she felt, too late to tell the jury what I learned, but not to tell you.

Some stories need to be told. They need to be told even if powerful people and powerful influences do not want the truth revealed because they stand to be embarrassed.

Some stories need to be told even if one of the powerful influences involved has already exacted a life-changing price from the storyteller and has threatened – in writing – to cause further harm if he tells the public what he knows.

Some need to be told even if telling could cost the reporter his friends, his job, and possibly, even his life.

Some stories need to be told. *Mack And The Boys* is such a story.

***

For most of her life, Ashley Alexandra Dupré was just an ordinary person. That changed in March 2008, when it was reported Dupré had been paid $4,300 for a two-hour personal encounter at the Mayflower Hotel in Washington with then-New York Gov. Eliot Spitzer.

When the news about Spitzer and Dupré broke, some – including the media – asked how one might come to be an escort. They also asked how it was possible for an elected official to find himself in a hotel room with a paid companion.

Reading this project, you will come to know how Mack's boys came to be in hotel rooms with senators, congressmen and other high-ranking individuals.

You will also learn that escorts and others in the business are not the scandalous, moral degenerates society often paints them as being. Most are ordinary people, much like you and your friends. They are someone's son or daughter, brother or sister. They too have hopes and dreams.

This report does not glorify the escort business, nor does it demonize it.

Listening to TV reports, I heard commentators talk about how Gov. Spitzer and other elected officials who have found themselves in similar situations violated "the public's trust."

For three years, my legally licensed referral business sent escorts to meet powerful and not-so-powerful men. In my opinion, the greatest violation of "the public's trust" I found did not take place in a Washington hotel room, but rather in the most-unlikeliest of all places for me – in Lexington, Kentucky.

That violation occurred when my employer – the *Lexington Herald-Leader* – demanded I give up my constitutional right to share this story with you in order to keep my job.

Protecting the First Amendment – especially freedom of speech – is a public trust given to newspapers.

By demanding I walk away from this project and sign documents promising never to tell anyone about it, the *Herald-Leader* tried to take away my voice, tried to take away the voices of all whose stories are told in *Mack And The Boys.*

The greater truth, however, is that the *Herald-Leader* tried to take away your right to read such a story.

Reading *Mack And The Boys*, you will come to know why I gave up the job I loved at a newspaper I cherished for this project.

I know I am taking a gamble publishing this report. I have weighed the possible personal benefits and outcomes. The results seem rather one-sided and not favoring the option I have chosen.

Making a case for changing how people think about others they might consider "different" is a mission I have been called to serve. To accomplish that task, I have come to tell you the truth about my experience in Washington, about what I did there and what I learned.

Reading this project, you will come to have a better idea of what it is like for society and "friends" to consider you an outcast, a freak, and how dying all alone in a shed might not seem the worst of all fates.

I hope after reading *Mack And The Boys,* you will be more accepting of others – those you might have once considered "different" from you – people like Deborah Jeane Palfrey, Ashley Alexandra Dupré and me.

Rest in peace, Deborah Jeane.

A note to readers

Mack And The Boys is an explanatory journalism project. Its purpose is to take you into a world that is very real, but one where few are allowed.

You are about to meet people whom society often looks down on, people who are not that different from you or those you hold dear.

www.MackAndTheBoys.com allows readers the opportunity to enjoy *Mack And The Boys* online, free of cost. In exchange, online readers are asked to contribute directly to one or more not-for-profit organizations that are somehow related to this project. This is done, in part, to honor singer/songwriter Harry Chapin who donated his time and effort to end hunger in America. As you will learn, he also granted permission for me to include his song lyrics – as long as others would benefit from what I wrote.

Reading this project, you will learn about the organizations and the work they do. It is my hope that you will include one or more of them in your charitable giving in the near future. All are worthy of your support.

DEDICATION

This project is lovingly dedicated to:

Max the Wonder Dog and the **Beautiful Miss Tilly.**
Through the turmoil of researching *Mack And The Boys,*
Max was there for me. Later, through the writing phase,
it was Tilly who put up with my craziness.

Pat Flannery, my freshman English professor at Southeastern
Christian College. She allowed me to step outside the norm to find the
inner me and encouraged me to write what I felt.

Nell Westbrook, my U.S. history professor at Southeastern Christian
College. Westbrook taught me about the founding fathers. She also
suggested I become a journalist.

Cecil Garrett, the dean and my Bible professor
at Southeastern Christian College. Garrett taught me photography
and how to publish a newspaper.

Carol Wright, journalism professor at Eastern Kentucky University.
Wright taught me how to recognize a story others needed to hear. She also
taught me to report what I saw accurately, fairly, and concisely.

John S. Carroll, former editor at the *Lexington Herald-Leader,*
the *Baltimore Sun* and the *Los Angeles Times.* Carroll taught the
importance of reporting stories that would benefit readers, even if
powerful influences and readers themselves didn't want the story told.

Henry Wright, one of the greatest copy editors and bosses ever.
Henry taught those of us who worked with him to check
every fact and that we always owed readers our best effort.

Bill Bailey (aka "The Duke of Louisville") and his co-workers at WAKY, the
greatest rock 'n' roll station ever. **Tom Kendall,** aka "The All-Night Night
Hawk," who worked the midnight to 6 a.m. shift at WVLK in Lexington
and **Herb Oscar Kent** who was on WLAP and later, WVLK.

Kowalski, who lost everything then found his own vanishing point.

Finally, to all of Mack's boys but especially
**Danny, Sean, Storm/Joey, Chase, Jonathan, Jesse, Drew,
Ryan, Michael, Zack, Mickey, Brendon,** and **Justin.**

Matthew Shepard, a student at the University of Wyoming. Shepard was beaten and left to die because he was gay. He died on October 12, 1998, three days after Capital City Boys ran its first ad announcing it would be representing gay male escorts.

Gene Pitney, singer and songwriter. In all, Pitney charted 16 Top 40 hit singles, four of which reached the top ten. He wrote "He's A Rebel" for The Crystals and "Hello Mary Lou" for Ricky Nelson. He was inducted into the Rock and Roll Hall of Fame in 2002. Pitney died on April 5, 2006.

For almost 30 years, **Herman Klurfeld** was one of the most influential newspapermen in America although his name was largely invisible to the public. Klurfeld was the chief writer for Walter Winchell, whose column appeared in more than 2,000 newspapers in the 1930s and 1940s and whose Sunday radio broadcast was heard by millions of Americans. Klurfeld died on December 18, 2006.

John Inman, British actor and one of the stars of "Are You Being Served?" While it was never said that his character, Mr. Humphries, was gay, we all believed so. Inman died March 8, 2007.

Tammy Faye Bakker Messner, ex-wife of Jim Bakker and co-host of "The PTL Club." She showed a tolerant attitude toward gays. I met her once. She was gracious and beautiful. She died of cancer on July 20, 2007.

Lee Hazelwood, singer/songwriter/producer, probably best remembered for his work with Nancy Sinatra but should be remembered for his entire career, which profoundly influenced generations of musicians and music lovers. Hazelwood died on August 4, 2007.

My mother, Margaret, the greatest story teller I ever knew. I came to enjoy hearing stories about other people from listening to my mother's stories. It is very possible, because of those experiences, that I developed my passion to tell other people's stories, including the ones in this report. My mother died on November 14, 2007.

He was born on Elvis' birthday in 2001 -- that was just one of the things that made **Bailey,** my son's dog, special. In the early days of the writing phase of this project, "Big Dog" would often jump up on my bed and listen as I read him what I had written. He was never critical and always supportive. Bailey died when he was struck by a vehicle on Sept. 30, 2008.

The Broad View

"Every journalist believes that he or she works, ultimately,
for the reader – not for the editor, or for the publisher,
or for the corporation, or for those opaque
financial institutions that hold the stock.

We all know journalists who have lost their jobs on principle.
They have refused to kill important stories, or to write glowingly
about politicians or advertisers who don't deserve it.

They have done this because their first loyalty is to the reader."

– WHAT WILL BECOME OF NEWSPAPERS
by John. S. Carroll

This statement is part of a speech delivered at the 2006 annual meeting
of the American Society of Newspaper Editors under the title
"Last Call at the ASNE Saloon."

Just So You Know...

Song lyrics used in *Mack And The Boys* are included to illustrate a point of view or to convey a feeling.

Lyrics are included for educational purposes only and copyrights remain with the rightful owners.

When lyrics use the word "girl" or "woman," you probably need to substitute the word "boy" or "man."

Not all the people seen in photos used in this project are escorts. Some just happened to be in a public place when the photos were taken or were friends. A few were hired as models for various projects of mine, including this one.

No one should assume that anyone featured ever escorted unless I make that point crystal clear.

Finally, please understand that whenever I use the word "boy," I am using it to define gender, not age.

Prologue

"Show me a man with no vices
and I'll show you a man with no virtues."
– President Abraham Lincoln
(Like me, a son of Kentucky)

"There are three sides to every story:
Your side, my side, and the truth.
And no one is lying.
Memories shared serve each differently."
– Robert Evans

Robert Evans was a self-proclaimed so-so actor who later
ran Paramount Pictures, taking it from ninth place to first.

"If you get an ear pierced, some will call you gay.
But if you drive a pick-up, they'll say, 'No, he must be straight.'
What we are and what we ain't,
what we can and what we can't,
does it really matter?"
– FEED JAKE
Artist: Pirates Of The Mississippi
Songwriter: Danny Mayo
SONY/ATV Acuff Rose Music (BMI)

"As long as a man
has the strength to dream
he can redeem his soul and fly."
– IF I CAN DREAM
Artist: Elvis Presley
Songwriter: Walter Brown
Gladys Music (ASCAP)

PREMISE #1

*"There are things inside you
that no one wants to face.
Things that you keep secret,
even from yourself.
But secrets are funny,
things that you try to hide
always turn out to be
the things you cannot forget."*

**– Georgia "George" Lass
DEAD LIKE ME**
MGM

Ride captain ride
upon your mystery ship,
on your way to a world
that others might have missed.
– RIDE CAPTAIN RIDE
Artist: Blues Image
Songwriters: F. Konte/C. Pinera
ATM Music (ASCAP)

"Beautiful Stranger"
Madonna
Peaked at #19 in 1999

Dirty little secrets.

Everybody has them.

Nobody wants them told.

Dirty little secrets. You have them, so do I. So do the rich and powerful and the weakest among us.

Nobody wants their dirty little secrets revealed, be they an individual, a politician, a family, a celebrity, or a Fortune 500 corporation.

For three years, I played a role in creating dirty little secrets for hundreds of Washington, D.C., residents and for those who worked in and traveled to the nation's capital. It is a role I chose and one from which I have not been able to escape, even though I left that world in 2001. It is a good bet I never will.

I have kept other people's secrets tucked away, deep inside me. These secrets have haunted me, not because of the role I played in them but because I have resisted telling the incredible story about them.

It is a story about senators, congressmen, lawyers, celebrities, media figures, and lots of ordinary people, including me. It is also a story about two of America's largest newspaper publishing companies at the time – Knight Ridder and Gannett. I worked for both of them.

All of them have dirty little secrets they do not want told.

Whatever the cost, whatever the outcome, the time has come for me to tell you about the secrets.

* * *

Sean was 15 minutes late when he finally knocked on my hotel door. The knock was soft but it did not matter. I was standing right behind the door, anxiously looking through the peephole. I would have heard the knock even if it had been on the door across the hall.

When I opened the door, I instantly knew he was not 19, as he had claimed. He was older. How much older, I did not know but I also knew it did not matter. He was cute, and I was alone in Washington, far from my home deep in the Bible Belt. I invited Sean into my room, smiling as if I never doubted anything he had told me in instant messages over the Internet.

Neither of us could have imagined what this chance meeting would mean for our futures. There was no way for either of us to know what our meeting would eventually cost and how it would change our lives and the lives of hundreds of others in Washington forever.

If I'm smart then I'll run away
but I'm not so I guess I'll stay,
Heaven forbid I'll take my chance
on a beautiful stranger.
– BEAUTIFUL STRANGER
Artist: Madonna
Songwriters: Madonna/W. Wainwright
Almo Music Corp (ASCAP)

Dorothy and her friends traveled to meet the Wizard of Oz. They eventually met the man behind the curtain. I came to Washington to attend a journalism seminar in nearby Reston, Virginia. I eventually became the man behind the curtain himself.

Hearing Sean's stories about escorting, and later, similar ones from an escort named Jeremy, intrigued me, but it was the whispering of the Beautiful Stranger I met later that enticed me to peek behind the curtain that shields Washington's secret world of gay male escorts.

Unlike Dorothy and her friends, my mission was not to find a way home but rather to tell you about the world of secret meetings, hush-hush financial arrangements, and life on the edge.

I came to Washington to investigate the world of gay male escorts. It is a great understatement to say I succeeded.

Sometimes, the only way to learn the truth is to play the game. I played the game, I learned the truth. I created, owned and operated what became Washington's most-successful gay male escort referral service at the time – Capital City Boys. I also eventually bought and ran what many consider to be Washington's best gay male service ever – The Agency.

Both referral services were legally licensed by the District of Columbia and were registered with the Internal Revenue Service. Neither, under my watch, took part in illegal activity.

Playing the game, I came to know the dirty little secrets of elected officials – Democrats and Republicans alike, lawyers and businessmen, church-going folks, entertainers and even a few in the news media – some whose names you likely know.

The fact that this project takes place in Washington was by chance. That is just where I happened to find it.

Even before the Rep. Mark Foley and Sen. Larry Craig scandals, Washington had a colorful past with prostitutes, escorts, whorehouses, and politicians who could not keep their pants on or zippers up.

I am a journalist. Accurately researching, reporting, telling, and presenting stories has been my life's work. This project turned out to be the biggest story of my career. Reporting it has forever changed my life.

I only wanted to look. I only wanted to report what I saw and learned. I never intended to get too close but, as often happens when you venture somewhere you shouldn't, I became a part of that "other" world.

Now I'm just looking,
then I'm gone with the wind,
endlessly searching for an original sin.
– ORIGINAL SIN
Artist: Taylor Dayne
Songwriter: (The master) Jim Steinman
Lost Boys Music (BMI)

Owning Capital City Boys and The Agency, I became known to

thousands who lived in and traveled to Washington as "Mack." Very few people knew my name was Malcolm. Even fewer ever heard my last name. That is how I wanted it.

I was foolish enough to think when this project was over, I could go back to my old life. That still has not happened. I know now it never will.

I lived and worked behind the curtain for more than three years. While I never sought the title or the job, for almost all that time I was the Wizard of Washington's gay escort world.

If you were a guy who wanted to escort in Washington, you most likely called Capital City Boys. If you passed the telephone interview, you were invited for a face-to-face meeting with me. If not, we probably never met, and maybe you worked at one of the other services or danced at one of the local male strip bars.

If you were looking for a quality gay male escort, you probably called Capital City Boys or The Agency, and if you called, chances are very good you and I talked. If we did not

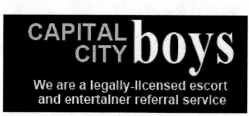

have the escort you were looking for, we would tell you and would suggest an alternative, even if he worked for a competitor.

National gay escort review Web sites spoke of Mack by name and mentioned his consistent practice of representing only the best gay escorts in Washington. Clients raved in reviews that Mack would never oversell a guy just to make a booking. It was true.

Storm, an internationally famous gay porn star, repeatedly remarked on my unique way of running Capital City Boys. "Somehow, you have managed to gain entrance into the strange world of escorting and brought with you respectability – something that up to now the escort world has seen little of."

Having worked for other services, including with Hollywood Madam Heidi Fleiss, Storm speaks with authority.

"The word is all over the escort community – to escorts and clients alike – Mack doesn't do drugs; that you take care of both your guys and your clients; that you take great pains not to lie to people; that you are dependable, reliable, and most of all, that you don't play games."

Let's face it, if one has to have a national reputation about running a gay male escort referral service, this one is not that bad.

* * *

As Mack, I came to know a lot more than I ever dreamed I might. I learned things I knew could end careers – political and otherwise. I came to know things that more than one person warned could get me killed. The warnings were well-founded.

I worked in Washington knowing someone with a dark past and a deeply hidden secret might come looking for me some night. Finding me would not have been that difficult of a task.

There was danger associated with owning and operating Capital City Boys and The Agency or any escort referral service in a town like Washington.

One cannot possess the knowledge and proof I had without knowing some danger comes with it.

That point was reinforced near the end of my time in Washington when Chandra Levy, a Washington intern who was involved with a congressman, went missing on May 1, 2001. She too had known things that could embarrass powerful people. Levy was found dead in Rock Creek Park a little more than a year after she disappeared.

The point was also reinforced by the execution-style murder of a Washington-based gay male escort service owner while he was in Richmond, Virginia.

I was never paranoid while in Washington, just cautious. I

knew I could easily disappear without anyone asking a lot of questions. For that reason, and others, I told no one the real reason I had come to the nation's capital. I also never told anyone I was secretly taping telephone calls and documenting escort visits.

* * *

Mack And The Boys involves people connected to the White House – both the real one and TV's "The West Wing." It involves people connected with the Senate, the House, the Supreme Court, lobbyists, and the national environmental movement. It involves drug dealers, the Metro Police, the porn industry, and Washington's gay community. It also involves people employed by some of the nation's largest corporations.

You will come to know how a mild-mannered Republican, Rush Limbaugh-listening, church-going journalist came to own two gay escort referral services and how I traded my career for a list of guys who would entertain clients for money. You will come to know how, in Washington, I no longer had to worry about checking facts and libeling someone. Instead, I had to deal with exaggerated claims of endowment and finding ways to fulfill all kinds of fantasies for all kinds of clients.

* * *

Telling other people's stories has been an important part of my professional life as a journalist. It has been since, as a college student, I traveled to hundreds of towns in Central and Eastern Kentucky in search of stories and photographs to be published in the *Lexington Herald-Leader*.

My training and experience as a reporter and photojournalist taught me to notice things that others might miss or look beyond. That training and experience convinced me that many readers would be intrigued by Sean's and Jeremy's stories, just as I had been. Experience had also taught me that some would never read such a project because it involves gay men and/or escorts.

Mack And The Boys is an explanatory journalism project. Explanatory journalism informs readers about a topic or situation they normally would not have access to explore or study on their own. Explanatory journalism demands I be accurate and complete but allows some flexibility in how I share my findings with you.

Mack And The Boys is a funny story. It is also a tragic one. It involves sex and money. It is about those who pay escorts for an hour of their time – including elected officials – and about hundreds of young, legal-age men – gay and straight – who escorted because they needed a way to survive in Washington or because they had certain other needs or desires.

"Escorting was a way to make a lot of money, feel important, and do something we wanted to do any ways – have sex," Storm explains. "It beat working in a coffee shop making $4 an hour and at the end of the week not having enough money for anything. You don't realize until years later," he says, "that each piece of yourself that you sold off actually died."

* * *

The title *Mack And The Boys* comes, at least in part, with apologies to the great author John Steinbeck. He wrote *Cannery Row* and its sequel, *Sweet Thursday*.

David S. Ward wrote the screenplay and directed the movie "Cannery Row." It was in Ward's movie that I first came to know and love Steinbeck's well-meaning but crazy characters. Ward chose actor/director Walter Houston to narrate the movie, a superb choice. In describing the main character – Doc – Houston, in that great gravelly voice of his, explains:

> *[Doc] had friends he didn't*
> *even know about and some*
> *he would never forget,*
> *friends like Mack and the boys.*
> *Mack is the elder and leader*
> *of a small group of men*
> *who have in common no families,*
> *no money, and no ambition*
> *beyond the time to discuss matters*
> *of interest but little importance.*

That narrative does not exactly describe the guys I came to know and work with in Washington but it is not completely wrong either.

Gay and straight men escort for a variety of reasons. Most do it for the money. A few do it for the thrill of doing something others will not. Some who escorted for Capital City Boys had fled their homes, seeking to be free from one oppression or another. Others had been chased away by their families because they were gay and "did not fit in at home" anymore.

Most of the people I came to know and work with in Washington were moral people who, for one reason or another, found themselves doing things some consider immoral.

Many of the escorts Capital City Boys represented were professionals in other lines of work. During the day, they were bankers, a dentist, an engineer, a photojournalist, and the CEO of a not-for-profit organization. At night, they entertained politicians, businessmen, college students, and lots of ordinary people.

Like the Tin Man, the Cowardly Lion, and the Scarecrow whom Dorothy met and went to Oz with, the escorts I came to know during the reporting phase of this project had one or more deficiencies. That did not bother me, I had my own. I brought along the baggage associated with having been molested soon after I turned 14 by a prominent Lexington, Kentucky, celebrity who happened to be a minor national one. Until now, I have kept that news a secret too.

We – these young freedom-seekers and me – had a lot in common. Each of us had a need. Each of us had a mission. Together, we changed the world of gay male escorts in the District, and in the process, many of us forever changed our own lives.

Most left enriched by having been a part of Capital City Boys, a part of *Mack And The Boys*.

> *What they didn't know was that*
> *their lives would be changed forever*
> *because they had been part*
> *of something great, and greatness,*
> *no matter how brief, stays with a man.*
> **– THE REPLACEMENTS**
> Warner Brothers and Bel Air Pictures

Some, sadly, did not.

I came to Washington to research this project. I learned a great deal about escorts and clients and the business. What I learned the most, however, was about myself, about who I am and what is important to me.

I gave up my newspaper career for this project. Until now, only a handful of people have known this. My employer, the *Lexington Herald-Leader* and its corporate owner at the time, Knight

Ridder Newspapers, were so ashamed of being linked to this project that they gave me an ultimatum: Walk away and never tell anyone about your involvement or we will terminate your employment. You now know one of the dirty little secrets.

The *Herald-Leader,* under the leadership of Editor John. S. Carroll, won national awards for standing up to powerful influences – people and organizations who did not want certain news published.

In 1999, the *Herald-Leader* and Knight Ridder promised to cause me more harm if I ever went public with this news. The *Herald-Leader* reminded me of this in December 2007, when I asked its publisher and human resources director to read this report, to submit the paper's side, and to raise any possible misinterpretations in my reporting.

Ten years have gone by
since I looked in her eye,
but the memory lingers.
– SUMMER (The First Time)
Singer/Songwriter: Bobby Goldsboro
EMI Unart Catalog (BMI)

Some will call me a fool for working a project such as this, even some journalists. Some people will say I made stupid decisions. Others will say what I did was repulsive, despite the fact my escort referral services always operated inside the law.

None of us have the ability to change our past. I cannot change what I did, I also cannot deny I did things some consider wrong. I have known all along there will be a price to pay if I share this project with you. That said, the cost seems small in comparison to the price others might pay if I do not come forward.

Telling what I know might have given Deborah Jeane Palfrey hope, might have renewed her determination to wage an appeal, or even to just live another day. It is too late for me to help Palfrey, but not too late to help others, maybe someone you know.

After years of trying to justify not doing it, the time has come for me to tell you about the Beautiful Stranger I met in Washington – the story of *Mack And The Boys* – the truth about the lovers, the dreamers, and me.

I walked in town on silver spurs

that jingled to a song
that I had only sang to just a few.
She saw my silver spurs and said
"Let's pass some time
and I will give to you, summer wine.
Ohh-oh-oh, summer wine."
– SUMMER WINE
Artists: Nancy Sinatra, Lee Hazelwood
Songwriter: Lee Hazelwood
Granite Music Corp. (ASCAP)

The Backstory

The Soho Tea & Coffee Shop in Dupont Circle was a major hangout for gays while I researched this project.

Soho attracted a diverse group of people. Patrons included people going to nearby gay bars, the club next door and those who just needed a place to hang out.

The scene became almost church-like when someone played a Madonna song. Everyone stopped what they were doing and either sang along or remained quiet and respectful, as if listening to a minister in church.

"Ray of Light" and "Beautiful Stranger" were hits during this time.

* * *

"Summer Wine" is one of my 10-most favorite songs. I love the combination of Nancy Sinatra and the husky-voiced Lee Hazelwood. "Summer Wine" was the B-side of "Sugar Town."

"Long Cool Woman In A Black Dress"
The Hollies
Peaked at #2 in 1972

Jeremy's life was forever changed the day his mother walked into his bedroom without knocking and found him kissing a male friend.

"Catching me kissing another guy would have been bad enough," he said, "but where my hand was left no doubt about what was going on."

His mother, Jeremy said, "freaked."

Jeremy's mother had worked hard to fix him up with the neighbor's daughter. "Trouble was," he said, "I was more interested in the neighbor's 17-year-old son."

His father's reaction, Jeremy said, was no different. The next few days convinced Jeremy that life at home was never going to be the same again.

Jeremy says his parents forced him to choose between "straightening up" and staying with the family or choosing to be with men and to leave.

Jeremy walked away from his home in Northern Virginia one morning while his parents slept. When I met him in Washington three years later, he had not been back.

The then 21-year-old said he was sure that he could leave home and have a better life. "I soon found out how stupid that idea was."

Jeremy stayed with friends for about a month then moved to Washington. It's "a great place to be if you're gay," he said.

Young, cute and on the streets, Jeremy said he was repeatedly approached by a guy who hung around outside of Mr. P's Bar on P Street. The man, Jeremy said, repeatedly told him about a "job opportunity."

"This guy kept telling me that he could get me work. All I had to do was to 'please' the guys he'd hook me up with."

Needing money, one night, Jeremy told the man he would "be around in case there was any work." An hour later, Jeremy walked into the (then) Radisson Barcello Hotel and went to a room on the third floor. A guy in his 40s opened the door and invited Jeremy inside.

"I sat down and we talked for 10 minutes. Then the guy suggested I come over closer to him, so I did." Jeremy says the man started kissing him then unbuttoned his shirt.

"Laying there on the bed in our underwear, the guy could tell that I was really nervous, Jeremy said. "He was a gentleman. I couldn't have asked for a better first time."

The man paid Jeremy $100. The encounter lasted about 45 minutes. Jeremy told me his story on June 13, 1998. I was in Washington, preparing to go to Rehoboth Beach, Delaware, the next day with Sean.

Jeremy and I met on a street corner in Dupont Circle. We were two strangers waiting for a light to change. I smiled and nodded at him, as I often do to strangers I meet. Jeremy smiled back.

We struck up a conversation as cars flew by, some seemingly coming very close to us.

"I sleep there some nights," he said, frowning slightly, pointing to the park.

Curious and a bit stunned, I said, "Really?"

Without hesitation, Jeremy told me he was a gay escort. "When I work I have enough money to rent a hotel room. When I don't, I have to find something on my own."

He tells me his real name is Jeremy but escorts under a different name. He is handsome and well-spoken.

The street light finally changes and we cross the street. I follow him into the circle, no longer caring about what I had planned to do. Despite the concrete being wet from a rainstorm a few minutes before, we sat at the fountain and talked about a variety of things, mainly Jeremy's life on the streets.

I tell him about my few experiences with escorts, including earlier that day with a guy named Jonathan.

I invited Jeremy to join me for dinner. Sean had plans that night. Jeremy and I did not. Over dinner, Jeremy told me he had worked with a couple of escort services in Washington and about what that was like.

At first, Jeremy says, he averaged a dozen jobs a week. Bookings eventually slowed as newer escorts became available.

Area where Jeremy and I sat near fountain in Dupont Circle
is a favorite for locals and tourists alike.

Jeremy said clients' expectations also changed. "That first guy
was happy just to cuddle and to do simple stuff," Jeremy said.
"Nowadays, clients want to do a lot more and I have to do it or I
don't work."

Do you like escorting, I asked?

"Not anymore," he said, looking away. "I just don't have a lot of
options right now. I wanted to study engineering but that dream
never happened. I guess it never will."

Ever think of going home? I asked, suggestively.

"No." Jeremy's answer came quickly and with great
determination. "Home was a lifetime ago," he said. "I don't even
know if they're still there."

Jeremy's pager buzzed. He went to return the call. Coming
back to the table, Jeremy said that he had an escort call and
would soon have to leave.

A few minutes later, Jeremy and I walked out of the
restaurant. It was an awkward moment for me. What does one
say to a stranger who has shared candid, intimate details of his
life? What does one say to a stranger you have come to care about
so quickly?

We stood there for what seemed a long time, neither of us
saying anything. "I have to go," he finally said. "Work is waiting."

And off he was, down the street, into the night.

Somewhere in a hotel room in Washington, a stranger opened his door and invited Jeremy inside.

Later that night, lying in bed, the lights off and sleep still far away, I could not help but recount what Jeremy had told me and wonder what life had in store for him in the future. I also thought about Sean and Jonathan. All of them were wonderful guys who – for one reason or another – found themselves entertaining men who would pay them for their time.

Each had a story to tell. Each of them could teach us something. It was then that I decided to research and write about the secret world of gay male escorts in the nation's capital. It was then that I decided to tell you about people like Jeremy and the man he met that night.

* * *

PERSONAL THOUGHTS: I never saw Jeremy again, though I looked for him the entire time I was in Washington. Not a single birthday comes and goes that I don't think about Jeremy, about the time we met while waiting to cross that street.

Life is strange sometimes. Lives can be forever changed by small things, like smiling and nodding to a stranger. Lives were forever changed the day Jeremy's mother opened that door and found him kissing his friend. Jeremy's was, maybe mine was too.

Sometimes I wonder what might have become of Jeremy's life if his mother had not walked into his room or, had she, if she had simply excused herself and closed the door. Sometimes, I wonder what might have become of mine.

Photo by Keith Stanley
Dupont Circle during snow storm. One of the great images posted on
www.kestan.com/travel/dc/dc_index.htm

Sen. Kevin Keeley: "Jackson's dead."
Louise Keeley: "Oh my God."
Sen. Keeley: "He died in bed? Whose bed? A prostitute's? A minor? And black? I don't believe this. I don't f**king believe this. I'm ruined."
Louise: "No, you're not responsible. Kevin, you cannot be held responsible for Sen. Jackson's private life."
Sen. Keeley: "Louise, I'm the vice president of the Coalition for Moral Order. My co-founder has just died in the bed of an under-aged black whore. Now wait till the media gets a hold of this."

– THE BIRDCAGE
United Artists Pictures

The seven-year-old's question was sincere and took her father and those nearby by great surprise: "Daddy," she said, "what's that hooker doing here?"

"Heads snapped up and people all around us turned just to get a look," my friend said, recounting what had happened the night before at his daughter's ballet recital.

In this case, the "hooker" was a clothes hanger that someone had left behind on a nearby chair.

Society has long had a love/hate relationship with hookers and their variously named counterparts. People love hearing about hookers and escorts and the people they meet, love to hear what they got caught doing and who was caught doing it with them.

My first real exposure to hookers came in the spring of 1975. That education came via a TV show called "HOT L BALTIMORE." The show, produced by Norman Lear, was a comedy on ABC about a couple of women who worked in a dump called Hotel Baltimore. The show also featured two gay characters but I don't remember much about them.

The "E" in Hotel on the sign had burned out and never was replaced. Those who visited HOT L BALTIMORE probably did not care about such things since their stays there were fairly short, and their interests something other than a neon sign.

When I came to Washington in March 1998, my knowledge about gay male escorts was very limited. I had come across a few guys in Lexington who "hustled" but had only participated in one encounter where money exchanged hands and, then, the money was given as a gift rather than a payment.

Paying someone for an intimate (whatever that means) encounter seems to be a line most of society considers crossing to be taboo. Most of those who pay escorts understand that position but feel differently.

One client, a man named Jeffery, says he has no problems

paying an escort to visit him. Jeffery, a client in his 50s, has hired Washington-area gay male escorts for more than 20 years. (Jeffery is not the client's real name but the one he asked to be called in this project. While the name Jeffery is not real, the client and the experiences he shares here and later in this project are.)

"It's like going to the grocery store. You get something there, you have to pay for it," he says. "There's no difference in playing blackjack or going to Disney World or hiring an escort."

Robert, another Washington resident who routinely hires gay escorts, agrees.

"A straight man invites a woman out for drinks, then dinner and maybe a show. At the end of the evening, the man has paid out a considerable sum of money and usually has the expectation that he is going to get 'something' in return," Robert says. "Gay or straight, with a date or with an escort, either way, if you're a man, you're going to pay for what you get. At least with an escort, there's a good chance you'll get what you want. A straight man with a date, well, who knows?"

Jeffery says he makes no moral judgments about the work escorts do. "They have their talents, I have mine." Jeffery makes no moral judgments about escorts but society often does.

"The gay escort and the so-called 'straight' escort have survived in two solitudes," says Dr. Maurice J. Smith, a psychiatrist and member of the American Gay and Lesbian Psychiatrists Association, a caucus of the American Psychiatric Association.

Dr. Smith works in Hollywood in the entertainment industry. His work includes counseling on script development, character analysis, and as a medical technical advisor.

Dr. Smith also assists actors who suffer a variety of gay, bisexual, lesbian, transgendered problems such as gender identity, "coming out," or living within a closeted life created by publicity needs to keep such news a secret.

"The straight escort is merely a holdover from the early European-based tradition of 'mistress' and 'gigolo,' female and male respectively."

Gay escorts, on the other hand, Dr. Smith says, fell victim to a vagueness in laws and enforcement by being categorized as "deviants" rather than as prostitutes.

Dr. Smith says law enforcement officials were caught in the

middle, being expected to enforce laws that never took lifestyle into account and were forced to handle complaints without clear direction.

"Both (gay and straight escorts) were and remain today widely acceptable in mainstream society with some pushback from the extreme right or religious zealots," Dr. Smith says.

"The sociological basis for the acceptance is based on a belief that (such) liaisons were a way of enhancing relationships within married couples. Partners with a straight escort were able to sexually relieve themselves of fetishes not provided by their spouses," Dr. Smith says. "It (also) protected the spouse from the wandering partner by keeping them satisfied, virtually ensuring the life of the marriage."

Dr. Smith says society has been slow to think gay escorts provide such a service. "Spouses entertaining gay escorts were perceived to have 'crossed over' the line into deviance and thereby forced the dissolution of the relationship. If the spouse were to accept the deviance then the couple would face collective banishment from society.

"We now know that the use of gay escorts was equally as rampant as with straight escorts yet virtually invisible to mainstream society," Dr. Smith says. "This was of course due to the very nature of fetishes. The desire to do something against norms and the innate bisexual tendencies of all people are found in most fetishes. Yet, for all of the previous reasons that led to marginalization there was still a need for a cloak or veil of secrecy and discretion to prevail."

Dr. Smith says this situation was further exacerbated in the 1980s with the arrival of the AIDS epidemic. "Due to the more rampant promiscuity naturally inherent in any isolated group, the epidemic spread more quickly among the gay population and society found a new reason to react. The deviants were now spreaders of disease!

"When the AIDS epidemic arrived, the veil was lifted and the gay escort was branded as a virtual 'typhoid Mary.'"

Dr. Smith says gay escorts continue to be discriminated against because the "disease carrying" or "deviant" labels are still applied to them.

* * *

"There are a lot of people in society who, the only way they can feel good is, to look down on someone else," Marvin, the owner of

Tops Referrals, says.

Marvin is quick to point out that sometimes, the condemnation comes from within the gay escort community itself. "A lot of escorts look down on other escorts, especially those who hustle in bars and (particularly) those who work the street."

Occasionally, escorts encounter condemnation and rejection from a client.

One of Marvin's clients forced an escort out into the hallway naked immediately after the client and escort had finished their business. "The escort tried to explain that he needed to put his clothes on before leaving but the client insisted he leave right then," Marvin says. "The client kept saying, 'You've got to go.'"

Pressed to explain why a client might do such a thing, Marvin says: "Many times, clients fell guilty about what they did on the call they just had, so they look down on the escort they were just intimate with. The client thinks: 'I had so much fun, (this) must be wrong.'"

Like Dr. Smith, Marvin thinks gay escort referral services can have a positive effect on some relationships. "Services like ours actually save marriages," he says. "We satisfy a need. We provide a very valuable service to society, and, when we provide safe, clean services, we can actually keep society balanced."

An escort referral service promotes the escorts it represents. It does not promote sex. That is how such a business can operate inside the law.

Like other marketing and public relations firms, Capital City Boys and The Agency sought clients – theirs just happened to be escorts instead of a grocery or hardware store or personal-injury attorney.

The product Capital City Boys and The Agency marketed was the escort's time and companionship – not sex. Put another way, Capital City Boys and the Agency offered "compensated dating," where clients – mostly men – paid generally younger (but legal-age) guys to spend time with them.

Sometimes, the call involved the escort to go out in public with the client. Most times, however, the call was conducted in a private sitting.

Marvin, the owner of Tops Referrals, speculates that some type of intimate activity happens in 95 percent or more of the calls a typical gay referral service books.

"Kissing is a form of intimacy," Marvin says. "Some escorts consider kissing even more intimate than giving a blow job." Asked to explain, Marvin said, "Some escorts will not kiss a client for anything. They reserve it for someone special in their lives."

Did escorts and the escort's client ever have sex? Sometimes, I am sure they did. But when sex happened, it was between two consenting adults, and the Capital City Boys escort did not charge for it – at least, he better not have.

"Sex is usually incidental to the appointment," Marvin says. That statement prompts the question no one seems to have a definitive answer to: "What constitutes sex?"

Sex used to be simple to define before a certain president gave us a second, much more restrictive answer – actually having some sort of intercourse.

"I have found that a lot of people agree with (Bill Clinton's) definition," Marvin says. "A lot of people, especially escorts."

* * *

The representation contract Capital City Boys had with escorts clearly stated the escort could not charge for anything beyond the cost of the time with the client.

Clients and escorts alike were told that a session was for a predetermined amount of money based solely on the amount of time a client wanted to book.

Both were also told that the price for a one-hour call was, say, $170. Both were told the price was the same no mattered what happened during the hour – if the client and the escort sat on a couch and talked the cost was $170; if they watched a movie or TV show it was $170; and if they baked cookies, cleaned out the client's garage, raked leaves or whatever it was still $170.

On the few occasions when there was reason to believe an escort had possibly violated the rule, Capital City Boys had a "Come to Jesus" meeting with the escort during which it was made crystal clear what the rule was and why it was enforced. It was a sermon that was never repeated – either the escort stopped making implied promises and continued being represented by Capital City Boys or he did not and the service terminated its representation.

* * *

An escort referral service is a matchmaker of sorts. Call one up and ask for a certain type of man or woman and they will match you up with someone who has your same interests.

If you are a "size queen" and want to meet someone with a large endowment so you can talk about such matters, just tell the service. If you are into leather and want to meet a "leather daddy" to discuss the latest leather accessories, just tell the service. It will match you up with dudes with such interests.

If you were to work the phones at an escort referral service for a week, you would hear a lot of things – some of which you would certainly never tell at church and some of which you might not even understand.

Such is the nature of the business. Capital City Boys had people call who never booked a session. After two or three calls, some even dropped the pretense of considering seeing someone. They just wanted to talk, so we talked and enjoyed each other's company.

Thankfully, there were a lot of good-natured people who called wanting to meet someone.

Some callers had particular topics they wanted to discuss with an "expert." The service matched their topic of interest with a qualified person. Some wanted to tell how their wives did not understand them or that their kids did not appreciate them. Capital City Boys matched these clients with appropriate "experts" too.

Then there were the more serious callers, generally in their late 30s, 40s and early 50s, who wanted to spend time with a handsome guy – usually younger than themselves – and were realistic enough to know that meeting an escort was the only way they were going to meet their "dream lover."

Capital City Boys appealed to all of these clients and more. Capital City Boys represented only quality guys with mainstream interests. You could take any one of Capital City Boys guys out to dinner in any fine restaurant and not be embarrassed. The same could not be said about certain other Washington-based services.

The majority of Capital City Boys' bookings took place in high-end downtown Washington hotels. Name a luxury hotel in Washington and it is a certainty that Capital City Boys sent escorts there. In some cases, lots of them.

"The doormen at those places have seen more hookers and prostitutes and escorts than the White House has seen Republicans," internationally known porn star Storm says. "It was so humiliating, when the doormen gave you that look that said 'we know why you are here and what you are about to do.' But they are not going to stop you because they don't know which of their important guests you are coming to see."

Sometimes, the client would meet the escort at the escort's place or somewhere Capital City Boys had arranged. These visits – known as in-calls – were popular with married men who wanted to meet a guy but needed to make sure there was no paper trail showing they had rented a room somewhere. The same was often true for an elected official or high-ranking government worker. Such documents could prove hard to explain later.

I once asked a congressional aide who happened to be a client if he knew how many senators and congressmen used straight or gay escort services. I asked because the number of such calls to Capital City Boys had declined.

"Very few, if any at all," was his quick reply. "They do not need to (call). That need is taken care for them now days." Pressed further, the aide said, "No one wants a repeat of the Wilbur Mills thing," referencing the October 7, 1974, incident in Washington involving an Arkansas congressman and an Argentine stripper named Fanne Foxe.

"Entertainment is provided to the people you mentioned in a safe, discreet and controlled way," he said.

"By whom," I asked.

"By friends. By those whose job it is to protect them," was all he would say. "Do you think all the big-shots got religion and are faithful to their wives? No way," he said. "You do not see one of these guys get caught picking up a hooker because they do not have to anymore."

> **Daniel McTeague:** *"What the hell's the matter with you? Do you not care about this hotel's reputation? You know, there is an old man shacked up in this hotel with a very young girl."*
> **Hotel Clerk:** *"Sir, most of these rooms have old men with young girls. This is Washington."*
> **– GREEDY**
> Universal Pictures

The client never wanted to talk about the topic again even though twice I tried to get him to do so.

* * *

I can tell you that – based on my research – it takes only a few choices or events before one might find themselves working in Washington's escort world or a similar one. No one ever told me they had aspired to being an escort when they were younger. I probably would not have believed them if they had.

Something in their past seemed to haunt each of them. It was this "something" that brought most who escorted to the point where spending time with strangers for money seemed a natural thing to do.

Escorting is not up there on the list of "What I Want to be When I Grow Up," not like being a beauty queen, a fireman, a law clerk or even a journalist. Yet, while in Washington, I met at least one of each of these types of people who had achieved their dream occupation and, for one reason or another, became an escort.

Since being back in Kentucky, I have chatted online with lots of ordinary people who are willing to "entertain" if you are willing to pay.

All are someone's son or daughter, perhaps even yours. Maybe he is the guy at the grocery, you know, the cute one; maybe she is the checkout clerk at the neighborhood pharmacy, you know, the one with the great smile.

One friend of a friend "entertained" gentlemen in Lexington for a few months. While working, the girl said she arrived at the client's home and just "danced," sometimes clothed and sometimes not. She says she once earned $800 for letting a Lexington man "suck her toes." I do not question that the man paid her for the encounter but I am suspect of the amount.

A friend I chat with online says a local man "gave" him $300 for a brief "encounter." Both "met" people via their MySpace pages. Both are yet to acknowledge what they did was escorting. They are not alone.

Many find the word "entertaining" more acceptable than escorting. The truth is, that, in this case, the different words have the same meaning.

An unscientific survey of those offering to "entertain" in Lexington found that female escorts charge between $150 and $300 for a "visit" while gay men generally charge between $50 to $100. As with any commodity, some "providers" charge less, some demand a lot more.

* * *

PERSONAL THOUGHTS: Is it possible for someone to run a gay male escort service with dignity, with integrity? I tried hard to do just that. John Steinbeck, in *Cannery Row,* shows us that it is possible for someone to run a whorehouse with honor.

A former student at Monterey Peninsula College in Monterey, California, wrote in an essay, that Dora (madam and working girl in Cannery Row's whorehouse): "is a great lady who has true human qualities because she does various things without considering virtue or vice."

Steinbeck illustrates Dora's goodness by showing her generosity and philanthropic mind.

The essay – *The True Message Of Cannery Row* – observes: "While some people who know (Dora) for her true kindness respect her, others hate her because of what she does. *Cannery Row* shows that even whorehouses, which are considered outcasts of society, can be places of benevolence and real human importance even more so than others."

Dora's operation and Capital City Boys' were a lot alike. Dora's motivations and mine were also a lot alike.

While I never connected any great association between *Cannery Row* and *Mack And The Boys* until wrapping up my writing and watching the movie yet again, I cannot deny there is an amazing correlation.

We meet Fauna in *Sweet Thursday*, Steinbeck's sequel to *Cannery Row*. She has come to run the whorehouse after Dora died. We are told that Fauna came to Cannery Row from San Francisco, where she had run a midnight mission.

"She didn't find her new profession very different from her old," Steinbeck tells us. "She thought of both as a public service." He also tells us: "Fauna regarded marriage with a benevolent eye. Not only was it a desirable social condition, but it sent her some of her best customers."

"Hello, It's Me"
Todd Rundgren
Peaked at #5 in 1973

I have loved music since I was a kid trying to figure out who I was and what life was all about.

When I first saw the movie "American Hot Wax" and heard Louise tell noted disc jockey Alan Freed, "I never had anything till I found the music," I knew exactly what she meant. The same was true for me.

Life is a rock but the radio rolled me.
Gotta turn it up louder, so my DJ told me.
Life is a rock but the radio rolled me.
At the end of my rainbow lies a golden oldie.
– LIFE IS A ROCK
BUT THE RADIO ROLLED ME
Artist: Reunion
Songwriters: P. DiFranco/N. Dolph
Crushing Music Co. (BMI)

Sitting in my bedroom, with the door closed and my two stepbrothers off somewhere, I often escaped into the world of rock 'n' roll music in the early and mid-'60s via Louisville's WAKY – one of America's premier rock stations at the time.

The songs I listened to taught me how others felt and how they coped with life's problems – problems I knew I too would

---

face. Songs gave me a lyrical roadmap to coping with life, love, and relationships.

I remember borrowing cassette tapes belonging to my future brother-in-law and listening to the great Gene Pitney sing "It Hurts To Be in Love," "I'm Gonna Be Strong" and "Twenty Four Hours From Tulsa."

I learned so much from Pitney's music other great artists like him – messages like the one in Tony Orlando and Dawn's hit song about how sometimes love disappears, *"slips right through your hands like summer sand."*

I love the imagery "Summer Sand" prompts. Couldn't you visualize sand slipping through someone's hands? Sure you could. That is the visual impact music has on many of us, part of the magic that helps us relate to others and events in our own lives.

* * *

My first "romantic" experience happened when I was in the fourth grade, just before Christmas break. When we went back to school, a girl I liked a lot did not return. She and her family moved away while school was out. I remember being sad that I would never be able to tell her how much I liked her and maybe learn she had liked me too.

Listening to the radio, I found – in the lyrics of the Cascade's one-hit-wonder "Rhythm Of The Rain" – that someone else knew exactly how I felt. It was through their words I found a way to express what I felt. I was comforted knowing that someone else had experienced the same hurt before me. They had survived, I would too.

I also remember having a candid conversation one summer day with my father about the divorce that broke up our family. The conversation took place during one of my annual weeklong visits with him. It was the deepest conversation we ever had – one that answered a couple of the dozens of questions I had for him.

Sitting in a restaurant in the small town where I was born and he still lived, my father told me there were a lot of things a kid my age would not understand – things I would better understand when I was older. He said he wanted me to know he loved my sister and me. He also said that he still loved our mother, something I had never heard him say before.

Then he told me about his favorite song. He said the song spoke to him because it conveyed a hope he had – the hope he and

The town (2006) where I was born and my dad lived.

my mother would somehow get back together.

He gave me a coin and told me to go over to the jukebox and to play Johnny Horton's "North To Alaska." I did. The two of us sat there – silent as the song played and I learned my father's innermost feelings.

Through the lyrics of the song, my father told me things about himself that, for whatever reason, he was unable to say himself, things like he was "*a lonely, lonely man*" and that sometimes "*a true love is so hard to find.*"

My father and I never connected like that again. He died a few years later as I neared the age where I would be old enough to ask questions – questions that usually would have started with: "Why?"

The artists who wrote lyrics included in this project gave this struggling teen a way to relate, gave me a way to express my feelings. Through their words, I connected to the world. I still do. Maybe you do too.

It is through words that we see into other people's hearts, and sometimes, our own. I credit music with helping create the best parts of who I am. For me, music has been both a teacher and a therapist. The songs I listened to taught me to respect the feelings, diversity, and plight of others. It is a lesson I live every day.

* * *

So, just who am I, and why do I feel compelled to tell you about Mack and the boys? I am a fairly shy person. That will come as a surprise to most who have ever met me. I do not seek the spotlight – never have, do not expect to in the future after the dust created by this investigation settles.

I have never been afraid to lead a group or to speak in public or to stand my ground. I am, however, shy about talking about myself and my personal life. I am not ashamed of who I am or what I have done, though candidly, long ago, I was.

I am a liberal-minded conservative white male who grew up in Central Kentucky. I was married for almost 10 years to a wonderful woman – at least, she was before we got married – but that's another story, perhaps for another time.

We have a great son. He has known since he was young that I never demanded perfection from him. He has also known he should not expect perfection from me either. It is an understanding the two of us have had for a long time, one that has served both of us well.

My son has known for most of his life that I demand just one thing from him – the truth, the absolute truth. Being a journalist, I have always dealt with the truth. I have little regard for those who don't.

Knowing neither of us is perfect – and always telling the truth – has helped my son and me get through rough times but never as tough as when I confided in him the dark secret about what I was doing in Washington and why I kept going there.

* * *

Lexington is a university town proud of its Southern heritage but equally proud of its Northern ways. It is also a "polite" town. Polite in that "proper folks" would never become involved in such a sordid activity as visiting a whorehouse or hiring an escort or hooker – at least few would ever admit it.

The same is true for some about being gay, though once a year – on the first Saturday in May – the entire Commonwealth stands up and proudly proclaims that all Kentuckians are homosexuals. We do this on worldwide TV just before the running of the Kentucky Derby. We do this while singing our state song and, describing what Kentucky is like, boldly declare *"the people are gay."*

* * *

One of Lexington's best-known historical residents is the legendary Madam Belle Brezing (1860-1940). Margaret Mitchell is said to have patterned her Belle Watling character in *Gone With the Wind,* after Brezing. Brezing ran a local "establishment." In this case, "establishment" is polite for whorehouse. Anytime there is an excuse to mention her in print, the *Herald-Leader* does so. Readers enjoy hearing such stories.

Jim Jordan, one of the *Herald-Leader's* best reporters, led his "The Buzz" column once with news that a woman had spent $4,500 "for a real if-it could-talk relic" from Brezing's home. Jordan wrote that the bed didn't come from Brezing's bedroom but from a guest room. He also wrote that after the excitement of the moment faded, the woman realized she had a problem – she didn't have a bedroom to put it in.

Other items also were sold at the auction though there was no proof they actually had any connection to Brezing's home. Someone even paid $5 for a brick.

* * *

I was in the first grade when the 1960 presidential election was held. I wanted Richard Nixon to win but do not remember why. My mother and her family were dedicated Republicans. I suspect my father and his family were Democrats, though I do not remember ever hearing any of them talk about politics. My father must have been a Democrat – he carried a card in his wallet that read: "I'll kiss your elephant, if you'll kiss my ass."

I passed the card along to my son. It seemed fitting since he is registered as a Democrat. For the record, most of the escorts who worked with Capital City Boys were Republicans.

Like a lot of Americans, I fell asleep watching the 1960 election returns. I remember being disappointed the next morning when my mother told me Nixon had lost. "Somebody ought to go (to Washington) and straighten those people out," I said.

It took years but when I finally got to Washington, it was not to straighten anyone out or to "out" anyone.

* * *

It is wrong to say I grew up lonely. It is wrong but accurate. I was the second-oldest of six kids in a yours, mine, and ours family.

I had lots of friends, and we had great times but I also kept to myself a lot. I had a best friend – Michael – but we lived in two different worlds. He was an only child; I had two sisters and three brothers. His family seemingly had lots of money; we had little. I went to church; he did not.

It also did not help that my family moved from one side of

Lexington to the other just as I was entering high school. Almost all of my friends went on to Lafayette High while I transferred to Bryan Station High. My friends, my peers, my support system, were taken away from me.

Jackie Paper had "Puff, the Magic Dragon" to escape with. I had great "friends" who visited with me via my radio. Radio personalities and music became my best friends. Literally, they were the only friends during my childhood and early teen years that I was able to keep.

Daily, I escaped into the world of rock 'n' roll music and its wonderful lyrics via WAKY – "790 on your radio dial. Broadcasting live from our studios in downtown Louisville."

There was Bill Bailey – "The Duke of Louisville" – the best radio personality I have ever had the pleasure of hearing. WAKY also had Johnny Randolph, Coyote Calhoun, Tim Tyler and others whose names now escape me.

Back then, I knew all their names and routines by heart. I knew because I imitated their on-air performances in the privacy of my bedroom. I dreamed of being there at the radio station with them. I secretly dreamed of being one of them.

These disc jockeys were my closest friends, though we never met, and there was no way any of them knew I even existed. Why listen to a radio station 90 miles away in another market? WAKY was that good. Why did I always dread dusk coming? Because WAKY was an AM station and the FCC required that it power down its transmitter at dark.

I'd sit alone and watch your light,
my only friend through teenage nights.
And everything I had to know,
I heard it on my radio.
– RADIO GA GA
Artist: Queen
Songwriter: Roger Taylor
Beechwood Music Corp (BMI)

Tragically, WAKY – the great one from my youth – ceased to exist in the 1980s. The station that meant so much to me and others was converted into one that played office music.

If you want hear what WAKY was like check out this tribute:
www.reelradio.com/jq/index.html#wakyremembered

Blasted government. How could the government allow this tragedy to happen? Didn't they know WAKY was important to me and thousands of others like me including future rocker John Mellencamp? Didn't they know that WAKY had played such an important role in who I was and who I would be the rest of my life?

Where was the freaking FCC, and what happened to its mandate of broadcasting in the public's interest? How could they allow this to happen? Somebody ought to go to Washington and straighten out those politicians.

* * *

OK, we have not directly talked about one thing you might be wondering about – am I straight or am I gay? You think you know? Well, you are probably wrong.

What makes one gay? Is it one encounter with another man? Is it two, or ten?

In the movie "In & Out," Kevin Kline's character – Howard Brackett – plays an audio tape to determine if he is gay or straight. He convinces himself he is straight until the voice on the tape tells him to resist the temptation to dance. Unwilling to resist, Kline's character breaks down and dances. From that point on, he knows he is gay.

In the movie "Billy's Hollywood Screen Kiss," Sean P. Hayes' character, Billy, says you can tell if someone is gay by his sense of fashion being years ahead of that of straights.

My former father-in-law, a nice man I respect very much, has a stronger opinion. "A priest who likes to suck on a d**k may be a priest but he's still a co*****er."

When once asked "Are you gay?" by an attorney handling a case related to this project for me, I answered, "No, I am not." My answer was accurate but not the absolute truth. I answered "no" because I'm bisexual, not gay. I know, it is a hell of a distinction.

Andrew, a character on television's "Desperate Housewives," handled this issue very well when asked by his family's minister if he was gay or straight. Andrew answered something like: "I like vanilla ice cream but every once in a while, I might also want to try chocolate." Simply put, that is me.

* * *

My mother, like lots of other people, was frightened by gays, maybe by a fear that I might be. My mother once caught me and a boy who lived down the street comparing certain body parts. We must have been five at the time. Had my mother caught me the day before, she would have found me with the girl next door, doing the exact same thing.

In the 1960s, it was commonly thought that being gay was a medical condition, a sickness. We now know that is not true. Still, those who are gay are considered to be "different" by many.

The image problem gays have suffered is partly the fault of the gay community itself – the fault of a lot of people like me who are afraid or hesitant to be identified as being gay.

For years, society has seen only the radical side of the gay community. Society's perception of gays was formed by what people saw on television or newspapers, mainly the extreme elements in gay parades.

Many are afraid to come forward because they know there will be a price to pay for telling the truth, for accepting themselves for who they really are. We know there is a price because we have seen others pay it. Ask former Rep. Mark Foley or Sen. Larry Craig. Ask the thousands of others who are gay but never chased teenage boys or tapped their toes in airport bathrooms.

In Lexington, one serious mayoral candidate torpedoed his campaign in 2002 by not showing up for a debate just before election day. It was widely rumored that someone was going to ask if he were gay. Many believe the decision not to appear cost him the election.

TV shows like "Will & Grace" have gone a long way to educate the public about the majority of gays with the characters Will and Jack. These were guys most would be proud to introduce as their friends. "Will & Grace" and other shows with "mainstream" gay characters changed how the public viewed gays and, in my opinion, helped open cultural doors.

Growing up in Lexington in the 1960s, I did not know a lot about gay men. The only gay man I knew anything about was a black man who would sometimes walk by my family's home on his way to see a man who lived down the street.

I do not remember much about him other than he seemed tall, had a soft voice, a gentle smile, and always wore a white shirt. I knew the man was gay because my parents told me he was. My parents usually talked about him in hushed tones because he was gay, because of his unusual name – Sweet Evening Breeze – and because it was rumored he was a hermaphrodite. Talk about eye-opening dinner-table conversation.

It would be years before I learned more about Sweet Evening Breeze, including that his real name was James Herndon.

For most of his life, Herndon worked at a local hospital. He was taken to the hospital for an eye injury as a child and was abandoned there. He later became an orderly and excelled at his job.

It is widely reported that after hours, Herndon often wore makeup and occasionally performed or appeared in drag on Main Street on Saturdays. Reports also claim Herndon had a "running mate" named Tripping Through the Dew. Lexington may be conservative at heart but, we have had some very colorful characters.

Herndon died in 1983 at age 91. When he died, he left his money to charity and his body to the University of Kentucky for scientific study.

I later worked with and became friends with the man whom Sweet Evening Breeze came to visit on my street. We worked together at the *Herald-Leader.*

Writing this passage, I realized I could document for history whether or not Herndon was a gay man, a transgendered person, or a hermaphrodite by asking my friend. I could but friends do not ask such questions, at least I don't. Besides, at the end of day, what does it matter? A lady has a right to keep some things secret, even a lady like Sweet Evening Breeze.

The only other person I thought might be gay – and it was never really confirmed – was Mr. Humphries on the British comedy "Are You Being Served?" The show came on our PBS station. I cannot tell you how many weekend nights I spent laughing at Mr. Humphries and those other marvelous actors. Gay or otherwise, Mr. Humphries was a class act.

Finally, I remember hearing my mother talking about actor Rock Hudson having once come to Lexington to film a movie. My mother talked about things she had heard and read.

It was not until later – while a student at Eastern Kentucky University – that I heard other stories about Hudson's visit. I heard from other students that Hudson was gay and while in the area had come to Eastern "cruising for gay sex."

I did not put a lot of stock into that story until Hudson, dying of AIDS, came forward to educate mainstream America about this horrible disease. May God forever bless actress Doris Day for standing there with Hudson, her friend and frequent co-star.

Those of us who live in Lexington were reminded about Hudson when the *Herald-Leader* published a Page One article saying *The Advocate* (a gay magazine) had ranked Lexington as being one of the 10-best places in America for gays and lesbians to live.

The March 27, 2007, issue of *The Advocate* ranked Lexington in fifth place, between Ithaca, N.Y., and Missoula, Mont.

Bob Morgan, was interviewed and quoted in the magazine article. Morgan told Andy Mead, another great *Herald-Leader* reporter, that Lexington has long been a magnet for young gay people from rural Kentucky. Now, Morgan says, it is attracting gays from larger cities.

Morgan, identified as being a local gay historian, told *The Advocate,* "Lexington has always considered itself a bastion of liberal culture. Young gay people now feel a sense of entitlement to prance the streets of Lexington," he says. "Or to be just as boring as heterosexuals."

Asked by the *Herald-Leader* to comment on the ranking, Lexington Mayor Jim Newberry issued a statement saying Lexington offers "something for everyone."

I know Newberry. You could say I work for him. I am a public information officer for the Lexington-Fayette Urban County Government. I often photograph the mayor at news conferences and major events. I then place his picture on the city's Web site. The mayor is a good man whom many suspect has his eye on a higher office. It is likely he will get there.

The ink is black.
The page is white.
Together we learn
to read and write
– BLACK AND WHITE
Artist: Three Dog Night
Songwriters: D. Arkin/E. Robinson
Templeton Publishing Company (ASCAP)

You have come to know how important music has been in my life and how I often use lyrics to convey what I feel. You may have already guessed that every segment in this project is the title of a song that has some special meaning to that segment and to me.

HBO's great hit "Arliss" did much the same thing. At the end of each show, a song always played that either captured what the episode was about or made fun of it.

For example, in the episode *The Art of Give and Take,* Arliss Michaels returns to his hometown where he is known as "Runaway Michaels" to redeem himself. True to the nature of the show, what Michaels claims greatly conflicts with reality. In this case, while boasting how charitable he is, Arliss gets a call telling him the money he is donating has already been given to another cause.

Realizing he is going to have to cover the donation himself, Arliss grabs the larger-than-life check and streaks across the ball field, once again running away from an awkward situation there. In the background, we hear Del Shannon's great hit "Runaway."

And so it is with the greatest of admiration of Robert Wuhl and the other writers of "Arliss" that I shamelessly adapt their tagline to introduce you to the heart and soul of *Mack And The Boys:*

My name is Mack.

I represented gay escorts.

These are our stories.

Remember when the music
brought us all together to stand inside the rain.
And as we'd join our hands, we'd meet in the refrain,
for we had dreams to live, we had hopes to give.
– REMEMBER WHEN THE MUSIC
Singer/songwriter: Harry Chapin
Chapin Music (ASCAP)

The Backstory

On Friday May 11, 2007, a new WAKY re-launched on 103.5 FM to the tune of the "Purple People Eater," the same song the great Louisville station played for 24 hours straight when it went live. The new WAKY covers North Central Kentucky & Southern Indiana. **www.waky1035.com**

"Society's Child"
Janis Ian
Peaked at #14 in 1966

When I opened my hotel door to Sean in Washington that night, I had no idea I would become a part of Washington's escort world or what being a part of that world would involve or require of me.

For all of the good and bad of the experience, I sometimes think I was born to live this story. In a crazy, mixed-up way, my being the man behind the curtain – even for a little while – makes perfect sense.

I have long felt comfortable being around less-than-perfect people – those society looks down on for one reason or another. I guess I take comfort in being around those most like myself.

I learned my first lesson in blind acceptance of others while in grade school.

On picture day one year I was chosen to sit in a chair up front because I was so well liked. I remember being embarrassed by what should have been an honor. With six kids, there was not a lot of money for new clothes after school started. That day I had worn a pair of jeans, the knees were torn from where I had played in them. When the class picture came back, my worse fear came to pass: My hands were desperately trying to hide the tears, to little avail.

The image of that kid trying to hide his shame is forever etched into my mind. There was nothing I could do about getting new jeans.

Blind acceptance lesson number one: Judge others only by what they can control, not by things they can't. It was a powerful lesson for me to learn. It was the first of many.

In junior high, the bus I rode to school made one stop on the way from our subdivision to school – in front of a battered house trailer. A modest-looking girl would get on, and then we would travel on to school. In the afternoon, the route was reversed and she would be the first one off.

Some on the bus made fun of where the girl lived because it was so different from our homes. I remember thinking how hurt the girl would be if she knew what others were saying behind her back. I knew how it would hurt her. I knew because I, too, had felt that kind of pain.

Being a child of divorced parents in the early 1960s taught me a great deal about the pain caused by what others sometime say or think. More than once, I overheard someone say, "Oh, Malcolm? He's from a broken home ..."

I hated hearing those words. Did my parents being divorced make me strange? Did it make me different? It must have, because others seemed to think so. I kept wondering why I was being branded with a label for something I had no control over.

One summer, there was a plane show at our local airport. I saw a friend from school there and he hung out with me for a while. Eventually, my mother openly suggested I try to get rid of my friend because people might wonder why he was with us. My friend was black. My mother's suggestion hurt both of us.

Singer/songwriter Janis Ian put into words what one teen felt when her mother told her she could not see someone because he was "different" from them.

The haunting lyrics of Ian's "Society's Child" conveyed how I felt about people judging others for something they had no control over – in this case, skin color. In the song, a white girl is talking to a black classmate who has come to visit her and about her mother's reaction:

> *Now I could understand*
> *your tears and your shame,*
> *she called you boy instead of your name,*
> *when she wouldn't let you inside,*
> *when she turned and said,*
> *"But honey, he's not our kind."*

Listening to "Society's Child" on WAKY, I had no idea that years later, the song about prejudice would take on a totally different – but just as important – meaning in my own life.

The shame of torn pants, knowing what others had said about that girl on the bus, being from a "broken home," and having to distance myself from my black friend taught me early the importance of blind acceptance and tolerance.

I promised myself that I would never judge someone because of their skin color, their beliefs, or other things they had no control over – things like being from a divorced family or being gay.

* * *

I must have been 10 or 11 when my stepfather, a good man, taught my stepbrothers and me to plow, plant, hoe and harvest corn and tomatoes from our two-acre garden. He also taught us how to sell the vegetables door-to-door.

In the fall, we would grow turnips and greens. On Saturdays, my stepfather would take us downtown into predominantly black neighborhoods where the potential to sell was greatest.

I knocked on the doors of shotgun houses and in Lexington's oldest housing project – a placed called Bluegrass-Aspendale. Most who opened their doors to me were polite and appreciated that I offered them the chance to buy fresh turnips and greens.

Selling door-to-door taught me a lot about people and has forever changed the way I judge people and events.

When a door was opened I could not help but see inside. Some of the shotgun houses and those in the government housing project were the cleanest I have ever seen – as a child or an adult. Naturally, there were also some at the other end of the spectrum.

The lesson I learned was, in most cases, the person who lived in the house had a lot to do with determining what the home would be like, not the place itself. The same is true in life. While we might not be able to determine the color of our skin or sexual orientation, we still have a lot of control over the person we are.

Had my stepfather not insisted on us raising those gardens, had he not taken us into those downtown neighborhoods, I never would have had this important, life-changing experience.

Like my own father, my stepfather had a drinking problem and, when he drank, he became a different person.

In junior high, I was once summoned to the office to take an emergency phone call.

"(Deleted) is drunk and threatening to beat you up when you get off the bus," my mother whispered to me. "Don't get off here. Go to the other end of the street."

What she did not tell me was that my stepfather had kicked in the rear panel of the side of my mother's car. She had bought it the day before. The sticker was still on the window.

That night, unable to safely sleep in our own home, my

mother, my two sisters and my youngest brother took refuge in the home of one of my mother's friends. We returned home when the drinking stopped and the immediate threat went away.

My mother and I became extremely light sleepers – we had to, our survival depended upon it. Multiple times my stepfather openly boasted that one night he would slip upstairs and kill either my mother or me or both of us.

Night after night, my mother and I fell asleep listening in the dark for a creaking stair – she in her room, I in mine.

Twice more we fled our home, fearing for our lives.

The last time I fled, my stepfather ordered one of my stepbrothers to go upstairs and get his rifle so he could shoot us. On this night – for the first time – my stepbrother complied and went upstairs. We left the house as he started back down, something dark in his hand.

I moved out of the house a short time later, having scraped together enough money to pay $175 a month for a furnished apartment on Lexington's north end. The next time my family had to flee, they came to my home. I never told my stepfather or stepbrothers where my apartment was. It was better for all of us that way.

Blind acceptance demands I recognize both parts of my stepfather, especially since the good in him far outweighed the bad.

I became able to slice his actions and my feelings for him into sections, much the way a customer might have sliced one of the tomatoes I had sold them. Just because one can't eat parts of a tomato does not mean the rest of it is worthless or needs to be thrown away. The same is true about people.

I have been able to "slice" things and people's behaviors ever since. This ability may explain why I look at my role in this project differently than some, perhaps, differently than you.

I continue to think kindly about my stepfather but have had little to do with him since the day I signed for that apartment.

The hurt of those threats; the need to flee the safety of our home; the shame of explaining why I was not living at home at times to friends; the listening for a creaking stair, all came with a high price.

It still does. That is why it is best not to be around me if Martina McBride's "Independence Day" comes on the radio. It is a sure bet I will go deathly silent as I relive what I have just shared with you.

No other memory of my life prompts as deep a reaction. My son experienced this once when he came to visit me in Washington. Driving up 16th Street in Northwest D.C., "Independence Day" came on the radio. I went quiet as memories of the abuse flooded my brain.

Unaware of what reaction I have to the song, my son continued to talk and asked me questions that I ignored.

Feeling that he was trampling on something sacred to me, I eventually yelled for him to shut up until the song was over. He had never seen me act that way – before or since.

Now he, and you, know why.

My teachers all laugh, their smirking stares,
Cutting deep down in our affairs.
Preachers of equality,
Think they believe it, then why won't they just let us be?

Society has long considered those who are gay, lesbian, bisexual or transgendered "different."

Once openly considered as "deviants," gays have become more accepted – some might even say fashionable to have around – since this project started in 1998.

"Over the latter part of the last century, homosexuals came 'out of the shadows' and entered into mainstream society through aggressive discourse," Dr. Maurice J. Smith says.

Dr. Smith says gays made these advances by challenging gender-biased laws and demanding equal rights and benefits. "This entrance on the social stage was immediately challenged by numerous special interests from the religious right to the military."

Dr. Smith says the AIDS epidemic was also used to suppress the entire gay community.

"The religious right broadened their deviant and disease spreading labels to encompass anyone who was a homosexual, irrespective of whether or not they were an escort or simply ill," Dr. Smith says. "This began a national, if not worldwide suppression of the homosexual community and created a bulwark to begin staving off legal advancements made by the homosexual community, and in many instances, reversing them."

Dr. Smith says the religious right was joined by the

establishment, primarily because of their power as a voting bloc.

"The establishment elements that should have moved with the times and overcome clear bias and prejudice, ignored the advice of most mental health professionals, sociologists, anthropologists, etc., and continued previous programs which marginalized all homosexuals.

"Several attempts have been made by the gay community to overcome their marginalization, with limited results," Dr. Smith says.

"Gay integration of the military failed, although clearly based on the same arguments used 50 years earlier to marginalize African-Americans from the same military privileges."

Keith Olbermann, host of MSNBC's "Countdown" show, illustrated this point perfectly on August 5, 2008.

Olbermann, citing a *Christian Science Monitor* report, said a shortage of Arabic and other Middle Eastern language translators was so severe that the Army was offering bonuses of up to $150,000 to those who stay in the service or sign up to join it.

Olbermann said the Army was paying the bonuses while having fired more than 300 gay Arabic translators, a move, Olbermann says, that could ultimately cost $45 million.

"We're kicking out Arabic translators who want to stay, while we're offering $150,000 to the ones who want to leave," Olbermann said.

"The only possible conclusion is ... the U.S. military, the presidential administration and our nation as a whole are officially more afraid of American gays than of Middle East terrorists."

* * *

Dr. Smith says gays continue to be "marginalized" but thinks attitudes and even society itself may be changing. "Slowly, gays are assimilating into the mainstream society. Gentrification of neighborhoods across the country is usually led by gays as they move into renewed communities and out of the self-imposed ghettos they created.

"Gay bars are closing by the hundreds as standard dating habits and gay escorting has moved to the Internet, eliminating the need to meet at public locations," Dr. Smith says. "This has limited the need for gays to have clandestine contacts in 'cruising' areas in public spaces which so unnerved the establishment and their law enforcement."

Dr. Smith says the Internet allows gay escorts to conduct their business without drawing public attention.

Dr. Smith says he, and most professionals, believe greater acceptance of the gay community will happen on two fronts: "First, through continued 'de-ghettoization' and Internet social networking. Second, and perhaps the challenge for all gays," Dr. Smith says, is the continuing need for the "closeted" gays to come out.

"National figures in entertainment, sports and politics who have come out either voluntarily or by being 'outed' have done more to advance normalization of the relationship of the gay population to the establishment than any other single factor," Dr. Smith says. "This applies to all role models.

"Gays must continue the pressure on their population to reveal their sexuality without reserve. It has long been suspected that the Masters and Johnston study that revealed a 10 percent population of homosexuals in society was simply a gross underestimation due to the sampling technique used."

Dr. Smith says the addition of the natural, anthropological evolution of masculine characteristics with women and feminine characteristics with men – the new "metrosexuality" combined with the acceptance of same-sex intimacy, regardless of gender identity – will cause society to evolve and change its outlook on gays and lesbians and, in the process, resolve the problem in the long term.

* * *

PERSONAL THOUGHTS: Society has come a long way in accepting gays but people still lose jobs and miss getting promoted because they are "different."

The kid with torn pants and from the broken home learned early the pain of being considered "different." It was a lesson he never wanted to repeat.

"Different" is not a code word for someone being gay. "Different" includes those who are physically or mentally challenged, or those at certain economic or social levels. "Different" also includes other standards of measurement like being overweight or too thin, or even how one dresses or talks.

There are thousands of people society considers "different," including people you know, people who dream of being thought of as "normal" or "ordinary."

In order to receive blind acceptance from others, you must give it. I practiced blind acceptance for years, not knowing my biggest need for blind acceptance was yet to come.

Growing up, the ending of Janis Ian's "Society's Child" gave the "flawed" me strength and courage to hold on for a day yet to come. It still does.

One of these days
I'm gonna stop my listening,
gonna raise my head up high.
One of these days I'm gonna raise up
my glistening wings and fly.
But that day will have to wait for a while,
baby, I'm only society's child.
When we're older, things may change,
but for now this is the way
they must remain.

The Backstory

"Society's Child" (Baby I've Been Thinking) was written by Janis Ian (seen at right). Ian was 13 when she began working on this, 14 when she finished, and 15 when the song became a hit.

"Society's Child" was published by Taosongs Two (BMI) and produced by the great '60s music storyteller Shadow Morton.

Working with her to obtain the right to use "Society's Child" lyrics, Ian came across as a very caring, generous person. A few months later, when I met her, I found out my initial assessment was correct.

Ian released her autobiography *Society's Child* in late July 2008. Buy the book. Buy the music CD "Best of Janis Ian, The Autobiography Collection." You will love both.

Here's wishing Ian continued success! And if you are fortunate eough to be close to one of her concerts, go and enjoy yourself.
www.janisian.com

"You Only Live Twice"
(Once for yourself and once for your dreams)
Nancy Sinatra
Peaked at #44 in 1967

People almost always seem puzzled when I boast that I am one of the few men who ever went into one of Lexington's strip clubs and came out with more money in his pocket than when he went inside. It was true. I owned an upholstery company, and Lexington's premier strip club was a client of ours. We reupholstered chairs and repaired couches damaged during lap dances.

Dropping off repaired furniture, I was amazed to see women kissing husbands, boyfriends, and babies goodbye in the parking lot and then going in the side door to go to work. I remember thinking what an interesting story one could write about those women and the lives they led.

* * *

Sean and I kept in touch through e-mails and long-distance telephone calls. I wanted to know more about escorting. I asked Sean questions and he told me stories. Sean told me – in great detail – about escort calls he had gone on while working for The Agency, Tops Referrals, and Dreamboys. He told me about clients and other escorts. He also told me about those who owned and ran the services.

I was amazed with the stories he told. I was convinced others would be too. As a journalist, I had been trained to find stories that appeal to readers. I was good at this.

In 1998, when I met Sean, I was the Internet news editor at what is now kentucky.com, having transferred from the newsroom at the *Lexington Herald-Leader.* Internet traffic on the site grew considerably under my stewardship.

Like most online news services, Kentucky Connect pulled reports showing what articles attracted the most traffic on our site. Articles about University of Kentucky basketball always fared well.

The reports also showed articles about sex or someone's sexual activities kept spiking off the chart. I mentioned this once in a manager's meeting. My bosses laughed that our readers were obsessed with reading about sex. The same readership pattern was true nationally.

My bosses were a bit puzzled when, during a slow time on January, I assigned my fledgling news staff to do new, original reporting on the 1959 plane crash that killed rock 'n' roll stars Buddy Holly, J.P. Richardson, and Ritchie Valens.

One editor questioned why anyone in Lexington would be interested in reading such a project. The answer was simple – in Lexington, few probably would be. But my audience was not limited to Lexington – my audience was worldwide – anyone anywhere could access our reporting.

An Internet news operation can serve niche audiences as well as broad-based ones.

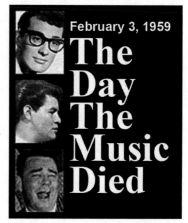

February 3, 1959

The Day The Music Died

It was never my idea to glorify the crash's 38th anniversary. I saw an opportunity to give my staff a live, deadline-driven training exercise on a national story.

The story also had a major Lexington connection that had never been reported. Bob Hale, the disc jockey who emceed the show and tossed the coin that put Valens on the plane had worked in Lexington as a TV anchor. Many in Lexington remembered Hale but did not know about his connection to the crash.

My story on Hale ran in the *Herald-Leader* and teased to our *February 3, 1959: The Day the Music Died* online package. The report, hastily put together but well-documented, was an Internet hit. Search engines found our project and linked to it.

Online readers came from around the world. Traffic was way up that week. The increased traffic pleased my bosses. Such things always did.

Our project came to be recognized as an authoritative source of information about the crash. People writing books and articles on the crash called or e-mailed us. Someone called wanting information for a one-hour segment on the crash for VH1's

---

"Behind the Music" series.

One great thing about a news project on the Internet is that you can launch it today and continue to develop it over time. I saw our project as a good start for reporting on the crash's 40th anniversary. We had two years to expand our package and strengthen our standing as the #1 online source about the crash.

Despite the spike in traffic and interest the project had generated, my bosses turned down my request to update the series the following year.

They quickly changed their minds, however, when a former *Herald-Leader* employee working in Washington sent an article from *The Washington Post* in which the *Post* recommended its readers check out our project. I was asked to scramble and update the series "somehow."

> **Lenny Richfield:** *"This thing about Buddy Holly, you know, I knew Buddy. We played pool together. In fact, he still owes me money. You gotta remember, well, let's face it, he's dead, he's gone."*
>
> **Artie Moress:** *"I know that, man, but his music isn't. Buddy Holly lives. Buddy Holly lives!"*
> **– AMERICAN HOT WAX**
> Paramount Pictures

* * *

I later suggested we do a series on an up-and-coming boy band consisting of two local guys and three from Florida. The group was growing in popularity, and, again, we had a strong local connection. No one else had done a major online report so we could become a major player on the Web.

I researched the band to see if such a project might make sense. I shot video outside of one of their concerts in Louisville. I wrote about the event. I saw how fans, teenage girls and moms alike, reacted.

My news staff was in the process of lining up more video and print interviews when our boss, David Reed, killed the project. "There won't be enough interest," Reed said.

The band – The Backstreet Boys – went on to stardom without us. I later noticed in *USA Today* that one Backstreet Boys Web site was the second or third most-visited site on the Net that particular week. That traffic – at least some of it – could have been ours.

* * *

Reed wanted original reporting for the Web site. His idea of original reporting was writing about a house fire or a bank robbery. Reed would have peed his pants (that's a Southern saying indicating that he was so happy/giddy) if we could have photographed someone being arrested, preferably a local attorney.

We did an extensive report on bourbon and historical road markers in Kentucky. Reed suggested both. Neither got much readership.

My idea of original reporting was much broader: find a topic that interests people and report on it. *February 3, 1959: The Day the Music Died* did just that. People wanted to know more about the crash that killed Holly, Richardson, and Valens.

A report on The Backstreet Boys would have done the same. It too would have drawn viewers from around the world. It would

> "It is the duty of a newspaper to comfort the afflicted and afflict the comfortable."
> – INHERIT THE WIND
> MGM

have enhanced our stature in the online news world – something everyone who worked in the New Media division wanted.

Fascinated by Sean and Jeremy's incredible stories, and knowing online readers' appetites for reading about all things sexual, I believed I had found a story people would want to read.

The Beautiful Stranger whispered to me that people should hear these stories, that I should tell them. I never expected the *Herald-Leader* to run this project, though I knew I would eventually offer it the chance. I did, twice – in 1999 and in again in December 2007.

Sean was to have been the project's tour guide. This project was to have been told through Sean's eyes and words. He was to have taken you deep into the world of gay male escorts. Sean was to tell you about the escorts and the men they met.

Experience had taught me I could not tell Sean about the project or risk missing the real story. If Sean knew I was taking notes and would be writing what he told me, there was a good chance he might filter what he told me to make himself look good and others look either better or worse than they actually were.

* * *

I was open to the idea of widening the scope of the project as I learned more about Washington's escort world. This is normal when investigating projects. Information obtained often leads a reporter to seek information not initially considered.

Sean's story led me to look deeper into the business side. The business side was an area Sean never ventured into but one essential to report this story completely.

Investigating government corruption, the *Philadelphia Inquirer* had two reporters run a bar in their city. The reporters then wrote about what they saw and heard and learned.

This process is called participant observation. Someone – in this case – a writer lives and experiences a culture, a community or a situation and then writes about what he or she saw and learned, giving their perceptions.

I found my story in Washington. I felt it worthy of being investigated and reported – not to uncover corruption but to explain the secret world of gay male escorts to you.

I decided to widen my project by starting and running a legally licensed gay male escort referral service in Washington. Doing so would allow me to learn firsthand what happens behind the scenes in such a company.

I knew working my project had the potential to create serious problems for me. I hoped I could explain my reasoning to my bosses and sell them on the project's merits, after all, I was working on the project totally independent of the paper. That never happened. Just as with the Buddy Holly crash story and the Backstreet Boys project, my bosses never saw the importance and readership appeal I did.

I never imagined it, I never intended for such a thing to happen but fate intervened and made *Mack And The Boys* my story, not Sean's. And, though I had chances to walk away, I chose to remain loyal to this project.

* * *

PERSONAL THOUGHTS: I first fell in love with Nancy Sinatra's "You Only Live Twice" in the summer of 1968. The lyrics were both familiar and enticing to me when the Beautiful Stranger whispered them to me 30 years later, trying to persuade me to tell you about Mack and the boys.

"You only live twice, or so it seems.
One life for yourself,
and one for your dreams."

Fate would soon intervene and force me to choose between being true to the Beautiful Stranger and walking away from most everything I held dear for a once in a lifetime dream.

"This dream is for you, so pay the price.
Make one dream come true,
you only live twice."

The choice was not an easy one, nor should it have been. In the end, the decision came down to doing what was easy or being true to myself. Being true to myself is very important to me. It always has been.

* * *

Did I cross a line I should not have? Did I follow the story too far? Did I allow the opportunity to explore the gay world to cloud my news judgment, or did I just fail at selling the project to my bosses? Late at night, when there is no one around and I am brutally honest with myself, I tell myself all those statements are true.

Thank you, Buddy.
Thank you for the music
and so much more.

The Backstory

"You Only Live Twice" was written by John Barry and Leslie Bricusse. It is published by EMI Unart Catalog (BMI).

"I Only Want To Be With You"
Dusty Springfield
Peaked at #12 in 1964

In order to write properly about Washington's gay community and those who are a part of it, I had to know what that world was like, I had to live in it, I had to be a part of it.

Publicly being part of a gay community was an experience I never had in Lexington. That was mostly a personal choice. I had gay friends and went to public places with them, just not "gay places." In the past, there was a price to be paid if you were gay in Lexington or even if people thought you were. Some will say there still is.

I found Washington's gay community to be very accepting of others. Those I met, invited me into their world, no strings attached. It is not an exaggeration to say that some members of Washington's gay community saved my life.

I liked hanging out with Sean. I liked it a lot. I enjoyed the luxury of "being gay" with him – something I had never really experienced with anyone else. I am not talking about sex. I am talking about doing things and going places – public things in public places.

The topic of conversation at the *Herald-Leader* on many a Monday was "You'll never guess who was seen at The (gay) Bar on Saturday night ..." Some people could not afford to be seen there. As a single father, I was one of them.

In Washington, no one cared where I had been or whom I had been seen out with; no one at work talked about me on Monday mornings. In Washington, I was just another person, I was free to be whomever and whatever I wanted to be. In Washington, I was free to be me.

One young gay male prostitute, a guy named Mike, described the feeling best: "It felt like I was home," he said. Talking further about how comfortable he felt being around other gay men, Mike said, "These people laugh when I laugh. They cry when I cry."

Though we never met, I know exactly how Mike felt. I, too, felt that comfort. My time in Washington gave me a host of memories money cannot buy and time cannot erase.

Jon Weece, senior minister at the Southland Christian Church in Lexington, quoted Mike during a sermon he delivered in late September 2007.

Weece told Mike's story. Weece told us about how the boy was forced from his home onto the streets because he was "different" than what his father wanted him to be – "different" because he was gay.

Weece told us how Mike became a prostitute to survive. I am sure Mike's story was new to many who heard Weece's sermon that morning. It was not new to me. I had heard the same story many times before. The stories I heard came with different names and different details, but they were the same.

I came to know and care deeply about dozens of people just like Mike. You have already met Sean and Jeremy, reading on, you will meet others.

While I never became a card-carrying member of Washington's gay community, I felt welcomed there. I felt I was invited to join in any activity I wanted to but never pressured to do so. As Madonna sang in "Ray Of Light": *"I (felt) like I just got home."*

* * *

I traveled to Washington on June 13, 1998 to interview Sean more formally. I also came to meet a "special" new guy at The Agency that Sean had told me about – a guy named Jonathan.

I asked Jonathan project-related questions during our time together.

"Where's home for you?" I asked. "Kentucky," he said.
"Really? Where in Kentucky?"
"Lexington."

The two of us shared a laugh when I told him I lived there.

Jonathan was known to other escorts in Washington as "Wild Turkey" in honor of a fine whiskey by the same name. Wild Turkey is made in Central Kentucky, not too far from Lexington.

Jonathan left Washington a couple of months after we met. He left after another escort called his mother in Lexington and told her "exactly what her precious son was really doing in D.C."

The call was made, three sources said, after Jonathan repeatedly refused to have sex with the other escort.

Attempts by The Agency to find Jonathan in 1999 and 2000 produced multiple tips that Jonathan had moved to Florida. It also prompted numerous stories from clients who claimed they had met Jonathan during his brief stay in Washington. All were glowing reports, some in far more detail than I cared to know.

The Agency's "Where in the World is Jonathan?" campaign produced an exchange with a man in California claiming to be a close friend of Jonathan's. The man told things I knew to be true – including one unique fact about Jonathan few would know. He also knew Jonathan's real name.

The man shipped me a copy of a gay porno Jonathan starred in – "Brandon's Big Weekend." The man also sent me a picture he claimed was himself with actor Mark Wahlberg. "I'm the old fart on the left," he said.

"I have a close friend (very heavy entertainment guy in Hollywood) named [Deleted]," the man said. "I think that you might have a few models that [Deleted] would like; I'm not his pimp, just (a) close friend.

The man suggested I come to New York for the big-shot's New Year's Eve party. Naturally, I was to bring a couple of my cutest boys with me. We did not go but I later read online that the Hollywood executive was in New York at that time.

* * *

PERSONAL THOUGHTS: Pastor Weece, in his sermon, told how Mike eventually was able to turn his life around. Many of the escorts I met in Washington did the same thing.

Weece told us Mike found God and eventually became a youth minister. Telling a church congregation about his past was the cost of Mike's redemption. Weece says the young man stood before the church and told them everything.

Weece went on to say that at the end of Mike's story a man in the congregation stood up and said he did not think it was fair for the church to have forced Mike to tell his story. The man, Weece said, pointed out that everyone in the church had something in their past just as bad as Mike's.

This project has stories similar to Mike's. *Mack And The Boys* will show you the people I met in Washington are not much different than you or those you care about, just different in names and a few other details.

It is my hope, through the telling of these stories, society can grow to be more understanding, compassionate and accepting of others.

I hope by reading this project you will come to have the courage and conviction to stand up – like that one man – and say, in your own words, that it is wrong to condemn this person or that one because he or she is "different" in one way or another.

That is what blind acceptance and this project is all about.

PREMISE #3

*"If you're going to work in a whorehouse,
then there's only one thing to be –
the best whore in the house."*

– THE BONFIRES OF THE VANITIES
Tom Wolfe

"She Works Hard For The Money"
Donna Summer
Peaked at #3 on Billboard's Hot 100 in 1983

Generally speaking, there are two types of escorts – those who work for an agency like Capital City Boys and independents who work on their own, finding clients online, through friends or, sometimes, on the street.

Those who mainly work the streets – openly looking to have sex with someone for money or drugs – are not called escorts. They are known as prostitutes or sex workers – a distinction those in the escort business are quick to stress.

No one knows how many escorts or sex workers are in Washington, D.C., at any given time – not the police, not the health department, not service agencies that help care for them.

No one knows the exact number because it is impossible to know. Even escort services cannot accurately tell you how many people are working for them at any given time. An escort who was available for work last night may have moved out of the area this morning without telling anyone, even the service he worked with. At the same time, two other escorts may have moved into the District but not yet signed with an agency or posted their availability online.

Then, there are those who escort only when they have a pressing need for money. This group includes college students and others whose ages generally range between 17 and 38. These are the people who lead what the media are fond of calling "a mysterious second life."

"Quite honestly it's almost impossible to ascertain how many

HIPS
Helping Individual Prostitutes Survive

Education
Empowerment
Support

You can learn more about HIPS and make a donation
via their Web site **www.hips.org**

escorts are working in the area without going to all the escort Web sites and paper ads and counting them," Cyndee Clay says. "Then (some) probably have multiple ads and some don't use the Web sites, so it's even harder."

Clay knows Washington's sex industry business very well. She is the executive director of Helping Individual Prostitutes Survive (HIPS), a not-for-profit service agency that assists sex workers in Washington to lead healthy lives.

"We don't even try to estimate the number of individuals trading on the streets in a given night," Clay says.

HIPS works from a non-judgmental harm reduction model, focusing on helping sex workers set goals and reach them to see the change they want to see in their lives, Clay says.

"For some, that is learning to reduce their drug use or work more safely. For some it's transitioning to legal employment or stable housing. For others, it's just the ability to access a supportive listening ear to help counteract the isolation they can feel as sex workers," Clay says.

HIPS makes 7,000 contacts a year with sex workers, mostly those working the streets. HIPS formally serves about 1,500 people a year, Clay says – 30 percent male, 35 percent female and 35 percent transgender women. She estimates that roughly 25 percent of HIPS' clients do both street and Internet work.

"HIPS' work with male escorts is greatly limited," Clay says. "It is a population that we do not have the resources to serve properly."

HIPS often gets referrals from other service agencies "for (gay escorts) in need of assistance." Clay says HIPS has helped male escorts with addressing domestic violence and chaotic drug use.

"Call Me"
Blondie
A #1 hit in 1980

There were three major gay escort referral services operating in Washington when I visited there in March 1998. There were also two or three minor ones offering two or three guys, and independent escorts working on their own.

The most-successful service by far was The Agency, a company owned and run by a man named Troy. Dreamboys and Topps Referral Service were the others. All three services thrived.

The Agency boasted having the best gay escorts in Washington. It was true. The Agency represented quality guys, ages 19 to the mid-30s. The cost for a one-hour session in March 1998 was $150. The service took $50 of that amount, leaving the escort with $100 and any tip he might get.

Tops Referral Service was a bit different from the other two. Its primary customer-base was locals who were looking for certain types who enjoyed more specialized entertaining. It still does.

Dreamboys advertised a host of guys ages 19 to mid-30s. They might have had such guys in the past but by summer 1998, Dreamboys was struggling to find people to send out.

"(Dreamboys' owner) once told me that 'when clients call me they're horny and they'll accept just about anything,'" Marvin, the owner of Tops Referrals, says.

Marvin went on to say, "And if they won't (go through with the call), they have to pay the ($50) cancellation fee, especially people in hotel rooms. I get $25 and the escort gets the other $25 – we both come out ahead."

Dreamboys was still operating under that philosophy but a different owner in 1998 when I visited Washington and later, when I returned to work this project.

Independent escorts were few in early 1998, usually only those brave enough to publish their home phone numbers or those savvy enough to have a pager or an AOL account. Back then, independents often charged somewhere between $50 and $100 an hour less than a service.

"I cannot begin to tell you how many beginners have come here, gotten an education about escorting and then went off on their own," Marvin says.

"There's no school for escorts to go to so they start out with a service, learn (my) tricks and then go out on their own before I can recoup my investment of time and knowledge," Marvin says. "Sometimes, they take clients with them. Either way, I get screwed over."

My "poor" experience with Dreamboys first put the idea that a properly run referral service could succeed into my head. It also made me want to know more about the operational side of Washington's gay male escort business.

Washington's gay male escort community changed a lot during late 1998 and 1999. The same was true for escort services across the country.

The changes came about with the ability for an escort to deal directly with a client and yet remain anonymous. Pagers and cell phones became cheaper and much more common. They also came with numbers that could be changed almost instantly in case a client became a problem. Hot Mail accounts and AOL screen names also let escorts and clients deal one-on-one without either knowing the other's true identity.

Using a referral service offered both clients and escorts great benefits. Services were in business to make money. Unless it was a shady operation, the service worked hard to maintain a good reputation.

That meant the client – within reason – usually got the escort he was expecting. It also meant the escort was professionally represented to clients. The client had someone he could call should there be a problem. There rarely was.

For the escort, working with a service meant someone else handled the prank calls and added levels of safety. Capital City Boys did an initial screening of clients and always knew where the escort had gone, when he arrived and, more important, when he left.

* * *

Several new services opened while I was in Washington. Most closed. When I left Washington in July 2001, Capital City Boys,

The Agency, Tops Referrals and a service called The Firm DC were operating. Two other services, Elite Escorts and Full Service Playhouse, were open at times and closed at others.

The number of independent escorts also grew dramatically. National Web sites promoted independent and agency escorts to viewers – many of them travelers – worldwide.

Independent escorts seemed to find themselves encountering more trouble than those represented by a service. Clients knew they could take certain advantages of an independent that they could not if they had gone through a service.

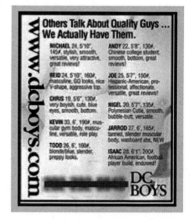

Clients who hired independent escorts often withheld some or all of the fees. "Who is the escort going to call?" a client named David told me. "Odds are good they aren't going to call the police."

One trick often played on independent escorts was to refuse to pay anything, then agree to pay half. The escort, thinking something is better than nothing, takes the reduced amount and leaves, vowing never to return.

* * *

The attacks on September 11, 2001, had a devastating effect on tourism in Washington. Restaurants that were normally packed had available tables. Hotel rooms, normally filled with people attending seminars and conferences, were empty.

The escort business also took a severe blow. DC Boys closed just shy of its first anniversary in 2002. Full Service Playhouse closed. So did Elite Escorts, though no one knows exactly when. Tops Referrals took a financial hit, closed its out-of-home office but remained open.

Both Capital City Boys and The Agency eventually closed. How much September 11 had to do with it and how much other factors were responsible is a matter of some debate.

The owner of The Firm DC was killed on June 7, 2004, in Richmond, Virginia, during a robbery. The man who took over the service said police were not sure what had happened but that the owner had been shot in the head, execution style.

It took years but Marvin says that Washington's escort

business eventually returned to pre-September 11 levels. He also says "surprisingly little has changed" in the world of gay escorts in Washington between the summer 2001 and the summer of 2008.

Marvin says the average age of escorts "has gone up some but not much." As for clients, "many of mine have been around for a long time. Not much changed there."

One thing that has changed is the price escorts charge. An informal, unscientific survey shows that most escorts in Washington now charge between $200 and $300 to visit your home or hotel room. Visits vary between 60 and 90 minutes.

The lowest price advertised I found was $175, the highest $320. Experience has taught me that some will visit for less than $175 and some will demand more than $320. Tops Referrals books most of its male models for $250 for a 90-minute session but some charge $300.

* * *

PERSONAL THOUGHTS: Both Tops Referrals and Capital City Boys were created because existing services in Washington were so poorly run that Marvin and I separately believed a better-run service could do well. Hard work and dedication to the clients and escorts we served proved we were right.

"Don't Mean Nothing"
Richard Marx
Peaked at #3 in 1987

Running Capital City Boys, I quickly became the keeper of secrets for hundreds of people – straights and gays, clients and escorts alike.

Republicans called me. So did Democrats. Senators and congressmen and their aides called. So did lawyers, celebrities, media figures including Washington-based reporters and editors. Lots of ordinary people also called.

The number of elected officials I knew who called Capital City Boys and The Agency was small. That said, the fact remains, elected officials did call.

Most clients shared at least one secret with me. Maybe they thought I had as much or more to hide than they did. Maybe some felt the need to tell someone their secret – someone who would not be judgmental. All who called needed me to keep secret what it was they told me. I have to think not a single one of them ever imagined they were talking to a journalist who had come to town to research a project.

Ready for the adventure or not, I found myself working behind the curtain of Washington's gay male escort world. For three years, I was the Wizard himself. As you might imagine, it was quite an experience.

* * *

The process of registering Capital City Boys with the District of Columbia went in stages. Twice, the clerk called out for the owner of Capital City Boys Escort Referral Service. Both times, people in the hallway seemed to stop what they were doing to see what dredge of society was going to respond.

Both times, I sheepishly went to the counter, smiling nervously, imagining that the same announcement had gone out all over the District over a giant PA system – the type used by rural communities to warn of impending danger. I remember wondering at the time if this vision might be an omen.

Capital City Boys ran its first ads in the *Washington Blade* and the *Metro Weekly*, the District's two gay newspapers, on Oct. 9, 1998. The ads, offering to represent gay escorts, caught the eye of several prospects, including one nicknamed "R-Street Robbie."

At the end of his interview, Robbie was asked if he knew any other guys who might be interested in signing with us. Without hesitation, Robbie wrote down eight names and seven phone numbers.

Calls were made, not knowing all the guys on Robbie's list worked for one particular service – Dreamboys. Robbie, I found out later, was looking to get even with J.T., the man who owned and ran Dreamboys.

One guy on the list called, wanting to know how Capital City Boys had gotten his number. He made it plain he had no interest in working with us. A second caller had a similar question and response, then a third.

A couple of hours later, Capital City Boys received the first of several anonymous threats. J.T. was now aware Capital City Boys existed. What he did not know was who owned Capital City Boys and how this new service had not only obtained his escort list but his secret personal phone number. Sean and I had left a message at that number too.

During one of the threatening calls, I told J.T. how Capital City Boys had come to have the names and phone numbers and we had no idea it was his list of escorts. J.T. demanded to know who had given Capital City Boys the names and numbers. I refused to tell. Until now, only three people have known that "R-Street Robbie" was the source.

J.T. paged everyone who worked with Dreamboys including Sean. Twice that night, we pulled into a gas station so Sean could call J.T. Twice J.T., not knowing Sean was involved with Capital City Boys, vowed to find the owner and "run him out of town after beating the s***t out of him."

This was not the first time in my life I had been threatened – just the first time the person making the threat had such good motivation to carry it out. It became clear J.T. was growing angrier as the night went on.

Sean and I were meeting strangers who responded to our ads. It would have been easy for someone to set up an interview, show up and beat the crap out of us. Interviews were switched from

Capital City Boys' hotel room to public places – very public places. Nothing happened. No one came after us but Sean and I were very careful with whom we met. We also looked over our shoulders a lot.

* * *

Capital City Boys officially opened on Saturday, Oct. 24, 1998. The service booked 15 calls that day – a company record that was never matched. Though the service had more than a dozen escorts interviewed and ready to work, none – including Sean – could be found or was willing/able to accept a booking that day. Capital City Boys could have generated $2,250 in business that day. The service would have earned a third of that amount – $750.

An on-call policy was quickly implemented and enforced. If an escort wanted to be promoted, he had to call and tell the service he was available. He also had to call if going off-duty before 11 p.m. While this procedure was never fail-proof, it did give the service a reasonable idea of who was available.

When clients called, only those who had called in or who had established such a reliable schedule that they did not have to call were pitched to clients. Still, the service had to deal with escorts who called in begging for work and then were nowhere to be found 30 minutes later after a client had been convinced he really should see that particular guy.

When told the recommended escort was not available, clients – used to having been messed over by services in other towns – would often call another service.

The harassing calls from Dreamboys continued into the next week. But it was not until someone woke me up one night, threatening to harm one of Capital City Boys' escorts that I felt the need to stand up and fight back.

The threatening late-night phone call rattled me but did not scare me off. I fired back, not with threats of my own but with the promise that if threats continued or if anyone working with Capital City Boys was harassed, I would go to authorities both in Washington and Kentucky, telling exactly what I knew about my competitors and that what I told would be extensive.

I overnighted one package addressed to Dreamboys c/o its apartment on Columbia Road NW, Washington. I overnighted an identical package to The Agency at its home on Ingraham Street NW. The return address on both was Capital City Boys, at an address on L Street NW.

The packages prompted totally different responses from the two services.

Troy, the former owner of The Agency called, saying that the new owner had nothing to do with threats but would investigate the matter and make sure they stopped. Calling from the Las Vegas airport, Troy said Kenny (The Agency's new owner) was flying him to Washington that afternoon to solve the problem.

"I am being dispatched out to D.C. I'm in the airport now and plan on having a meeting with the office staff (in Washington)," Troy said.

"I plan on having a meeting with J.T. I have had to deal with him before and I don't mind dealing with him again. I think most of the problems are coming from J.T. and not our company."

Continuing, The Agency's former owner explained, "I love taking care of s**t and whooping ass, so if I have to go and fire everybody there (at The Agency) I'll do it. I don't give a s**t, I'll take care of it. I just wanted to let you know we appreciate you writing a letter to let us know what kind of problems you are having and we will have them taken care of."

In a follow-up call, saying the message had been sent to J.T., Troy said Kenny had one request of me — not to work a certain escort named Eddie. "The Agency's owner has, at great expense, sent Eddie to work in D.C.," Troy explained. "The Agency's owner would greatly appreciate it if you would consider this one escort off limits."

Having already interviewed Eddie, I understood why The Agency wanted to protect its investment — Eddie would be a great asset to any service. I also understood I had made a friend, one who had great influence and power. Capital City Boys never represented Eddie, though he asked us to do so several times.

The reaction at Dreamboys was totally different. Storm happened to be in the office when my package arrived. Storm said J.T. and Tristian — one of the guys helping J.T. — were thrilled when they received my package, thinking I had slipped up and had given them my address.

The two of them piled into a cab and raced to the address, where they expected to find someone from Capital City Boys working in Suite 307.

Instead, they found a Mailbox Etc. location. Box 307 was assigned to Capital City Boys. I was in Kentucky but they did not know that – yet. It would not take them long to find out and when they did, they struck back, struck hard.

Having accessed registration papers I filed with the District of Columbia government, J.T. and Tristian found out my real name, my address and other personal information.

Somehow, J.T. and Tristian were able to pull a credit report on me and discovered where I worked. Tristian called the *Herald-Leader* and told them I was running a gay escort service in Washington. He recommended they check out the Capital City Boys' Web site on the Internet.

Tristian later bragged to me about having made the call. He laughed when he told me how shocked the people he talked to were by what he said.

Two guys seen at the 1999 Pride festival are symbolic of our clients and escorts – mostly conservative in public, a bit more "colorful" in private.

* * *

Sean and I ran Capital City Boys from its opening until I moved to Washington the following August. It was not an easy task. Being disciplined enough to run a business was not part of Sean's makeup.

Sean often stayed up until dawn then slept until 4 p.m. or later, which meant he could not get to the bank in time to make a deposit. He was not much better at answering telephones and following through with clients' requests.

Sean had a difficult time collecting from escorts because he rarely went out to collect until after 10:30 p.m. Few escorts were available then. Half were home in bed because they had to work the next morning while others had gone out to a club or were socializing with friends and did not want to explain why they were giving money to a stranger.

Capital City Boys paid its way during the fall of 1998 and spring of 1999 but generated little profit. Still, it managed to stay open and survive – something few services in Washington were able to do.

Time showed Capital City Boys was serious about being in the business and was not into bad-mouthing competing services. When a client called Capital City Boys and mentioned another company, the person working the phone was under instructions to reply "They are a good service" and then quickly stress even better points about Capital City Boys.

When someone called asking for a competitor's phone number, it was given. When Capital City Boys did not have the exact type of guy a client was looking for, it recommended the caller contact one of its competitors. That approach cost Capital City Boys some business but it also generated good will. No one in the business felt threatened by Capital City Boys. Clients felt they could trust the service. This was mentioned several times on escort review Web sites.

* * *

I first met Marvin, the owner of Tops Referrals, at Annie's Restaurant on 17th Street soon after Capital City Boys opened. I quickly came to like Marvin. Almost from the start, we agreed that while competitors, we could be of help to each other; that both companies would benefit from a friendly relationship.

Kenny, The Agency's owner, had also expressed an interest in having a good working relationship. Kenny and I met a few times when we both happened to be visiting Washington.

J.T. and I kept our distance. That would later change and we became good friends.

* * *

Though struggling, in the spring of 1999, Capital City Boys continued to bleed off both clients and escorts from the other services, especially Dreamboys.

As is the case in any city, there are only so many clients and so many escort candidates to draw from. And, unlike Dreamboys, Capital City Boys actually represented and sent the guys it advertised. Having matched Dreamboys' $150 price, and being reliable made a huge difference.

It was also at this time that the escort world really began to transform from a predominantly service-based industry to one where many of the best escorts started promoting themselves. I am not sure any of us recognized this major shift was happening at the time.

The Agency began to have serious problems. Having an absentee owner, being forced to move to a house near the Maryland border and raising its prices and fees took a toll. Tops Referrals, which had been closed for a short while because of a legal problem not related to the service itself, reopened.

The Agency eventually increased its price from $170 to $200. Tops increased the cost of its 90-minute call to $225. Capital City Boys raised its price to $190.

It quickly became clear clients were slow to accept the new pricing. Capital City Boys dropped its price to $170 and bookings increased. The math was convincing and easy to understand – Capital City Boys and the escorts it represented made more money at $170 than at $190 because the service was able to book more calls. Capital City Boys would have to book and collect on six additional calls every night to make up for the referral fee it made off one call at $170.

Increased bookings gave Capital City Boys an edge in attracting the best escorts. Business improved after I moved to Washington. So did collections. Both made Capital City Boys stronger. It also continued to take its toll at the other services.

Kenny, The Agency's owner, told me over lunch one day he was not happy with how his service was performing. He blamed the poor performance on his not being there, running the service himself. The Agency had gone through a progression of managers, none of whom seemed to match the abilities of Troy, The Agency's previous owner and founder.

Sensing my interest, Kenny told Rich – who was managing The Agency at the time – to stop eating and go across the street to the Safeway to pick up something for him. I sent a puzzled Sean with him.

Kenny restated that The Agency was not working as well as he hoped and, because other business interests would soon be demanding more time from him, said he would consider selling The Agency to someone who "would continue its legacy." I told Kenny I had such an interest and would like to explore such a venture further.

Kenny and I talked off and on about the possible sale of The Agency during the fall of 1999. Kenny reportedly paid $60,000 for The Agency in July or August of 1998. The Agency was not as successful as it had been when Kenny bought it, and even less since Capital City Boys had opened.

Rich confided there were "two sets of books" for The Agency when I asked about The Agency's finances and delighted in telling me I could not see either one. Rich said I already knew all I needed to know about The Agency.

The Agency had value but without knowing about its revenue I had no way of knowing what that value might be. Capital City Boys had become #1 in the market. Like most, I assumed, The Agency was #2. That assumption later proved false.

Beginning the pricing dance and speaking in general terms, I proposed a structured settlement over a period of five years. "Not interested in any such deal" was the message that came back. I then proposed a structured, more generous settlement over a period of time based on The Agency's future performance. "Not interested. I want one settlement."

Not wanting The Agency so badly I would sink $60,000 in cash into the deal, I backed off, thanking Kenny for the opportunity of having tried to buy his company.

Kenny called me sometime later, wanting to "find a price that works for both of us." Wanting to own The Agency purely for personal reasons, I discreetly started asking detailed questions of a select group of escorts about what they knew about The Agency and its operation. This included asking people inside Kenny's inner circle.

Only one knew I was considering buying the company. Most just thought I was curious about my competitor. In strict confidence, I was told how poorly run The Agency was and how few calls were being booked. The most shocking news came from two escorts who worked with Capital City Boys who had spent an entire week "partying" at The Agency's house.

"Nobody's working, Mack," one reported back. "They can't. They're all doing drugs, doing drugs big time."

I e-mailed Kenny, detailing what I had learned, saying I was no longer interested in buying the service. Kenny never denied the report.

Kenny eventually called. "Name your price," he said. "Just make it reasonable." I offered the lowest price I thought I could without insulting him. He countered, then I countered, restating what I had been told.

Kenny suggested $15,000 cash, assuming financial responsibility for The Agency's credit card machine (a debt of about $2,500) and the lease on The Agency's house near the Maryland border.

Someone had woefully overpaid for the machine but I reluctantly agreed to assume the debt anyway. I refused to assume the lease. Kenny was paying $3,000 a month in rent. Capital City Boys could not justify taking on that expense.

On December 7, 1999, I became The Agency's third owner. It was then I came to know what I had actually bought. Things were as bad as I had suspected. Legal rights to the name, a few assets like photos, two Web site addresses, a list of clients and their phone numbers, and information about past Agency escorts and those who had applied to be part of The Agency was all I received in the sale.

You might recognize some of the escorts' real names. You certainly would recognize some clients' names.

The business plan was simple: I would continue to run Capital City Boys and research this project. Sean and an escort named Austin would run The Agency as a separate company. That plan was scrapped two days later when it became clear Sean was more interested in spending time with Austin than running a business and that Austin was not any better.

Only one of the few "working" escorts that The Agency had on its list expressed any interest in continuing to work. After missing three meetings, it was decided The Agency would not represent him.

Eventually, two of The Agency's former escorts came to work with The Agency under my ownership. Both were very reliable. One of them was a straight guy named Brian, the other, a gay guy named Ryan. Both entertained gay clients. Brian also entertained female clients.

* * *

J.T. called me in March 2000, wanting to meet. Ryan, Sean, and Austin warned me not to go, saying such a meeting could be dangerous. This was a possibility but J.T. had left both me and Capital City Boys alone for a long time.

I went. It was a very candid meeting, one that held a dramatic, unexpected ending. J.T. admitted he had arranged for friends to call Capital City Boys to see what it might say about Dreamboys. "I was amazed," he said. "Not once did you talk bad about me or Dreamboys, even though we tried to get you to."

He apologized for his actions after Capital City Boys opened. J.T. also apologized for Tristian having called my employer in Kentucky. "That wasn't my idea," he said, "but then, I didn't stop him either."

Then J.T. told me he intended to close Dreamboys. There was nothing left to the company but its wonderful name. I offered to buy Dreamboys for $500 but J.T. turned down my offer. The offer was not higher because there really was not anything to buy. The service had died because of its horrible reputation.

J.T. did not own the legal rights to the name Dreamboys. Multiple checks with the District of Columbia showed no one owned the name. I had known for sometimes I could register "Dreamboys" and force J.T. to cease using the name. I never did, knowing there is great benefit to not kicking a sleeping dog.

* * *

Tristian and I crossed paths again later. We met because he and a friend were preparing to open two escort services in Washington – one females for males and one males for males. He and his backer – a man who worked at America Online in Northern Virginia, and who had cashed in nicely on AOL stock – hired me to design Web sites for the services.

They also hired Marvin, the owner of Tops Referrals, to advise them about how to run a service properly.

I met with Tristian and his backer at their newly leased apartment at The Lexington. The irony of that name did not escape me.

Having seen how Dreamboys' owner reacted when Capital City Boys opened, Tristian said he thought it wise that the three of us have a "friendly" working relationship.

No one in business likes having a new competitor but Tops and Capital City Boys welcomed newcomers. Neither service was into breaking legs or making threatening late-night phone calls. Besides, the odds were good that Tristian's new services would not last long – most did not.

The two services did fail. Tristian bragged he and his backer had so much fun "interviewing" escort candidates that their girlfriends became "livid" with them. Tristian said his backer was given the choice of walking away from the services and Tristian or being dumped. The backer walked away.

A month or two later, while eating lunch with Marvin at a restaurant on P Street, I noticed a man outside asking strangers for change. It was Tristian. I pointed this situation out to Marvin. He had seen this type of thing before, I had not. I remember wishing I had brought my camera to record the moment.

* * *

PERSONAL THOUGHTS: You cannot own an escort service and not anger people from time to time. Those who found themselves in certain situations or were close enough to witness Mack handling a problem would never describe me as shy or timid. Likewise, no one I worked with outside the escort world could ever imagine how owning a service sometimes required me to act. I have to admit, though, occasionally, I provide glimpses.

Although there are a lot of similarities between Mack and me, there were also major differences. The one trait of Mack's I still possess is his lack of patience dealing with those out to cause harm to those I care for or with those who play games.

"Rainbow Connection"
Kermit the Frog
Peaked at #25 in 1979

Tops Referrals opened in the early 1990s. It is the oldest-operating gay male escort referral service in Washington. Scores of other services have opened and closed since Tops opened.

The credit for Tops' longevity belongs to its owner, a 56-year-old man named Marvin.

Marvin, once a major in the Marines, opened Tops somewhat out of desperation and personal need. It was also somewhat by chance. Marvin and a couple of close friends, hired local gay escorts from time to time, but were disappointed by both the quality and reliability of the guys they met.

"There was a horrible lack of service," Marvin says.

Marvin had just completed a contract human resources job and had gone to dinner with his friends to mark the occasion. One of the friends asked Marvin what he was going to next with his life.

"I told him I really didn't know," Marvin says.

The friend took five $100 bills out of his wallet and handed them to Marvin. "Take this money and find us some escorts you can refer on to us," Marvin says the friend instructed. Other friends also put in $500 each and Marvin began his mission to find quality guys who would entertain his friends. As with his other endeavors, Marvin worked hard to accomplish his task, never compromising on quality.

Marvin placed an ad in a local paper stating a desire to hire escorts. Marvin then "met" with those who answered the ad. After completing each encounter, Marvin decided who was worthy of recommending to his friends and who was not.

"At first, no one paid a referral fee," Marvin says. The $500 each had paid covered that debt.

The friends were pleased with Marvin's selections and apparently told others of his success. Eventually, others came to Marvin and asked him to recommend escorts to them too. When

Marvin replied he only referred escorts to his friends, one asked: "How do I get to be your friend?"

Seeing the potential for success, Marvin set up a different arrangement and expanded his business, calling it Tops Referrals. "I never planned to get into this business," Marvin says. "It just sort of happened. I never planned to continue doing it, it just has."

Thousands of "friends" have asked Marvin for referrals over the years. And, just as he did in the beginning, Marvin continues to take that responsibility seriously.

It is because of Marvin's dedication to clients that Tops has survived when so many other services came and went, many of them, quickly.

"Most people treat running a service as a toy," Marvin says. "They don't realize it is a business that demands a lot of attention and a lot of hard work. Most new services fail because their owner isn't committed to making the investment in time that it takes."

* * *

After he started the service, Marvin says he came to understand that he made good matches one-third of the time, made a tolerable match a third of the time and missed the mark the rest of the time. "I may missmatch people from time to time," he says, "but I will always send the person I promised or I will pick up the phone and call the client and tell him the person he wanted to see is not available and offer a replacement. Most clients appreciate that approach. They don't always get such service elsewhere."

* * *

Tops has its escorts collect their fee at the end of the session, "Just like at a restaurant," Marvin says. "Occasionally, when a client doesn't feel he got what he expected, I have to get involved and find a compromise."

* * *

Marvin grew up in rural North Carolina, exactly where, he

---

never said and, as a friend, it never seemed right to press the issue.

"I grew up not knowing what being gay was," Marvin says. In fact, Marvin did not have his first gay experience until after he and his first wife separated.

Marvin recalls his father's "non-reaction" when he told his father he (Marvin) was gay.

"He really didn't understand what I was saying. Finally, (my father) leans forward and says, 'Look, your mother and I don't talk to you about our sex life. Why tell us about yours?'"

Marvin says he had a separate conversation with his mother. "She never blinked," Marvin says. "Moms always know."

Asked how his family reacted when he broke the news to them that he was running a gay escort referral service, Marvin says, "Again, it was a non-reaction."

Marvin, trying to explain what his referral service offered, said something along the line that his business helped people."Oh," Marvin says one family member said, "Like a Boy Scout helping little old ladies?"

Asked if the work he and I did in Washington qualified us for the label of "pimp," Marvin had a quick and simple answer: "No! There is no way we fit the model of a pimp. A pimp is a guy on the street. He takes everything the girls working for him earn. A pimp controls every aspect of their prostitutes' lives. He gives the best performers a nice hotel room and jewelry, but if she leaves, he takes it back."

* * *

PERSONAL THOUGHTS: Today, Marvin lives in a beautiful fifth-floor condo apartment in an up-and-coming part of Washington. Looking out his living room's wall of glass, you can see a spectacular view of Washington, especially at night. On one side, there is the Capitol, on the other, the Washington Monument. In between, if you look hard, you can see the flag that flies over the White House.

* * *

Marvin says he knows of only one time when an escort and a client turned what usually is a once or two-time encounter into a longtime relationship. "That happened more than 10 years ago. They met, fell in love right away, dated and became a couple. They are still together today, still very happy."

Career-wise, several who escorted for Marvin went on to be

lawyers, a couple became doctors and at least one became an architect.

"The sad stories outnumber the good ones," Marvin said quietly, then turned to look out his beautiful wall of glass. Neither one of us spoke for a couple of minutes. Neither of us said a word. We didn't have to, we knew only too well the other was remembering associates who, for a variety of reasons, qualified as being one the "sad stories."

Helping Our Brothers & Sisters

Marvin has opened a not-for-profit organization to educate the public and help those who are forced out of the military for being gay. Eventually, the organization may expand to assist others who are gay.

Helping Our Brothers & Sisters
Post Office Box 53477
Washington, DC 20009

Check www.MackAndTheBoys.com
for the Helping Our Brothers & Sisters Web site

"It's a job.
It's not who we are.
At the end of the day, we decide who we are."
— THE RECRUIT
Buena Vista Home Entertainment

"(We Are The) Boys"
From the Broadway musical "Big River"

Escorting is a profession that generally cares more about a person's age, looks and open-mindedness than what educational degrees they might have. Like hospitals, banks and lawyers, there are so many escorts because there is both a need and a demand.

The gay escorts I met while researching this report are not what you probably assume an escort is like. Most are just like you. Most are good people. Like you, they care about doing well, they have needs, feelings and opinions. Some go to church, some do not. In Capital City Boys' case, he could have been your banker, lawyer, dentist or even the undertaker who buried Aunt Sadie last year.

* * *

Gay men escort for a variety of reasons. Some say they do it for attention and for the thrill of doing something that others would not. Others say they do it simply for the chance of having what they consider "exceptional" encounters with strangers. All will eventually admit the real reason they escort is money, easy money. Like with horse racing, without money being involved, most would never participate in the sport.

Capital City Boys escorts came from a variety of backgrounds. Many were professionals. Two were bankers – one a branch manager. One was a dentist – he drove a Mercedes. One was an engineer – he drove a Cadillac. Two worked for law firms – one handled paperwork for cases going to the U.S. Supreme Court. Several were college students, one studying international economics. One ran a not-for-profit foundation, another was the son of an attaché at a foreign embassy in Washington. Two were in advertising sales. One was a photojournalist for a Washington newspaper.

Several of our escorts worked at beauty salons. Two were undertakers, one was a model, two worked at medical clinics. At least three were in the military. Another was the son of a high-ranking official in the Connecticut State Police.

So that you do not get the mistaken idea all of Capital City Boys' escorts were saints, one escort the service represented was into hiring boys in Northern Virginia, – ages 18 to 21 – to drop their pants and masturbate while he filmed them. He then sold the footage without the boys' knowledge.

Why did these people escort? All had a need. All had a desire that they could not meet on what their regular jobs paid.

Capital City Boys had guys who escorted to save money for the down payment on a home or to finance renovations to a home they already owned. Capital City Boys also represented guys who had no jobs and uncertain housing situations. These guys escorted just to survive till the next day.

Many had come to Washington in hopes of finding something better than what they had left behind. Some came because they had nowhere else to go.

Dave came to Capital City Boys soon after it opened. He was still working, though not much, when I sold the service. Dave, who had a professional daytime job, started escorting because he had a financial goal he wanted to meet. After a while, he told me he continued to escort because he came to enjoy "spreading good cheer" throughout the District.

Trevor was working for Dreamboys when Capital City Boys opened. He first became a friend then an escort for Capital City Boys. In his 30s when we met, one of the first things Trevor told me was that he was going to escort "just a little while longer and then retire." That was 1998. When I called Trevor in 2004, he told me the same thing. Like Dave, Trevor had a regular job and his feet firmly planted in reality.

Magenta came to Capital City Boys early in 1999. Flamboyant and into dressing in drag, Magenta offered Capital City Boys clients a walk on the wild side of tame. Not into escorting for anything but the money, Magenta could be counted on to show up dressed like a nurse, a female hooker, or a handsome male freshman college student, if that was what the client requested.

Rob was very quiet. Quiet until it came to the "personal" part of a call. Then, the quiet blond boy from down South could make the most-conservative Republican in Washington squeal with delight. Sunday nights were never the same after he left town.

Marcus was a cute, 19-year-old, blond, straight, boy who thrilled many of our clients near the end of my stay in Washington. I never got around to asking why clients liked him so much, but knew they did.

I first saw Ian dancing naked at Wet, a gay strip bar. I was sure clients would like meeting him. For the most part, I was wrong. Being shy, Ian was not into small talk and came across as being "cold." That really was not the case. Once Ian got to know you, he was very outgoing and charming.

Living outside of Washington and not being available on any set schedule did not help Ian's escort career either. It was impossible to set up a call for Ian the next night because no one had a clue when he was going to be available. Ian did not last long.

Aion was a firecracker. The first time we met he insisted he take his clothes off, right away. After his interview, he went down the hall, naked as the day he was born, passing a couple of my roommates who just smiled at me, amused by what they saw and me shaking my head.

Shortly before Aion "left" Capital City Boys, three clients in a row "failed to pay" for their sessions. Only one other client had ever "failed to pay." In that case, the escort called the service from outside the client's home. Aion waited a day or two before reporting that the out-of-town clients he had seen had refused to pay.

I decided to no longer represent Aion after Charles, Drew and I bumped into him at a coffee shop in Dupont Circle one Sunday afternoon. Aion came over and bragged he and a client he had seen the previous week had come in for coffee after going to a movie.

When I asked when he would be by to pay his referral fee for the time spent with the client, Aion said: "But we just spent time together." "That's exactly what we charge for," I reminded him, giving a look that no one could mistake its meaning.

* * *

While escorting sometimes took a mental toll on those in the business, it also rescued some.

Escorting allowed Tim, then a manager at a local retail store, to regain his self-esteem and get on with his life after having been dumped by his partner for a younger guy. "Tim came to me saying he needed to escort to help pay his mortgage," Marvin, the owner of Tops Referrals, says. "The partner had left and now Tim had to pay the entire amount, not just half."

Pleading his case, Tim told Marvin he would take any call at any hour. Tim kept his word and in the process helped heal the wounds he suffered in his breakup.

Tim "had been made to believe he was an ugly duckling," Marvin says. "Escorting restored his confidence, his self-assurance."

Tim explained to Marvin: "Guys are paying $200 to be with me. I can't be that bad, can I?"

Tim is not the only one interviewed for this project that says escorting rescued him.

Jay was in his late 20s when he started escorting. "There was a major void in my life," he says. "I

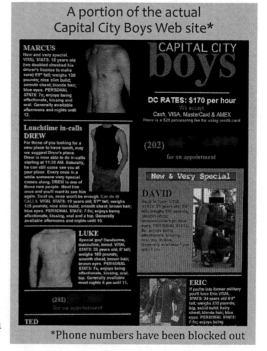

A portion of the actual Capital City Boys Web site*

*Phone numbers have been blocked out

became determined to find what would fill that need." Escorting was one of the paths he tried. For Jay, escorting was a way to move from an unhappy life to one where he felt good about himself.

"I had sex with lots of different people and I got paid for it," he says. "This gave me a sense of 'You have worth, you have value,' to others.'" Jay escorted in the Washington-area for 10 years, having started in the late 1980s.

In addition liking the money, Jay says he found escorting intriguing, exciting and an answer to being "horny all the time. Plus," he says, "escorting cut out the socialization aspect" of finding someone to be intimate with.

"As my life came more in balance, I found escorting less rewarding," Jay says. Asked if he regrets having escorted, he says: "Just the opposite. None whatsoever." Today, Jay has a Masters degree and has completed some work toward a doctorate. He works for a major corporation based in Northern Virginia.

* * *

Capital City Boys once represented two guys who were dating. Neither knew the other was escorting. Neither wanted the other to know. I came to know when one of them showed me a picture of his boyfriend. It was a handsome face I recognized as one of Mack's boys.

One night, one of the guys called to say he was coming right over to drop off a referral fee. A couple of minutes later, the other one called saying he had "found a couple of spare minutes" and wanted to do the same. I answered the door for the first guy and suggested he come upstairs, where we could talk privately. Charles waited downstairs for the second guy, collected his money, then sent him on his way. Charles never said, but I am sure there was a dreamy smile given to the escort somewhere in there.

Charles then came upstairs and handed me the money, a sign that I could wrap up my conversation with the first escort. I can say with great authority that a dreamy smile was given to that escort. I know, because I was the one who gave it.

Capital City Boys once had three roommates who worked with the service. All had moved to Washington from Richmond, Virginia.

All were cute. One, Brent, was immensely popular. The other two could have been. One worked about a month and quit, saying escorting "just isn't my thing." The third was shy and hardly ever called to update us on his availability. When he worked, he got good reviews and seemed to enjoy himself. One day, we realized he had not called in weeks. He never called again, either.

Max the wonder Dog was especially close to one escort, a handsome, red-headed 23-year-old named Tyler. Max's passion grew out of Tyler almost always bringing him something to eat and paying him some attention.

Max also took a special liking to Charles. I jokingly accused Charles of cheating on his boyfriend with Max (he didn't). And when Max would cough, I would accuse Charles of having shared a cigarette with him. Both would just smile, neither confirming nor denying my allegation.

* * *

Like other businesses, Capital City Boys carefully decided who it would and would not represent. Like any other business, choices were made for a variety of reasons – a hunch, a need, an outstanding personality, or because they offered something completely different than the rest.

Capital City Boys accepted almost every blond who applied. Blonds were always in great demand. On the other hand, Capital City Boys generally represented only one red-haired guy and no more than two Asians at a time because demand for them was light. The same was true for blacks.

Clients preferred guys with a smooth chest over guys with a hairy one. Escorts came to understand that preference, and some who did not have a naturally smooth chest would shave or "Nair" on nights they worked.

New escorts were always in demand. Many new escorts start out making big money their first couple of weeks and are surprised when the number of calls they go on and their income decline.

"When times were booming, a new escort could make $2,000 his first week, his part," Marvin says. "The second week, $1,500. By the third week, he could be down to $1,000. If you are good, you'll reach some happy plateau."

Marvin says Tops keeps about 50 escorts on its roster. "10 to

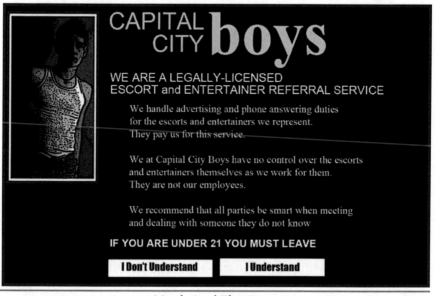

15 get work on a regular basis, the others just occasionally," Marvin says. Tops' list also includes escorts who have certain specialties whose services are requested only every once in a while.

Capital City Boys kept fewer active escorts on it list, probably about 20.

* * *

Capital City Boys represented escorts – much the same way a talent agency represents an actor. The escort hired the service to represent them. The escorts – in almost all respects – were the boss. They – and they alone – decided if they would accept a booking. The service did not make this decision.

Escorts certainly could sever the working relationship with the service at any time and for any reason.

Capital City Boys took great pains to inform clients that it was a referral service paid by escorts to promote them, much the same way a newspaper or radio or TV station advertises a company's services or a Realtor markets a home.

Callers were told they were being charged for the escort's time and travel – not the promise anything sexual would happen.

If a caller got rude or crude or insisted on having the service promise he would receive a sexual favor, Capital City Boys would interrupt the caller and sharply state this was not what the service provided. Then, the operator would hang up. This procedure cost us money but kept us legal.

The same routine was applied to callers who asked if Capital City Boys had anyone who liked to party – a euphemism for doing drugs. Other services were not nearly as strict.

* * *

The application and interview process to be represented by an escort referral service is much like any other job – at least up to a certain point. Some services require prospective escorts to demonstrate how they might handle themselves on a call. Capital City Boys did not.

One guy interviewed at Capital City Boys but who was passed over said he had won a Grammy. A later check proved he had.

Another candidate claimed he had worked at the White House and said he was a close friend of Chelsea Clinton's and was "on good terms" with her mother.

Having heard a wide variety of claims during interviews – including a black man who claimed to have blond pubic hair – the candidate was told about some of our clients and that some even used U.S. Senate-issued credit cards.

"I can beat that," he said. Standing, he whipped out his wallet and pulled out a White House credit card with his name on it. I love credible people.

* * *

Two of Capital City Boys' escorts once felt they deserved "a break away from things." They checked into Washington's Four Season's Hotel for two days. Their room cost $887.37 per night. They spent $653.95 on room service the first night, $729.60 for breakfast the next morning, $787.20 for room service the second night, and $562.96 in mini-bar fees. In all, they spent $4,885.63. They charged the bill to an unsuspecting man in Maryland whom they knew (not a client).

* * *

New associates were always told escorting was not for everyone. Then they were told, "Only you can decide if it's right for you." Almost without exception, the interviewee was sent off to think about whether escorting was right for him. He was always told to call the next day with his decision.

I never wanted anyone to say Mack had forced him to do something he really did not want to do. Not sending the escort out that first night was my way of ensuring that mistake never happened. Only a few never called back. Most did.

New escorts were closely monitored after each of their first five calls to make sure they felt OK about what they were doing. Most did. A few did not and quit somewhere after their first call and before their fifth. If an escort completed five calls, he would likely stay with the service for a while. Generally speaking, most escorts averaged working about six months.

Some who continued to work struggled with meeting strangers and what they sometimes did on calls. Sebastian was one of them. Sitting in a darkened hotel room late one night, Sebastian confided that some times after a call that he would come back "feeling dirty." "Mack," he said, "there are lots of times I come back and sit down in the shower and scrub myself like crazy, trying to get the dirt off of me."

That said, Sebastian was one of the most dependable escorts who ever worked with Capital City Boys.

* * *

"I am not proud of what I do,"one escort candidate, a guy named Steven, remarked during an interview. "I do what I have to do to survive. Society has turned its back on me and others like me. We get punished because we are not society's ideal version of a human being because of the work we do, yet in private, these same people treat us like royalty.

Steven said he once met a client in his room at the Willard Hotel. "[The businessman] kept telling me how much he cared for me and begged me to stay with him all night so I did. The next night, I happened to be back at the Willard for another call. I saw the man in the lobby. The [man] quickly looked away and wouldn't even look at me."

* * *

Some escorts would drop out after a couple of calls because they were afraid of what their friends would say if they found out.

In the "Law and Order" episode *Church*, a woman pleads guilty to murder rather than have her church congregation learn she had once escorted or that her preacher husband secretly had an affair with a gay escort. The night before, on CBS's "Shark," a woman's testimony was discredited because she too had once escorted. It would be easy to dismiss both cases as being just TV shows, but both are factually accurate.

* * *

Boyfriends were bad for business. With few exceptions, a boyfriend meant Capital City Boys would soon be losing the escort. As if following a script, the escort and I would almost always have "the conversation." The escort would say something like, "Mack, I'm sure this is the guy I'm meant to be with. I have to be faithful only to him."

With few exceptions, the escort would always come back – usually after finding their "true love" in bed with another guy. The "other guy" almost always happened to be younger or cuter or more muscular than themselves.

Sometimes, the prodigal escort would cry on my shoulder

when he came by to see if he could work again. He was always welcomed back. Never once did I mention I had expected he would eventually return.

* * *

Escorts who called on and off and who paid their referral fees in a timely manner were promoted aggressively. Escort candidates got told this fact twice during their interviews. The service benefited from stressing that those who helped the company the most got promoted the most.

The same was true in the service's print and online advertising. Capital City Boys ads promoted escorts who generated the most money for the company or who was a unique draw. New escorts also got promoted. New escorts always generated interest with clients, and interest often times converted into booked calls.

Only a handful of escorts blew their chances of success with the service by never paying their first referral fee. No new escort was given a second job before he paid for the first.

The best escorts knew it was in their own interest to pay the fee right away or at least by the next afternoon. Some earned the right to hold the fee until after a second call. Only a few earned the right to hold off paying beyond that.

The chances of collecting the company's referral fee dropped off tremendously the longer it took for an escort to pay it.

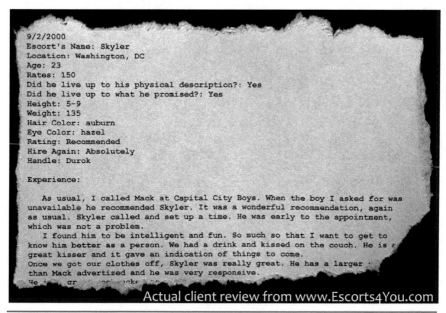

```
9/2/2000
Escort's Name: Skyler
Location: Washington, DC
Age: 23
Rates: 150
Did he live up to his physical description?: Yes
Did he live up to what he promised?: Yes
Height: 5-9
Weight: 135
Hair Color: auburn
Eye Color: hazel
Rating: Recommended
Hire Again: Absolutely
Handle: Durok

Experience:

    As usual, I called Mack at Capital City Boys. When the boy I asked for was
unavailable he recommended Skyler. It was a wonderful recommendation, again
as usual. Skyler called and set up a time. He was early to the appointment,
which was not a problem.
    I found him to be intelligent and fun. So much so that I want to get to
know him better as a person. We had a drink and kissed on the couch. He is a
great kisser and it gave an indication of things to come.
Once we got our clothes off, Skyler was really great. He has a larger
than Mack advertized and he was very responsive.
```

Actual client review from www.Escorts4You.com

* * *

PERSONAL THOUGHTS: Occasionally, when I question myself about having gone to Washington and if having been Mack was worth what it cost me, I remember certain conversations and events, or read e-mails I kept, like this one from Jonathan:

> *"You were like a father – not a daddy,*
> *not a sugar daddy. And that's exactly*
> *what a lot of guys needed. You'd listen,*
> *then decide what to do, and helped us*
> *in anyway we asked.*
> *Most of the time, you were right."*

For the record, no job evaluation I have ever received anywhere else means more to me than that one.

> *I will be your father figure*
> *put your tiny hand in mine.*
> *I will be the one who loves you,*
> *'til the end of time*
> **– FATHER FIGURE**
> Singer/Songwriter: George Michael
> Chappell & Co. (ASCAP)

Nov. 20, 1998: Brendon's First Call

Every escort's first call is a major event for him. Those who claim otherwise either don't remember it or are lying.

Those who had Capital City Boys represent them knew they always had someone watching their back and someone there for them.

Here is a transcript of the phone call I had with Brendon about his first call. Brendon's is typical of most first-time calls.

MACK: Are you out of your movie?
BRENDON: Yes, I am. Just walked out.
M: OK — you have a pencil and a piece of paper?
B: No, I don't. Can I, well where is it?
M: I don't know. You have to call the guy first.
B: Oh crap. Can you page me the number?
M: Sure I can. I can do that.

B: And then it will be pretty much out of your hands after that?

M: Well, no. Here's how it works. You will call him and talk to him, and if you guys agree to meet, call me back and tell me you are going.

B: OK.

M: And I'll get the address from you.

B: Gotcha.

M: And then, you go, you do your thing, and when you get out, you call me back.

B: OK.

M: So that I know you are safe. Now, let me tell you what I know about this guy. You nervous?

B: Ugh, hmmm. Yeah, sure.

M: It's only natural to be.

* * *

B: [laughs] I think I've got it set up.

M: OK.

B: I have to call him back in five minutes. He's checking on his cash flow. I think I may have to walk with him to the money machine.

M: Be safe. Always remember: Don't do anything you're not comfortable with, OK?

B: Mack, I'm scared I won't, I won't be able to, ugh, sing. [laughs]

M: I understand.

B: Five-eleven, 200 pounds, that sounds big.

M: Five-eleven, 200 pounds? Well, he will probably wears it well.

B: I hope so. That will help me. [laughs] Now, I am getting nervous. [laughs]

M: Just keep breathing. That will help you. Where is it you're going? I need it for the records.

B: [gives address]

M:: Listen. I want you to know, 'cause I want to tell you so you don't think otherwise — if you get there and it's just not right, then get out of there.

B: Yeah.

M: You're not going to make me mad at all. I'm going to be mad if you ever put yourself at risk. That's the only time I'm going to be mad at you.

B: Right. I won't put myself at risk. I will put myself in an awkward situation

M: [laughs] Well, we all get in awkward situations.

B: Right, exactly. I figure I'll just grin and bear it for an hour.

M: That's it. Then get out.

B: Exactly.

M: Watch the clock. I mean don't keep looking at your watch. Give him an hour and 10 minutes if you have to, but after an hour, say we've got to be wrapping this up.

M: Are you sure you want this?

B: He's, no, like... look, I've told you plenty of times, I realize I can't cherry-pick. I'm just afraid this guy is going to be so, oh, you know.

M: Listen. Listen. I rejected a 435-pound guy who wanted to see you.

B: Thank you!

M: I thought to myself, as much as I want to send the kid out tonight, I am not going to have this be his first. I'm sorry, I don't care.

B: Oh my God. Well, I guess I will call you back in a few seconds. After I verify. He may [drop off]. I don't think he'll change his mind, but he may, just because it's this late and he doesn't want to walk to the money machine. Blah, blah, blah, or whatever, you know?

M: Yeppers.

* * *

For the record, Brendon did the call and enjoyed his time with the client. What exactly happened during the call? I don't know. When asked what song he sang, Brendon said "a favorite show tune."

Brendon left Capital City Boys a couple of months later, but, like most escorts who left, remained a friend.

I first met him on a Friday night in March 1998 as someone called Rent20. I met him after reading his ad in the *Washington Blade*. Talking on the phone, I learned he was an independent escort. He asked me as many questions as I asked him.

Rent20 may have the unique distinction of being the longest-working gay male escort in Washington. I met him twice in 1998. He is still working in Washington today but under a different name.

Rent20 arrived promptly at the agreed upon time. The first thing he did was to phone a "friend" to let him know he had arrived and all seemed well. Rent20 introduced himself to me. I think he called himself Brian but I cannot swear to it. Rent20 was his screen name on AOL. That name has stuck with me.

Rent20 was all business. He carefully went over his rules and made certain I understood them. The primary thing I had to understand, he said, was that I was not paying him to have sex – if indeed that is what might happen – because that might be unlawful.

Rent20 explained I was paying for his time and travel expenses. He went on to explain that if we had sex, it would be because we – as consenting adults – decided that is what we wanted.

"I like to be extremely detailed and up front about things and cover all potential bases before meeting," Rent20 says. "Communication is extremely important in this business. It is very easy for misunderstandings to develop."

Rent20 was not into telling stories about his adventures but I learned a lot about the escort business – how it should and should not be run and about how an escort should and should not conduct themselves.

Later, when I opened Capital City Boys, I incorporated a lot of the things I learned during our encounter. Things like having the escort call in to say he had arrived and was safe. Understanding its legal importance, I also adopted Rent20's strict policy about a client paying only for an escort's time and travel.

I contacted Rent20 twice about this project. He agreed to answer questions I e-mailed him but never did. Respecting his privacy while balancing what can be learned from his experience, I will continue to call him Rent20. I have known his real name since 1999. I will not reveal it here. The quotes you will read are from information he has shared elsewhere and personal conversations we have had in the past.

* * *

Rent20 offers clients the opportunity to back out of the call, if, for some reason, the client wishes to do so after he first arrives. Few escorts offer such a generous cancellation policy.

"It is a sad fact that many so-called 'escorts' send out fake/misleading pictures, lie about their age and/or physical description in a attempt to get business they normally wouldn't get," Rent20 says. "These same 'escorts' will promise anything to the client he wants to hear just to get the call."

Rent20 says he enjoys escorting and the money he earns. "Working your typical college part-time job for $10-$15 (an) hour is not that appealing. I would much rather be my own boss."

Escorting has been pretty lucrative for Rent20. He currently charges $220 for a one-hour visit, $1,200 for an overnight visit and $2,300 for a weekend. If he meets with a couple, then the hourly rate almost doubles.

If Rent20 averages nine calls a week for 50 weeks a year, he earns $99,000 plus tips. If he averages seven calls a week, he makes $77,000, plus tips. If he averages only three calls a weeks, he earns $33,000 a year, plus tips.

No one but Rent20 and possibly his "friend" knows exactly how much money he makes. Rent20 is shy about saying. Using numbers he once shared and information about the Washington escort market over the past 10 years, I estimate Rent20 has earned between $450,000 and $700,000 since he and I first met in 1998. Again, that range is only an educated guess.

* * *

Based on postings published on national escort review Web sites, Rent20 still excels at making sure clients enjoy their time together.

(He) "arrived at my hotel room on time," a professional in his mid-40s wrote in his review. "He was definitely a (sight) for sore eyes. Very cute, boyish and sharply dressed. When he stripped down to his tight briefs, his slim smooth body was gorgeous and curved in all the right places. Absolutely HOT would be an understatement!"

Other clients echo that sentiment.

"He did not watch the clock and provided the most enjoyable hour I have ever spent with a young guy," an older client wrote.

One 57-year-old client wrote: "This was the best experience with an escort that I have ever had. I did not feel that empty feeling at the end with (Rent20). I knew that my pleasure was his business. I really believe he enjoyed our time too. (Rent20) is the Smithsonian of DC escorts."

* * *

"Some clients label me cold and just interested in business," Rent20 once told me when I mentioned he had not talked much during our time together. "That's how I am. I am shy and don't like getting all social. So when I see someone I am right down to business, and you know I am good at that. :-)"

* * *

PERSONAL THOUGHTS: I have admired Rent20's attention to his client's feelings and his business since the first night we met. I continue to admire his ability to maintain his popularity in one place for 10 years. In the escort world, such success is rare.

I kept an eye on Rent20 the entire time I ran Capital City Boys. I have continued to keep an eye on his Web site, advertisements and reviews since returning to Kentucky, seven years ago. I remember ever seeing only one bad review about Rent20. As an expert in the field, I can tell you, even with the best of escorts, there is always going to be one.

"Opportunities"
(Let's Make Lots of Money)
Pet Shop Boys – Peaked at #10 in 1986

Being an escort is a lot like being a real estate agent – you can make a fortune if you are good at it, or you can starve if you aren't. Having owned and operated an escort referral service and having managed a real estate advertising sales team, I am in a unique position of knowing about this correlation.

* * *

Luke came to Capital City Boys toward the end of the research phase of this project. He quickly became a star.

Luke followed the service's simple rules – he called in when he was available, was prompt for his appointments, and paid his referral fees on time. In return, Luke was heavily promoted. He and I were the perfect example of what the Pet Shop Boys sang about in "Opportunities": *"I've got the brains, you've got the looks, let's make lots of money."*

Luke made a lot of money for Capital City Boys. He made even more for himself. It was a win-win situation, one that lasted until I left Washington in July 2001.

Unhappy with the new owner of Capital City Boys, Luke decided to become an independent escort. He placed his own ads in the *Washington Blade* and on certain Internet sites. Following what he had learned while working with Capital City Boys, Luke says he was able to take as many bookings as he wanted – usually five a week.

Since he only wanted one call a day and was in demand, Luke was able to increase his booking price to $200. Working on his own meant he got to keep all of it. Luke said he was making $1,000 a week. Working 50 weeks a year, Luke earned somewhere around $50,000. If Luke was like most, the $50,000 was tax-free.

Like weight-loss plans you see on TV, Luke's income experience was not typical, though it was also not unique. Luke handled escorting as a business. He had a financial need and the money he earned went toward that project. Other escorts could have been at Luke's income level but most never took escorting seriously – just a means of getting to tomorrow. Even while facing a personal financial crisis, there was no certainty that some escorts would be available to work.

Female escorts are able to handle more calls a day than their male counterparts. Generally speaking, in Washington, the good ones also charged more, some charge a lot more.

Former New York Gov. Eliot Spitzer reportedly paid some $80,000 on high-priced call girls. Wiretaps reportedly caught Spitzer detailing exactly what he wanted from his time with "Kirsten." He reportedly paid $4,300 for two hours of time.

An IRS agent who testified in the Deborah Jeane Palfrey case said her business generated about $2 million in revenue over a period of 13 years. He also said the money was divided "about evenly" between the escort and the service. (Female services traditionally take a larger fee than male services.)

A female escort, working on her own in the summer of 2001, could easily bring in $800 a day doing three calls. Working five days a week amounts to $200,000 or so a year.

The call girl whom Sam Seaborn met on TV's "The West Wing" earned $3,000 a night. Guess how many times a week she might have worked, deduct 40 or 50 percent for her service and then multiply that by 50 weeks. Whatever numbers you use, it is big money.

* * *

Capital City Boys earned a $60 referral fee for every $170 booking. Tops earned $90 on a $225 call. In 2000, Capital City Boys and The Agency generated $353,720 in combined bookings. This earned the company $120,915 in commissions and fees. This was an increase of $124,325 in bookings and $42,685 in commissions and fees over 1999.

Capital City Boys could have doubled that amount if it had "provided" drugs to clients and had run a special unit of guys who were into "partying" with clients. Certain escort services – gay and straight – in Washington did. Capital City Boys could have also boosted sales if it had worked harder to close deals and forced guys to take calls they did not want to take. Other services did that too.

Advertising was Capital City Boys' largest expense, followed by rent and utilities. Phone bills were high but Capital City Boys did have a lot of lines. Phones are the lifelines of an escort service. If the phones do not work, no one goes out and no money is earned by anyone.

* * *

Jesse, a handsome, well-fit, bi-sexual escort, was once on a call with a repeat client when things went more than a bit crazy. "The client had me get into some red underwear he wanted me to model," Jesse said. Such a request was pretty common.

Jesse and the client had pretty much completed their hour together when, Jesse says, the client insisted he go into the next room and get a bag of drugs from the top drawer of a dresser. Jesse refused. The client became agitated with him.

"The next thing I know there's a knock on the door and a friend of (the client's) shows up expecting to party and have a go with me," Jesse said.

Again, Jesse refused. This time, the client and his friend both became angry and berated Jesse until, the hour up, he finally left.

The client had paid for his session with a credit card, one he had used at Capital City Boys on other occasions. Credit card transactions were handled at the start of the call, not at the end, like with clients who paid with cash.

Two months later, Capital City Boys received a notice from its credit card clearing house that the client had contested the charge, saying he had not authorized such a charge on that date.

That charge back was one of five Capital City Boys experienced in its three years of operation, a small number for an escort-type business. Two came from clients with New York City addresses. The other three were locals.

I challenged all five charge backs and officially lost all five times.

I lost the first challenge because we did not have a signed sales slip. That was my stupidity. The client involved had not been pleased with the escort he met. I sent a second, one of our best, at the normal rate minus the service's referral fee. The client paid cash for the first call and charged the second. Looking back, I think the client intended to contest the charge right from the beginning.

I lost the second charge back because the client claimed the card had been stolen while he was in Washington. That, and we did not have a perfectly clean imprint of the card.

The third charge back was the one from Jesse's client. Jesse had obtained the client's signature on a sales receipt but failed to get an imprint of his credit card. The client contested the charge, I believe, because Jesse refused to do "extra" things the client wanted.

The fourth charge back was also filed by a repeat client. The client had charged for sessions before and I thought I was safe. The client claimed someone stole the extra card he had given his sister. Marvin had warned me not to accept checks from this client, saying the client was into stopping payment on them.

Attempts to get the client to pay were unsuccessful until I posted the man's first and last name and his address (minus apartment number) on Capital City Boys' Web site.

The man soon called, asking how he could get his name removed.

"Pay me for the call," I said. "Send me a money order to ..." I told the man, on good faith, I would go ahead and remove his name but that I expected payment in a few days. I received a money order a couple of days later. I remember wishing I had tried that approach earlier.

The client later called and saw other escorts. The client and I came to have an understanding: he would always pay cash and at the beginning of the session. That arrangement worked well for both of us.

The fifth and final charge back was filed by Gary, also a repeat client. Gary made arrangements on April 2, 2001, to see an escort shortly after midnight.

The escort arrived but could not get Gary to open the door. Capital City Boys had a $100 cancellation fee, which we waived when there was a good reason for not going through with a call. Falling asleep, which is what Gary said happened, was not a good enough reason, especially when the service had already paid the escort $60 for attempting the call.

I would have posted Gary's name and address on the Web site except that I was busy trying to decide what to do with my life and the business. We never sent anyone else to see Gary after that.

In each case, Capital City Boys suffered the financial loss, not the escort. Capital City Boys charged each client using a credit card a $25 early payout processing fee. This fee covered costs associated with offering a credit card service and losses from charge backs.

Capital City Boys got stuck holding four bad checks. One, for $600, was made out to an escort who did an overnight call with a client named James on Aug. 18, 1999.

The escort had been instructed to collect his fee up front and to make sure the client did not "steal" it back, a trick that was sometimes played during overnight calls. The escort failed to collect his fee up front and, the next morning, the client paid him with a check. When the escort took the check to the man's bank, the check was stamped "Account Closed."

Capital City Boys gave the escort $200 and promised to attempt to recover the remaining $400. All attempts failed. Capital City Boys "ate" the $200. The escort had made a mistake that cost him the additional $400 minus the referral fee due the service. I could not, in good conscience, ask him to suffer a total loss on the call.

The other check, for $425, was accepted and cashed out while I was out of town in July 2000. The check, written by a repeat client, came back because there were not enough funds to cover it. Despite repeated promises by the client, we were never able to collect.

The other two checks were written by Tom, Capital City Boy's best customer. (You will read more about Tom and his checks in a coming segment.)

* * *

Bookings and commissions at Capital City Boys and The Agency declined during the first six months of 2001. There were two major reasons: George W. Bush became president, and I was torn about leaving Washington. No one at Capital City Boys cared about the business side the way I did, and I was trying to decide what to do next with my life.

A friend in Washington warned me business would fall off if a Republican were elected president. I dismissed the theory as an attempt to get me to vote for Al Gore, as he was going to do. The prediction proved true.

Asked if the falloff was because Democrats were more likely to be gay than Republicans, my friend shook his head and said no. "Republicans like d**k just as much as the Dems do – they're just too tight to pay to meet someone. They'll buy a porno and run it till the tape breaks from overuse. Democrats, on the other hand, will buy two pornos this week and another on payday."

* * *

Having watched "The Untouchables" on TV as a kid and having loved hearing Walter Winchell's wonderful narration, I learned that G-Man Elliot Ness could not convict Al Capone on the real crimes he allegedly committed but was able to jail him on tax evasion.

Then there was Leona Helmsley. Helmsley reportedly said when charged with tax evasion: "It's only the little people that pay taxes."

Helmsley was convicted in 1989 on tax-evasion charges. She had been accused of using hotel employees to work on her country estate and writing off their pay as business expenses. She earned the nickname "Queen of Mean." She also earned 18 months or so behind bars at the federal prison in Lexington, Kentucky.

With these two tax cases in mind and because I once had spent more than two years being audited by the Internal Revenue Service over an office-in-the-home deduction, I decided it would be in my best interest to pay any and all taxes due. The choice was simple. It was the right thing to do. It was also the easiest.

Capital City Boys could have "doctored" the books and hid booking fees somewhere in the house but then, what if someone came in looking for money and stole it? Capital City Boys could have also given the money to someone else to hold but as happened in John Grisham's *The Partner,* that person could make off with the money too. A third option was to declare the company's actual income, pay taxes on it, and spend it any way I wanted.

I never feared the IRS. While it was very thorough in my audit, overall, it was fair. In a letter dated Monday, April 17, 2000, I informed both the IRS and the Kentucky Department of Revenue the exact nature of this project:

"Capital City Boys is a legally licensed
gay male escort referral service located
in Washington D.C. My involvement
with Capital City Boys is connected
with my being a journalist.
"I am researching the world of gay male
escorts. I plan to write about that lifestyle.
The company is legally registered with the District
and operates within the law."

* * *

PERSONAL THOUGHTS: This project was never about sex. It was never about making money. Keeping accurate records and paying taxes was a part of the research. My project demanded I keep accurate records for the IRS but, more important, for you.

The Backstory

"Opportunities" was written by Christopher Lowe and Neil Tennant. It is published by SONY/ATV Tunes (ASCAP)

* * *

Leona Helmsley died on August 20, 2007.

"Everybody Hurts"
R.E.M.
Peaked at #29 in 1992

Author's note: If you were a man living in or visiting Washington between December 1998 and March 2000, you might have met Christian. Well, at least that was his name to a select group of men who booked one or more sessions with him through Capital City Boys. Here, pretty much in his own words, is Christian's first-person account of his time as an escort in the District.

* * *

My real name is not important, at least not to this story, and, not at this time. What is important, however, is what I have to share about my personal experiences as a male escort in Washington, and how I came to be a part of Capital City Boys.

Let me first tell you a little about me and how I came to be Christian. I was born and raised on Long Island, New York. I moved to a small town on the east coast of Florida with my mother when I was 14, just after my parents divorced. I was a product of an absentee father and an overbearing mother.

If you were to look at my childhood, you would see a boy with a "normal" upbringing – mid- to upperclass neighborhood, mother, father, sister, brother, aunts, uncles, cousins, grandparents and many friends. What could possibly be wrong?

Like others, I always felt different. How, I didn't know, and well, probably still don't, but I was different. At age 7, my parents wanted me to be part of a local swim team. I wasn't interested in swimming but stayed on the team because I enjoyed being in the locker room after practice. Cute boys in Speedos, hot damn.

I had a few experiences with boys my age back then. At the time, we all thought it was just something boys did. My first, and only real experience with another teen boy (at least for a while) happened shortly after I moved to Florida, while I was in the 9th grade. I went through junior high and most of high school dating girls.

I dropped out of high school and started a car detailing business. I made excellent money for a 16 year-old but had no sense of responsibility. I didn't then and still don't like paying bills. As my debt racked up and my credit got off to a bad start, my sister thought it would be a good idea for me to move to Northern Virginia, so she could help me get things back on track. I saw an opportunity to escape from all my problems and I took it.

Did I mention that for the past 11 years I had been repeatedly sexually molested by my grandfather? Did I mention I had been raped by a complete stranger on a Florida beach, gagged, tied up to a palm tree and f**ked up the a** dry? Well, all that happened, and more.

I packed up what I could fit in my car and drove to Virginia. I moved in with my sister and her girlfriend. I was free at last. No more molestation, no more fear of being raped. I was free to do whatever I pleased.

My sister told me I should feel comfortable telling her I was gay, if, in fact, I was. I told her I wasn't. My sister also told me not to venture into D.C. without her until she taught me about the "safe" and "dangerous" parts of the city. I didn't listen. I knew there was a gay area in D.C. from previous vacations. I just didn't know exactly where it was.

The next day, I got in my car and drove into the city. I went and found the gay area I had been looking for. I found a gay bookstore on Connecticut Avenue, just off Dupont Circle. I walked in and felt as if everyone either knew I was straight, unsure of what I was or just thought I was lost.

I finally realized that everyone might be looking at me because I was "fresh meat" in the big city. Scanning the books in the bisexual section, I felt a tap on my shoulder. I turned around and saw a beautiful black man. He introduced himself and, nervously, I did likewise.

He then asked me a series of questions. Questions like, "Are you new in town? Are you gay? How old are you? Where are you from?" His next question took me by surprise: "Wanna get out of here?"

"Sure," I said. I had no clue what was going to happen next. Was he going to take me to lunch? Was he going to take me into a back alley and make me perform sexual acts on him? Was he going to take me back to his place, tie me up, rape me and kill me? I had no idea.

He took my hand. As we walked past the counter, the clerk said, "Goodbye, Tony." I was relieved to know he had not lied about his name. Someone knew him, so apparently he had been there a few times.

Other people greeted Tony as we walked toward Dupont Circle. We went into Starbucks and he bought us iced coffees. We walked into the circle and met up with a group of people.

Tony introduced me as "his friend." I remember feeling at ease, feeling welcomed by Tony's friends. I didn't understand why Tony's friends were being so kind to me. I also didn't understand why, with all the friends he had, Tony felt he needed another.

After an hour or so, it came time for me to head home. Tony walked me back to my car. We exchanged phone numbers and, just as I was about to get in my car, Tony kissed me. This was my first time kissing another man. I loved every second of it.

Confused as hell, I drove home.

Tony became my first boyfriend. He also became my "first." He was kind, gentle and passionate in every way. Well-hung too, I might add. Our relationship went on for a while but I wasn't ready for what he was looking for. He was looking for a long-term relationship; I was looking for someone to explain what was happening to me. We remained friends for a while, then just drifted away. I will never forget him, ever.

* * *

So, exactly how did I come to meet Mack you might ask? One night, I created the screen name PrettyBoi18 and checked out the chat feature on AOL. I created that name despite never considering myself pretty or a "boi." To me, a "boi" was a cute blond-haired, blue-eyed, smooth-chested individual.

I knew the name would gain attention. What I didn't know was what I was getting into because I had never used AOL chat before.

After searching a few profiles and turning down multiple IM's from people wanting sex, I received an IM from Mack. We chatted for a while. I believe it was my mentioning I was looking for another job that prompted Mack to pop the question: "Have you escorted or thought about escorting?"

I didn't even know what escorting was. Too embarrassed to ask, I found a definition online and answered him with a "no."

Then, I told him "there was a first time for everything." I think we chatted a few more times before we set up a meeting. Scared as can be, I met Mack and I became part of Capital City Boys.

Mack did not talk me into escorting, I talked myself into it. Mack talked me through it. He guided me and helped me through the fear of being alone with strangers who paid money to spend time with me. Eventually, the fear faded and my work at Capital City Boys became a job.

While most escorts worked for money to buy drugs, to pay for that night's bar tab or maybe to just pay some extra bills, I escorted for other reasons. I felt good that people wanted to see me so much that they were willing to pay to have me come over. While I never considered myself pretty or good looking, I always felt that way when I was with a client.

Did the extra money help? Of course it did. Did I make a lot of money? Yes, but we all know the more you make the more you spend.

I escorted because I felt needed and wanted for the first time in my life. I enjoyed the money, but I hated myself for escorting. Growing up, I was taught that such behavior was wrong.

Working with Capital City Boys, I was taught that I set the rules, not the client. In fact, the escort deciding what happened during a call was company policy. Mack never forced us to go on calls if the client wanted something we were not comfortable with. I think I can speak for all who worked with Capital City Boys when I say that this policy was one of Mack's many ways of showing respect for us.

No two calls were ever alike. All were unique in their own ways, like a Social Security number, a fingerprint or a snowflake. Some calls were "good," some were "bad," some were just "OK." Some were damn fun.

One client, a guy named Tim, had me bring boots along on one call, on another, rollerblades. Tim's fetish was not being with guys, it was not being with me, it was not the act of calling an escort – a complete stranger – one whom he could do certain things with for the hour he booked. His passion was the boots and rollerblades.

Tim had no interest in sex. He just wanted to bend someone over his knee and spank them, while fantasizing about the rollerblades and boots.

Weird? To me, yes, but then who am I to judge? Tim enjoyed

boots, rollerblades and the spankings. Being a part of that is why I was there.

Looking back now, I realize I got paid to be a part of his fantasy, wearing nothing but boots. Good money I might add. He was a good tipper as well. As I write this passage, I get a good chuckle about those times. These calls were some of the "OK" ones.

I remember being at the Gay Pride celebration in June 1999, with Mack and some of the "boys." A call came in asking what escorts might be available that day. Not many were. I think I was one of maybe three who were available.

Mack noticed the look I gave him that said I was interested in taking the call. I never asked, but I'm sure it was a relief to Mack knowing he didn't have to track down an escort on Gay Pride.

Escorts were notorious for being nowhere to be found on holidays, gay events or when the clubs opened. I know what you are thinking, and the answer is yes, an escort was much more likely to go out on a call if you were around Mack during business hours.

Most call it favoritism. Helping out with the phones on occasions, I know otherwise, it was strictly business. Sometimes an escort would call in, saying he was available, then be impossible to reach. When this happened, the service often lost the call, not a good thing on a slow day. As with any business, a certain number of "sales" had to be made in order to pay the overhead.

You should know one thing: Mack was not a pimp. He legally owned and operated a male escort referral service.

Anyway, back to my call. Mack handed the phone to me and the client asked me what my stats were. I told him: six-foot tall, 178 pounds, brown hair, brown eyes, medium build, moderately hairy but well groomed. I would normally tell you my endowment about this time but I think I'll keep you wondering. I told the client, a man named Bobby, and he was delighted. The client booked the call.

I told Bobby I would have to take a shower before he could come over for his in-call. I had been outside at Gay Pride events and was sweaty. Bobby abruptly stopped me and asked when I had last showered. I told him that morning. Bobby said he preferred I not shower again, that he wanted to just come right over.

It became obvious Bobby liked sweaty guys. I just went with it. I laughed and told Mack that the client wanted me to run home. I asked Mack if my running home was part of the client's hour. As courteous as ever, Mack said: "No kid, we don't charge for travel time." We both smiled and I was on my way.

The call only lasted a half hour. Bobby still paid for the full hour (again, company policy) and didn't even question it. This time, the client wanted to enjoy the sweat on my body. In one hour I managed to please a client, earn $100, shower and got back to my friends at Pride. Not a bad day. That was a "good" call.

One time I got to a client's hotel room and, when the door opened, I thought I was at the wrong place. I was just about to apologize for the inconvenience when he said, "Christian?" I said, "Yes." The client invited me into his room. I was both shocked and relieved at the same time.

The client was from another country, which one, I don't know. He was tall, lightly bronzed skin, slender, toned, and hot! He was only 22 and was in D.C. on business. We had a blast! I felt guilty for taking the money that time. That was a "great" call.

I also had my share of "not so good" calls. I once had money thrown at me and was told to "pick it up, like a good little whore." I was once told to get down on all fours and beg for the money owed to me. I was once walked around inside a gorgeous mansion on Capitol Hill, wearing a dog collar and leash. I was, once, at client's home, tied up, gagged and whipped beyond my liking. A repeat client, a man named Patrick, once slapped me across the face just before I left. The slap was unexpected, especially since he had been a perfect gentleman right up to that moment.

When I tell you these were "not so good" calls, I mean mentally. These calls brought me down and made me feel dirty. These calls made me feel like a whore, not an escort. I felt degraded.

I held these feelings inside me, deep inside me. I felt the client had behaved the way he did because it made him feel good, or powerful or something else. I knew he didn't mean to make me feel bad. I simply saw that behavior as part of the game.

I didn't like how these clients treated me but I never said anything, not even to Mack. How would I benefit from saying something? I knew I wouldn't, so I stayed quiet.

Clients liked me. I know they did. You can tell when someone isn't having a good time.

Regardless of if the call turned out to be "good" or "bad," I always made the client believe I had a great time, even when that was not the case. This feeling was important to many of my clients, and therefore, important to me. I was always very courteous and considerate of my clients' needs.

My favorite client was a man named Tom. We became the best of friends, became lifelong friends. Tom was special to me for many reasons but especially because he treated me as an equal, the way one treats a special friend.

* * *

More than half of the men I met were straight, at least I guess they were. They wore wedding bands and confided in me that they were. Some said they had never been with a guy before and wanted to see what such an experience was like. Others admitted they had seen guys before me and then usually added that they had to keep this part of their life a secret because they had a family or girlfriend or fiancée.

Most of my calls took place in downtown hotels. I liked these calls. I always felt safe. I never had to worry if the place was going to be clean or dirty. I also took comfort in knowing that the people downstairs knew who the client "really" was. He may have lied to Mack and me about his name, but the people downstairs knew who he was.

Was I ever intimate with a client? Yes I was. To me, being intimate with a client meant the client treated me with respect, from the time he opened the door until the time I left. Respected me by doing simple things like asking, "How was your day?" "Did you have any trouble finding my place?" In other words, by asking questions and actually caring what I said in return and not by saying, "Come in, take your clothes off and get started..."

When the client and I had sex, we were two consenting adults, doing what we chose to do during that paid hour of time. Let me make this one point clear: I never got paid to have sex or to perform any sexual acts.

* * *

I never considered myself to be like most other escorts. There was good and bad in feeling that way. Yes, I went on calls, met strangers who paid me to, well, let's just say, make them happy.

I was often jealous of the other escorts I met. They had a lifestyle that went along with escorting – doing a call then going out with friends to spend the money you just made. Being at

Mack's, I would often hear an escort tell someone on the phone, "yeah, I'll be there," meaning they would be heading out somewhere to meet up with friends. Many times, these escorts would meet up with friends at Badlands or Nations (nightclubs).

Driving around the Dupont circle area, I would see escorts in the circle or at Soho's or at Annie's. They hung out after their calls. I always got in my car and went home, to be alone.

I was never friends with other escorts. I was never in a group, never in a clique. Looking back, I didn't want to be in a clique. I wasn't into popping pills or snorting coke. Maybe it was my fault, maybe I just felt like an outsider, maybe I just felt like I didn't belong in a group.

My brother, my sister and Mack were my social circle. Escorting allowed me to widen that circle some with clients who became friends. I never had friends my age, they were always older. Even today, I don't have friends my age. For me, friendships never lasted long. Friends came and went.

Self-esteem issues caused me problems. I kept thinking, "cute boys are out of my league." It seems the ones that wanted me, I didn't want, I had no interest in. But those I wanted were either with someone or, in my head, way out of my league.

* * *

Mack made it clear that escorts were not to date. "It's bad for business," he'd preach. I listened and followed his instructions.

The one time I strayed was with an escort named Junior. The whole Junior thing is something I'll never forget. Mack and I were staying at the Carlyle Suites Hotel. A Capital City Boys escort named Junior had been thrown out of the house in Northern Virginia, where he had been staying.

Always willing to help the boys, Mack told Junior he could stay in the room with us. At some point we turned out the lights to go to sleep. I was in one bed, Mack was in the other and Junior was on the loveseat.

Mack got a call and had to go out to see someone. Getting dressed, Mack gave Junior and me a few instructions and, just before leaving said: "behave."

It was a simple request but one we ignored. When Mack returned, his key unlocked the door but he couldn't get in because we had fastened the chain lock. Mack exploded. He hadn't wanted to go out, didn't want to leave us alone and now that he had returned, we had locked him out of his own room.

Oh, did I mention the lights were off? Did I mention Junior had moved over into my bed? Did I mention neither of us had any clothes on?

Behave. It was a simple request, one I knew I should have followed.

Banging on the door, it quickly became clear Mack wasn't going to laugh about this situation. Eventually let into the room, Mack didn't hesitate to make that point clear. Using words, Mack beat up on me. I felt horrible. I felt so bad for disappointing Mack it almost made me feel like I had become "one of them" (just another escort). It was as if I had thought "Everybody else takes advantage of Mack, why shouldn't I?"

Seeing how upset he was, I knew I hadn't only disappointed Mack but also Malcolm. It was as if I had disappointed my own father. I remember thinking, "This is the first time I disappointed you, my first time to hook up with another escort. This is first time ..."

This was my first time but not the first time Mack had faced such a situation. At the time, I had no way of knowing why my hooking up with Junior upset Mack so much. I learned later.

* * *

Toward the end of Mack's time in Washington, I came to realize the loneliness and the frustration he was facing. I would call Mack from time to time after I left Washington. He was always out on street meeting somebody, always busy, always having fun.

When I called him in the spring of 2001, I instantly knew something had radically changed. There were no street noises, no sounds from a TV. I asked him, "What ya doing?" when he replied, "I'm at home," I knew something was seriously wrong.

Mack said he couldn't get a moment's peace because of all the drama going on around him. Having been around Mack a lot, including a monthlong stay in Lexington, I knew how much he enjoyed peace and quiet. Mack desperately needed someone to help answer the phones so he could have a life in D.C., so he could go out to dinner or for a drink with friends. Mack did not have that.

I could have been there for him. I would have loved to have helped more. Because of certain decisions Mack made, that did not happen and I eventually moved far away. I moved, but I never lost touch with Mack. I stayed in touch because I felt a connection with Mack right from the start. We were alike in so many ways.

Do I have any regrets, am I sorry I did this? No. What I've done in my past defines who I am today. I got into this business and I was nervous but as I got into it, I became comfortable. After all, I was used to getting paid to do things from my grandfather who molested me.

I knew at some time I would have to face my demons. I have. I went through some severe depression because of being molested and my time escorting. I am a stronger and better person today because I'm not wasting my future reliving those experiences. I have put those things behind me. I have learned that everybody has their own story, their excitement, their own past, their own thrill.

Along the way, I learned not to be so judgmental. Escorting opened up a whole new world for me. I met a lot of people I otherwise never would have.

Do you think when Tim, the client, goes into a 7-Eleven to get a coffee that the clerks know he likes seeing a naked guy wearing rollerblades or boots? No way. I got to know a totally different side of him and others, a side that if others knew, they would probably damn them to Hell.

I learned I couldn't judge him – he has his special interests, I have mine, and you have yours. Mack calls this blind acceptance. Having previewed *Mack And The Boys* ahead of you, I know you will come to know more about blind acceptance and why we should all practice it more. I can tell you from personal experience, it will make you a better person.

Now that you've taken the time to hear my story, I would like to introduce myself to you, my real name is Danny.

* * *

CHRISTIAN'S PERSONAL THOUGHTS: Mack, of all the

guys/boys who have come and gone in and out of your life with Capital City Boys, you and I are still friends 10 years later. Maybe I didn't get to live with you or work with the company as long as I might have liked, but maybe that was meant to be – maybe that's why we're still friends.

* * *

MALCOLM'S PERSONAL THOUGHTS: Not inviting Christian/Danny to move into the Capital City Boys house was the biggest mistake I made associated with this project. Sean did not want Christian/Danny there. I gave in to his demand/wish. I knew right away I had made a mistake but did nothing to correct it. Somehow, Christian/Danny looked past my lousy decision and remained my friend.

I also handled the Junior situation badly. I shouldn't have cared if he and Junior had messed around. No one in Washington knew running Capital City Boys was a research project. I took my work as a journalist seriously. I guess I foolishly thought everyone should. I had a lot riding on this project, taking time to make sure someone around me got to mess around was not high on my priorities.

In the early days, while still living in Lexington, I would invite Capital City Boys' top-revenue producers out to dinner when I would breeze into town.

The three times I did this produced the same result: the boys and I went to dinner then went our own ways. Later, when clients called wanting to meet one of my dinner guests, remarkably, no one was available.

I stopped hosting group dinners after one of the guys confided in me that the escorts paired off after the dinner and went out for the evening, enjoying each other's company. They got a date out of the dinner, the company got stiffed. From then on, I took only one or two escorts to dinner at a time and made sure one or both stayed close by afterward.

* * *

Christian/Danny courageously told you his real name. Later in this project, in a segment called "Danny's Song," I will tell you more about this thoughtful, wonderful guy, someone I am truly proud to call friend.

Working the phones at Capital City Boys, I came to know a host of dirty little secrets. Though I never intended to, I came to know who liked having oral sex with another man and who had a passion for young boys.

Capital City Boys never represented anyone under age 18 and rarely anyone under the age of 19. In Washington, the age of consent is 16. Anyone who "looked young" had to produce a valid ID showing his age or he was not represented.

I never found nor heard of a licensed service in Washington that provided under-age boys to clients. Those in the business knew whatever financial reward that might be gained was not worth the risk.

Still, young boys were apparently available, at least, I kept being told they were.

One man, looking to meet a 15-year-old boy, said he had previously met such a boy through a man who hung out with a group of boys at a coffee shop near Dupont Circle. The caller said he had met the boy during a trip to Washington earlier that year. Now that he was back in town, the client wanted to see the boy again or to meet another under-age boy.

The man did not remember the name of the coffee shop. He called to see if I did. The caller offered two other important pieces of information: The man and the boys were there only late afternoons and only on weekdays.

I spent afternoons the next couple of weeks cruising through the coffee shops near Dupont Circle, trying to document the man's story. The closest I came was just to observe suspicious behavior at one particular place.

It was there that I found a group of teen boys, usually numbering between seven and 10. They met there after school with a dark-haired man who looked to be in his mid-40s.

The boys and the man stood out for three reasons: The coffee shop was not very busy at that time of the day; a 40-something man hanging out with boys looking like 14- and 15-year-olds is a bit unusual and gets noticed; and the man was usually the only one drinking anything. The boys generally just sat there.

I sat and discreetly watched the group for about an hour at a time on multiple occasions. The boys seemed to be close – laughing and talking as friends often do. Occasionally, the man would go outside, usually out of sight.

Every time the man returned, the boys got very quiet. The man would sometimes call one of the boys outside. When called, the boy would almost always reluctantly push their chair back, smile slightly to the others, and then walk outside. A cute, tall, dark-haired boy was called outside a lot.

Sometimes the boy and the man would return, sometimes just the man.

There was never any indication anyone at the coffee shop was involved in whatever was going on with the man and the boys.

No matter what was going on, the behavior was strange. What was the man doing with the boys? Where did the boys go when they left? I never found out in part at least because I never figured out an effective way to investigate without endangering this project.

I knew police ran sting operations in Dupont Circle from time to time, mostly for drugs. Maybe this time the sting operation was to trap someone wanting under-age boys. Who would have believed that I was just asking questions for a project and not trying to hook up if I had asked the man about his friends and if they met older men for money?

I casually asked a couple of the guys who worked with Capital City Boys if they knew what was going on – they did not. I directly asked one guy to see if he could find out. He found the man and the boys but said, like me, he too could not figure out a good way of asking since the boys never left the group unless having been called outside by the man.

Finding out more about the man and the boys got put on a list of things to check on later. I never saw the group of boys nor the man again.

* * *

The out-of-towner was not the only one who called Capital City Boys asking to meet an under-age boy. Perhaps our name attracted such calls.

One caller persisted. "Name your price," he said several times, "and I'll tip both you and the boy very well." Capital City Boys repeatedly hung up on him.

The client called several times, always with the same request and always with promises of lots of money. Capital City Boys never sent anyone, even when he asked to see a 19-year-old it represented.

The man kept calling, pushing the service to find him an under-age boy. When it became clear he was not taking "no" for an answer, I did something I never repeated with any other client – I rattled off the caller's name, his address and where in Roslyn, Virginia, he worked. I knew this information because I had investigated the caller.

I told him that – based on my own experience – his employer would be even less thrilled to hear about his repeated requests for an under-age boy than mine had been to learn I owned a gay escort referral service. The line went dead. Capital City Boys never heard from him again.

* * *

Escort clients were not the only ones having sexual encounters with under-age boys in Washington.

One 14-year-old blond boy was repeatedly observed being allowed into Badlands, then a gay club near Soho. I ran into the kid around 2:30 one morning. I was coming out of the gyro restaurant on P Street as he was walking by. On this particular night, the boy was shirtless and his hair, face, chest and arms were covered in some sort of a blue coloring.

The boy told me he had been to Badlands. When I asked how he was able to get in, the kid laughed and said all he had to do to get in or to get a drink was to let someone who worked there put their hand down his pants. "They get to touch me and I can have anything I want," he said. "They never get any further than touching even though they beg" for more.

There was no indication that anyone but the one Badlands employee was involved in this situation.

It was not uncommon for under-age guys – just not as young as the blond boy – to be allowed to drink in bars and other gay clubs in hopes of the favor leading somewhere.

* * *

Lexington, Kentucky, has also had its share of men seeking

under-age boys for sexual pleasures.

One of the city's most-famous cases happened in May 1984, when a police undercover operation targeted at male prostitution in the city's downtown area went awry. A local attorney picked up two boys – one 16 years old and the other, 14 – and took them to his home, police said, to have sex.

The 16-year-old, later identified as Speed Ramey Jr., was wearing a listening device issued to him by local police during the encounter.

Police listened while the 14-year-old "sold himself" for $20. Police followed the boys to then Lexington lawyer William Wessell's nearby home. Police "broke in" after Ramey told them the attorney and the 14-year-old had gone into another room to have sex. Wessell was convicted of sodomizing the 14-year-old. It was reported that Wessell was put on probation for five years and fined $500.

Lexington's police department was heavily criticized for using minors in the sting operation. A $12.5 million lawsuit was filed by the 14-year-old's mother. It was reported that the city eventually settled out of court for $145,000.

Ramey "always knew what he was doing was wrong," Barbara Lawrence, a social worker with the Crimes Against Children Unit, told the *Herald-Leader* in January 1989. "He just wanted a fast-buck and life in the fast lane."

Lawrence told the *Herald-Leader* almost everyone who knew Ramey found it difficult not to like him. "The women adored him; the men he solicited adored him."

Ramey died December 31, 1988, at the age of 21. He died while in a minimum-security prison in Kentucky on an unrelated conviction.

Craig Stacy, a close friend of Ramey's, said Ramey was not gay. "He always wanted you to know that," Stacey told *Herald-Leader* reporter Kevin Nance in January 1989. "For him (it) was just for the money."

The Wessell case is not the only sex case involving minors in which the Lexington-Fayette Urban County Government has been involved. Another involves Ron Berry who founded a youth jobs program designed to encourage disadvantaged youths to participate in public service work.

The *Lexington Herald-Leader* reports that Berry was convicted of 12 counts of sodomy with 12- to 16-year-old boys in

2002. Berry completed a three-year prison sentence in 2005.

More than 160 people filed lawsuits against the Urban County Government, claiming the city continued to fund Berry's program even though officials knew Berry was sexually and physically abusing children in the program.

The lawsuits allege that officials allowed the abuse to occur because Berry, once a prominent and powerful black leader, could deliver votes. The city has settled some of the suits, others are still pending. The *Herald-Leader* reported that one payout – in 2002 – was for $2.4 million. The money went to 17 plaintiffs.

* * *

NEWS UPDATE: In August 2008, Kentucky Gov. Steve Beshear restored Ron Berry's right to vote and hold office. A spokesman said the governor, as a matter of policy, automatically approves the partial restoration of civil rights if applicants have served their sentence, paid restitution and have no outstanding warrants. Prosecutors can object to the partial pardon but, for some reason, Berry's paperwork apparently got lost and no one opposed the action.

* * *

PERSONAL THOUGHTS: The tall, dark-haired boy I repeatedly saw at the coffee shop appears in one of the photos I shot of Chase performing at Soho one night – he was one person in a room crowded with people. I did not know the boy had been there that night until I edited my photo shoot the next day. I had been that close to getting an answer to the mystery about the man and the boys, that close to knowing the truth.

* * *

I met William Wessell once. Our chance encounter occurred sometime between 1994 and 1998, long after the incident involving Speed Ramey. It was not until after he told me he used to be an attorney but had gotten into trouble with a minor that I realized the stranger I was talking with was Wessell. I knew all about his case, having put many of the articles and photographs about his case into the *Herald-Leader.* I kept that fact a secret.

Wessell and I talked briefly about his experience. "No one wanted to hear my side," I remember Wessell saying. "All they heard was that I had paid a 14-year-old boy to s**k (him)."

Almost every escort had two names – a real one and a made-up one. Rarely does an escort use his real name. Although made-up names do not offer a lot of cover, they are widely used because they give the escort deniability in case someone "stumbled" onto a Web site and thinks he recognizes a friend.

Capital City Boys allowed guys to choose their own escort names. If someone chose something weird, they would be counseled to choose another. Love Child and Pharaoh were among the strangest names chosen. Experience indicated neither would be successful. They were not.

Most chose ordinary names like Joe, Mike, Jim, Andy, Glenn, Eric and Rob. Maybe the plainest of all was a handsome 22-year-old named Earl.

Some chose names with great pizzazz, names like Jayme. Having model-quality looks, Jayme changed the spelling of his name three times until he was happy.

The service offered a list of names to choose from. Some names, like Max and Mack, were off-limits. No need for any confusion. Only one guy could use a name at a time.

The first escort signed to be represented by Capital City Boys was Sean, so every name was available to him. First he was Sean, then Shaun, then Shawn, then Sean again. He chose the name Sean because it was his friend's name and he thought it was cute to use his name. A friend of Sean's worked for us too. He chose to use Sean's real name as his escort name. He thought that was cute. Sean did not.

Services often "retire" a name for a few months after the guy using leaves to avoid a mix up. If a client calls asking for a certain guy soon after a name is reactivated, smart services make sure the client is asking for the new guy, not the old one.

Capital City Boys occasionally ran into a problem when a client would ask to meet Hunter. Hunter – who was small in size, had a smooth chest and black hair – had worked at The Agency before this project started. The Agency had once had two Hunters – both small, smooth and with black hair. One came back to work with The Agency while it was part of this project. We ran into trouble a couple of times when a client who met "our" Hunter was looking for the "other Hunter." The Agency got good at asking "which Hunter" after the second mix-up.

The most provocative name of any escort we represented was Will. It proved to be a great name for an escort – simple, direct, suggestive.

One guy insisted on being called Sean Peter. After much discussion about the possible meanings and ramifications of an escort using the name Peter, we let him. He was a hot 22-year-old Italian and we did not want to lose him to another service. Sean Peter did not stay long. His girlfriend got jealous of the attention he got from clients and made him quit.

Another great name one escort used was Cravin Morehead. That name prompted several humorous exchanges with a client named Bob who suggested we represent drag queens so we could use names like Anita Dick, Iona Traylor and Rachel Tensions.

Clients also used made-up names for the same reason escorts did – it gave them some sense of protection.

What names did clients use? How did they come up with the name they used?

Former New York Gov. Eliot Spitzer used the name of a friend/supporter. Spitzer's choice was not so out of character for most clients.

The Good, the Bad, and the Really Ugly episode of Warner Bros. Television's "Big Shots" did an excellent job of explaining how such a thing happens:

Duncan Collinsworth: "The night I pulled into that truck stop, the night I hooked up with Dontrelle, before we completed our transaction, she asked me my name. If there was one thing I knew it was not to give her my real name."

Brody Johns: "Well, that's good thinking."

Duncan Collinsworth: "You would think so, right? The problem is, it was late and I was tired, so I gave her the first name I came up with ..."

Brody Johns: "Which was ..."

Duncan Collinsworth: "Yours."

"Dream You"
Pirates of The Mississippi
Peaked at #68 in 1993

In an effort to capture the business traveler and to satisfy a desire to write, Capital City Boys developed what became a successful marketing campaign called "Up Close & Personal."

The campaign featured a conversation with Mack in which he talked about certain escorts, telling interesting things about them. Naturally, the piece was written in a way that encouraged the reader to meet with the featured escort.

Here are three such articles:

MEET RAND

The first thing you will notice about Rand is his smile. You can't help but notice it. It's wonderful. It's intoxicating. But most important, it is genuine.

The next thing you'll notice is how cute he is. His smile is an important part of his cuteness, but there's a  lot more to Rand. Talk to him and you'll see that he has depth.

Spend an hour or two with him and you'll see how wrong you were if you ever thought he was the least bit shy and reserved.

Rand is a well-traveled kid. He grew up in Virginia but has lived and spent time in a lot of places, including South Beach, Florida, and Paris. (Smiling, he is quick to point out that he meant Paris, France.)

There's that smile again. Did you notice it this time?

Asked what he wants to accomplish in the future, Rand is quick to smile and answer that he wants to own a club.

Nice dream, kid. As he elaborates on his idea, it becomes clear that his would not be just another club. No way! Not with this guy.

"Overall, my club would be a melting pot," he says. "There

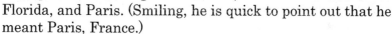

would be go-go boys and go-go girls. Some nights there would be sumo wrestlers or Japanese schoolgirls dressed in cute uniforms rapping to techno music."

Well, now. Rand certainly paints quite a visual image, doesn't he?

Smiling again, Rand conveys what he believes will be the key to his club's success: "People would come [to the club] every week just to see what crazy thing I came up with."

The detail he offers about his idea reveals he has thought long and hard about this dream.

Asked if he has a boyfriend, Rand smiles again and says no. "I tend to do better with guys somewhat older than me," he says. "I feel much more comfortable that way."

Asked to explain, he smiles (slightly this time) and says, "I'm just not into guys my own age or younger. I don't want to be anybody's father – at least not just yet."

Well now! Reader, is that a smile I see on *your* face?

MEET ZACK

If you like a down-to-earth kid who has his head on straight, then you'll love Zack. If you like a kid who can listen and carry on an intelligent conversation, then you'll love Zack. And, if you like a kid who genuinely enjoys himself and his work, then you'll definitely love Zack.

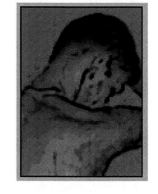

Listening to Zack, you begin to see the person deep inside of him. You'll come to know just how wonderful and mature this kid really is.

"I'm into music," he says. "That's what I want to do with my life – record and sing."

When most 19-year-olds talk about their dreams, the dream is usually something way off in the future. Many times, it has just a shot in the dark of ever coming true. But listening to Zack talk about his love for music, I leaned back in my chair and thought that maybe, just maybe, his dream wasn't so far off, so far-fetched.

His musical influences are Mariah Carey and someone called Babyface. OK, so he didn't mention The Backstreet Boys or Meat Loaf. I can forgive him for that. I must admit, I did not have the nerve to ask him if he had ever heard of my favorite music writers: the great Jim Steinman (the power behind Meat Loaf) and the wonderful '50s and '60s rock 'n' roll team of Jerry Leiber and Mike Stoller.

Asked what might set him apart from other escorts, Zack smiled and, for the first and only time during the interview, was stumped. He thought for a while longer, then smiled and said he didn't know.

Fair enough answer. You see, I don't yet know what sets him apart from the others either. I just know that there's something very special there.

Meet Zack once and you'll see what impressed me. Meet Zack once and you'll come away knowing you've met someone who isn't like all the rest. Meet Zack once and I am certain you'll want to see him again. And again. And again.

MEET AARON

Aaron is not your typical escort. No way. Everything about him is special. Everything about him is classy.

Look closely and you will see the difference between Aaron and other escorts. Meet him once and you'll know for sure that what I say is true. Meet him a second time and you'll never forget him. Ever.

"I'm a laid-back guy," he says proudly. He is. And that's part of his charm. It is a part of what sneaks up on you and grabs you and captures your imagination as well as your heart, even before you know you've lost either one of them.

If you love voices, you'll love Aaron's. It's intoxicating. Aaron is well-spoken. The words and phrases he uses show you that he is well-educated. In fact, he has a master's degree. But unlike some with that level of education, he isn't stuffy. Just the opposite.

From the time you meet Aaron until the time he leaves, you will enjoy yourself. His gentle smile will offer you a glimpse into the real man inside of him. His gentle smile will warm your heart. His gentle smile will put you at ease.

A Class Act. That's Aaron.

So why would a guy like Aaron escort? Once you come to know him, his simple explanation makes sense: "I don't mind a guy that's affectionate and shows interest in me."

Aaron does enjoy attention – both getting and giving. In his private life, Aaron enjoys traveling, cooking, white-water rafting, and being outdoors "I have an adventurer's streak in me," he says. "I'd love to go skydiving."

Ask him what his favorite song is and his class shows through again. "I'm not into just one type. I like eclectic, dance, hip-hop, classical, new age, and rock. There are certain artists in each category that I get into."

Aaron had his first serious sexual encounter with another man when he was 17. The other guy was 24 or 25. "In term of my experience, I'm pretty much relationship-oriented – laid-back, traditional, conservative. But on the flip side, I also have a really odd, wild side."

Hmmmm.

"In terms of sexuality, I really have done most things. Everything from really vanilla sex to group sex to leather. I have been very open in terms of trying other things."

I told you – Aaron is special. Everything about him is classy. Look closely and you will see the difference between him and other escorts. Meet him once and you'll know for sure that what I say is true. Meet him a second time and you'll never forget him. Ever.

The Backstory

The Pirates of The Mississippi, a country music group, was founded in 1987. The **"Dream You"** video has something for everyone: A sexy woman, a cute, shirtless boyfriend, someone dressed as a policeman, someone dressed in drag and someone banging on a piano while it is burning, at least, that is what I recall.

The group's biggest hit, **"Feed Jake,"** topped out at # 15 in 1991. That song, used as one of the four statements in this book's prologue, references people assuming someone is gay because he wears an ear ring and someone is straight because he drives a pickup.

www.thepiratesofthemississippi.com

"Suddenly Last Summer"

The Motels
Reached #1 on the U.S. Billboard Album Tracks chart
and #9 on the Billboard Pop chart in 1983

OK, so it was Atlanta, not Memphis.

It was March and not summer.

And, all right, I was the lonely boy far from home, not him.

But in so many ways, when Pam Tillis belts out Michael Anderson's "Maybe It Was Memphis," she conveys exactly how I felt about Drew, one of Capital City Boys premier escorts:

"Maybe it was you, maybe it was me,
but it sure felt right."

When I first met him, he was David. That name was as far away from the truth as Drew would be. He came to my hotel room in Atlanta and forever set the standard by which Capital City Boys would judge future escort candidates.

No one ever surpassed him. Few even came close. In my opinion, David/Drew was perfect. Perfect in every way. He spoke so softly. He was so beautiful. He was so Southern.

During our time together, he convinced even me, an expert cynic, that there was nowhere else in the world he wanted to be. I knew his was an act, but I also knew it was well played, something few escorts are able to successfully pull off. It was an act I and others who met him will remember for years to come.

I told David about owning Capital City Boys in Washington. I gave him my name and phone number and told him to call if he ever came to D.C. and wanted to work.

Sixteen months later, the call came. He and his "friend" had moved into the area, and both wanted to escort. His timing was perfect. Capital City Boys needed a new star as its top-producer went into a personal tailspin. Drugs and entertaining for free at Washington's Crew Club – a gay bath house – were taking a toll on him. Both were bad for business. So was his refusal to leave drugs outside our house when he needed to stay overnight.

That night, David – renamed Drew – was introduced to Capital City Boys' A-list clients. This select group of clients almost always got to meet new escorts first. This perk kept clients loyal to Capital City Boys – at least as loyal as calling Capital City Boys first the next time they wanted to see someone.

Washington came to love him. Drew quickly became a legend. Time after time, clients would call Capital City Boys after having met with Drew. Time after time, clients related stories about being under his spell. I understood exactly what clients meant, even those who had trouble finding the right words.

Mel Carter explained this situation in "Hold Me, Thrill Me, Kiss Me" when he sang:

"But they never stood in the dark
with you, love."

* * *

I was closer to Drew than anyone else in Washington in part, because like me, Drew was an outsider. Having met Drew in Atlanta, I considered him someone from the "real world." Drew was the only person to hold that status. I could be different with Drew – I could be Malcolm. With everyone else, I was Mack. That difference – invisible to everyone but me – felt good. It meant Malcolm was still alive.

When a small group of Capital City Boys escorts and I would go out to a bar or club I was also treated differently than the rest. I was older and my role as owner of the service was different than theirs. I did not live in the escorts' world, and while a few were kind enough to include me in outings from time to time, it was always clear I was not one of them.

Neither my age or notoriety mattered to Drew. He was not shy or ashamed about being seen with me. Being an outsider gave Drew a cover socially active local guys did not have.

* * *

In July 2000, Drew's "friend" went home for three weeks. Drew and I made the most of his newfound freedom. I was far more social during those three weeks than at any other time while in Washington. It is not an exaggeration to say many of these days are among the best of all my days.

Drew and I went out to dinner sans phones – a luxury I rarely experienced. The number of calls Capital City Boys booked dipped dramatically during this time. I did not care. OK, I did but I coped.

Charles could not work the phones every night so some nights I worked at the office until 10 or so. Drew and I would then cruise through the bars on P Street. Sometimes we would stay a while, sometimes we just walked through. Some nights we played pool at Mr. P's, sipping on drinks we both swore had been mixed with low-grade lighter fluid.

A few times we went to Wet or LaCage to watch cute guys dance naked on the bar. Drew never met a drink he did not like nor one that lasted very long around him. Where we went did not matter to either of us. The things we did, the fun we shared was more than enough to ease the pain of being so far from home, so far from the real world.

Once, we went to the White House at 2 a.m., stood there in the dark and marveled about its beauty and what an incredible job the founding fathers had done. We also stood there and talked about our lives, about who we had become and how far away from the "normal" lives we both independently desired we were.

For a few precious minutes, two friends shared something special, something no amount of money can buy. It was times like this one, when I was able to totally escape from being Mack. It was times like this one, that I could be the real me.

* * *

Drew never indicated he wanted more than a friendship and I never expected more than that from him. I never once mistook what we had as love or anything like it. It was not. It was something far more important – it was my life fantasy come true.

I grew up in the Bible Belt in a Christian home. I was a youth leader in my church. How could I be gay or bisexual or anything but straight? I turned 21 in the summer of 1974. That was not a good time to be gay or bisexual, but until recently, when possibly was?

No one I knew was openly gay. No one I knew was that brave. I honestly do not know which, if any, of my friends were gay. I did not know I was. I might have wondered, I might have had certain interests but I certainly was not going to label myself as such and I sure was not going to ask anyone if they were.

I did not get to be gay when I was 18, when many gays now "come out." I did not get to be gay when I was 21 and could socialize at a bar or a club either. Considering the times, it was probably a blessing.

I have long wondered what it would be like to be 21 and to have the freedom of being gay – not in 1974 but in today's more accepting world. My time with Drew that July gave me that opportunity. Since the difference in our ages did not matter to Drew, it was not an issue for me. For those nights, in my mind, I was Malcolm, and Malcolm was magically Drew's age – 21.

Martha Davis and The Motels conveyed this feeling in "Suddenly Last Summer" when they sang:

"It happened one summer,
it happened one time.
It happened forever, for a short time. "

Escorts and clients alike questioned what was going on with me. For the first time anyone could remember, Mack was not around much. Some, when they found out Drew and I were spending time together, got mad. Others rolled their eyes and speculated I had gone off the deep end.

They just did not know how special this time with Drew was to me. Not even he knew. And until I explained the situation to Charles late one night, I had never revealed my fantasy to anyone. Telling you this now is only the second time I have ever shared this secret with anyone.

Drew flew to Atlanta a few days later to join his "friend." When they returned, it became clear the special time I had spent with Drew was over, my fantasy had ended. Once again, Malcolm stood onstage but in the shadows, outside the spotlight. Mack was back, totally.

* * *

Drew and I remained close. He often invited me to join him and his "friend" at JR's or at the Fireplace on Thursday nights. The Fireplace offered free drinks to guys who took their shirts off. Drew and his "friend" did and drank for free. I did not and had to pay. The company was good and certainly the view was worth the cost of the drink.

When the free drinks ended, the crowd – including the three of us – always left. Drew and his "friend" would either go to Badlands or go home. I was never invited to go with them. When asked what I had planned, I would explain I had somewhere to go and somebody to see. It was a line I often used in Washington when I found myself in an awkward situation. Awkward, because it was clear I was not being invited. The statement was also true. Mack almost always had someone to see.

Then, with all of us standing there quiet and smiling, Drew and his "friend" would say "good night" and then head off in one direction and I would turn and go in the other.

Drew and his "friend" continued to work with Capital City Boys until I sold the business in July 2001. They opened their own escort referral service – DC Boys – three months later. They ran the service for almost a year before closing it and moving away.

I handled Web site production duties for DC Boys. I also counseled Drew about business issues. It was good knowing Drew faced some of the same problems and situations I had and he, too, was bothered and amused by them.

* * *

PERSONAL THOUGHTS: I was wrong to think time and distance would eventually fade the memories of having once lived out my fantasy those summer nights in Washington with a boy named Drew. They haven't.

The Backstory

"**Suddenly Last Summer**" was written by (The great) Martha Davis. It is published by Dimensional Songs of the Knoll (BMI).

"**Maybe It Was Memphis**" was written by Michael Anderson. It was published by Atlantic Music Corp. (BMI).

"**Hold Me, Thrill Me, Kiss Me**" was written by Harry Nobel. It was published by EMI Mills Music (ASCAP).

"I Want Candy"
The Strangeloves
Peaked at #11 in 1965

Chase was dirty and tired-looking when Capital City Boys rescued him from the unforgiving streets of Washington. Chase was sleeping in Dupont Circle at night, having been chased from his home because he was gay. His was a strict Christian family, he said – one that could not accept that he was "different."

His family found it more acceptable to push their son onto the streets than to embrace his sexuality. It is a situation one sees over and over again in Washington. The same is true elsewhere.

When Chase was introduced to Sean and Christian, they had the same reaction – "You've got to be kidding!" Neither thought Chase was worthy of being a Capital City Boy. At the time, he certainly was not.

Two days later, after making sure Chase had a safe place to stay, several hot baths, a haircut and styling, a manicure, hot food, and new clothes, Chase was reintroduced to Sean and Christian. Again they had similar reactions: "Wow. I never would have imagined that was possible," Sean said.

"It's 'Pretty Woman' come true," Christian said. At the time, none of us knew how true a statement that was.

Chase later revealed he liked to dress in drag. When in drag, Chase was known as Candy. No one at Capital City Boys could have predicted Candy would make as many public appearances as she did. We also did not know Candy was "hated" by a large number of young gays who hung out at Soho or that "she" would intensify those feelings to the point people would often leave the coffee shop when Candy arrived.

* * *

Clients were attracted to Chase just as Capital City Boys had expected. It, however, surprised all of us that Chase was not the least bit interested in working and bluntly told clients he was with them only because they were paying him.

Most escorts feel this way. Most are smart enough never to admit it to a client. A reputation like this is a career killer.

Escorting was not the problem for Chase – his fear of being close to someone was. Even 20-year-olds who stayed overnight with Chase after having met him at a club complained about Chase being "cold."

All but a few clients complained about him. Chase once did a weeklong call with a repeat client who confided he was about to go to prison on tax-evasion charges. Chase and the client clicked and the man was thrilled to have spent the week with Chase.

* * *

Chase moved into Capital City Boys' house on P Street with us in November 1999. Actually, he found the house for us. Having rescued Chase and believing that he would be an important case study for this project, I wanted Chase close by. Everyone, including Chase himself, agreed it was best he have a safe place to stay.

* * *

Almost from the beginning, it became clear Chase had a problem following simple house rules; rules established to protect all who lived or stayed there.

Chase was forever bringing people home with him on Sunday mornings after spending the night at a club or an after party. Bringing people into the house unannounced was a serious breach of company policy. Not just anyone could be allowed in the house. It was not safe, and keeping the house "safe" was a primary function of Capital City Boys or any service. There was enough danger lurking out there for us, we did not need a roommate inviting trouble inside.

"Mack," Chase almost always would say, "these are my longtime friends. It's safe to let them stay."

Chase knew that hard-nosed Mack did not like being awakened to let him inside but would not turn away anyone needing shelter. Anyone. After eyeballing Chase's guests and deciding they did not pose a serious threat I would go through a routine of scaring everybody by asking why I should let any of them in – including Chase. That scene played, I invited the guests inside, and found pillows, sheets and blankets for them.

Almost without exception, when the "longtime friends" got up the next morning and was asked how long they had known Chase, they would confide they had met him the previous night.

A few apologized for not being as forthcoming hours before while standing on the porch. The repentant sinners were always forgiven and told, "You're not the first one to say those words, and probably won't be the last." Then they got a smile that let them know the transgression was forgiven.

* * *

Word spread on escort review Web sites about Chase's reluctance to warm up to clients. As would usually happen with bad escorts getting bad reviews, calls for Chase fell off.

He also became a bigger problem for others living at Capital City Boys' house. Everyone else was working and bringing money in for the company. Chase mooched off everyone. This became a serious problem as it became clear Chase was not going to change or become more productive.

I never pushed the issue with Chase other than to stress he had to be available to work. When he failed to do that, he was moved into a smaller bedroom downstairs. The much better room upstairs was assigned to someone else, someone who was working and brining in money for the company. Chase considered this a personal insult and swore he was not going to work at all anymore. Weeks having passed since Chase had last gone on a call, no one viewed this as a major threat.

A couple of weeks after being moved downstairs, Chase left to spend time with his "new, rich boyfriend" – a guy he had met three days earlier at Soho. The "new, rich boyfriend" turned out to be a recruiter for a Web site based in Maryland that featured "barely-legal boys." Two weeks later, the "new, rich boyfriend" dumped Chase. Once again, Chase was living on the street and sleeping in Dupont Circle.

Capital City Boys considered taking Chase back in but decided against it when there was an outcry by those living at the house. "He's a threat to the company, to all of us," Sean said. Ryan agreed. "He's proven that."

Chase came back to the house only to visit and for dinner from time to time. He never worked with Capital City Boys again.

Chase later told me men at "the farm" took photos of him. "Photos I didn't like."

* * *

PERSONAL THOUGHTS: Chase called from New York City once just before Thanksgiving and said he wanted to go home to Virginia. I bought him a bus ticket. A week later, he was back in

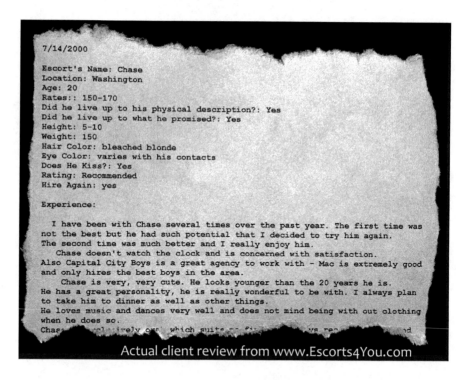

7/14/2000

Escort's Name: Chase
Location: Washington
Age: 20
Rates:: 150-170
Did he live up to his physical description?: Yes
Did he live up to what he promised?: Yes
Height: 5-10
Weight: 150
Hair Color: bleached blonde
Eye Color: varies with his contacts
Does He Kiss?: Yes
Rating: Recommended
Hire Again: yes

Experience:

   I have been with Chase several times over the past year. The first time was
not the best but he had such potential that I decided to try him again.
The second time was much better and I really enjoy him.
   Chase doesn't watch the clock and is concerned with satisfaction.
Also Capital City Boys is a great agency to work with - Mac is extremely good
and only hires the best boys in the area.
   Chase is very, very cute. He looks younger than the 20 years he is.
He has a great personality, he is really wonderful to be with. I always plan
to take him to dinner as well as other things.
He loves music and dances very well and does not mind being with out clothing
when he does so.
Chase

Actual client review from www.Escorts4You.com

New York City. A couple of months later, he called again, saying he did not have money for food or a place to stay. I arranged for Drew – who had moved to New York City – to give Chase $100 cash. I then reimbursed Drew.

Though not publicized, all of Mack's boys were entitled to being rescued. Any time one of them wanted to go home and did not have the money, Capital City Boys or I paid his way.

Chase got two rescues. Early one morning while I was living in Louisville, Chase called wanting a third. He did not get it. The man he was living with had beaten him but Chase refused to call the police as I urged. I remember telling him, "I can't help you if you won't help yourself."

It was a long time before I heard from him again.

"Larger Than Life"
The Backstreet Boys
Topped out at #25 in 1999

He breezed into the hotel room on time for his interview in November 1998, soon after Capital City Boys opened. My life has never been the same since.

"My name is Storm," he said with authority. "And who might you be?"

I was never in control of the interview; he was. Our relationship has been that way ever since. I would not have it any other way, even if I could.

Storm said he was already working for two other services but wanted to leave because both were being poorly run. "You think you can do better?" he asked me.

Turning pale and my voice cracking, I managed to utter, "Yes."

"Good," he said. "D.C. needs a well-run service, one clients can rely on."

Smiling at what he had just said, I invited Storm to sit in the chair facing the loveseat where I was sitting.

"Mind if I record our conversation?" I asked. "I might want to write a book someday." "Yeah, you and everybody else in this town. Sure, go ahead," he said. "Just remember, I know who you are, and I'm Sicilian."

Storm and I talked about escorting and what each of us wanted from our working relationship. Forty minutes later, when he left, the room began to return to normal. I knew Storm was someone special; I just did not know how special. Time would show me.

Not being into porn, I had never heard the name Storm nor had seen any of his movies. I thought having an internationally famous porn star working for Capital City Boys would be a plus. Actually, it was a mixed blessing.

Some clients, especially out-of-towners who knew of Storm, wanted to meet him. If he was not working that night, the clients usually said they would call back the next day, never a good thing for a referral service wanting to book a meeting that night.

For these clients, a substitute was out of the question. I understood how they felt. Out of the hundreds of escorts I met or knew about in Washington, none was like Storm.

Washington residents – for one reason or another – tended to shy away from him. Some clients confided that they would never meet a porn star, no matter who he was.

For that reason, Storm was the only escort I ever allowed to work under two different names – Storm and Joey, his real name. That arrangement worked well, though a few times clients had a hard time deciding if they wanted to see Storm or Joey.

Storm also did something that only one other person – Mickey – did on a regular basis. Storm called every Sunday morning, always offering good ideas for the service. Capital City Boys implemented some of them and passed on others.

If something was happening in Washington, Storm knew about it. Storm's information was always solid and useful.

Once, Storm called on the way to shoot a movie. He talked about a really hot, blond boy he had met and was seeing. "Mack," Storm said, "he's so cute. When you come back, I'll introduce you to him." That never happened. He and the boy had a major fight and broke up before my next visit. I did, however, meet the boy later, and Storm was right – the kid was special. He eventually became Capital City Boys' legendary Jonathan.

Storm never lied to me, and the only thing he ever exaggerated was himself. That was OK because, you see, Storm was always larger than life to me. He always will be. I need him to be.

When it became clear I would be moving to Washington, Storm insisted Max the Wonder Dog and I move in with him. We did, along with a Capital City Boys' escort named Christian. Living in a rented bedroom with my friend, the internationally known porn star, next door and Christian down the hall in Toby's room (Toby was Storm's roommate) was something like I had never encountered. This new arrangement took a great deal of adjusting on everyone's part but we all managed.

I came to see and learn things about Storm I had never known – things like how gifted he was at writing beautiful poems. One night, when he got angry at Toby, Storm took a marker and wrote a deep, dark but wonderful passage on his bedroom wall. I remember being very moved by it.

* * *

Joey was raped at age 15 by a man who worked at the same bar in Newburgh, New York, that he did. (Storm says New York law allowed 15-year-olds to work there, doing cleanup duties.)

"At that time, I had (been with other boys) only two or three times," Storm explained, "never with anyone older."

Joey was clearing glasses from tables when the attack happened. The man "did what he wanted to do," Storm said. Joey left the bar after being raped, his clothes torn by the attacker.

The man who had come to give Joey a ride home that night blamed Joey for the attack. "What did you expect," Storm said, quoting the man giving him a ride. "You're wearing tight leather shorts. You got what you were asking for."

* * *

I was also moved by a collection of photos Storm had hanging on the opposite bedroom wall. They were family photos. A few of them were of a cute, young, happy boy.

"That was me when I was 17," Storm said quietly as I stood in his room one afternoon, staring at the handsome boy. "That's the year my mother kicked me out onto the streets because I liked boys instead of girls." Storm's words hung in the air.

Joey was forced onto the streets. "On my own at 17, I did not have a lot of options," he said. "I did what I had to do to survive." To survive, Joey turned tricks under the name Storm, a name his grandmother used to call him. "It's strange to explain," he said, "but Storm took over and protected Joey. Joey is alive today because Storm was there for him when no one else was."

* * *

There were nights when Storm would stay up all night chatting with people on AOL and keeping everyone else in the house awake. My moving in had prompted the need for Storm to locate his computer in a hall closet near the bedrooms.

* * *

There was a paranoid side of Storm, one all who knew him had to deal with. Having finished reading *Hanibal*, I lent the book to Storm to read. A couple of nights later, he rushed into my room upset that he knew "the truth" – that I had written *Hanibal* under the name Thomas Harris. My first reaction was, "Don't I wish that were true!"

Storm said he knew I had come to Washington "undercover" to

write *Hanibal* and that the chapters he had not read yet were all going to be about him. "Your name is Stallons. The FBI agent's name is Starling," Storm said making his point. "They're awfully close."

* * *

Storm was also forever hearing clicking noises over his telephone. Storm was afraid the National Security Agency or others more nefarious were listening in on his conversations.

One night, Storm called, swearing a hit squad had taken up position across the street and was getting ready to launch an assault on our house to kidnap him. The "hit squad" turned out to be two plumbers who had arrived in a white Ford cargo van to work at a neighbor's house.

Storm was very paranoid about white cargo vans, especially Fords. Christian is fond of telling the story of how one day Storm went flying down a highway at a high rate of speed, weaving in and out of traffic in order to get away from a white cargo van.

Storm later confided to me why he was afraid that someone in a white van would grab him. After sharing his secret with me, I came to understand the basis for Storm's fear. The reason is very credible.

Those of us who lived in the house with Storm believed he allowed his paranoia to get the best of him from time to time. That said, none of us – to this day – are able to explain what happened one particular night after we had all gone to bed.

The house was dark and quiet. Storm was in his room, Toby in his, and I was in mine, the door to the hallway opened. Fifteen or so minutes after we had all settled down and without anyone around, Storm's computer powered up by itself, and, as Storm and I stood there and watched, signed itself into an AOL chat room.

"It was D.C.," Storm said after previewing this segment. "Strange things happened there."

* * *

Storm was the only escort I ever officially "terminated" for anything other than nonpayment of referral fees. The dismissal came while I was living with him. Storm became personally involved with one of the guys working with Capital City Boys. The guy happened to be staying at the house at the time.

Storm ignored warnings not to "mess" with my guests. I overreacted and told Storm that Capital City Boys would no longer represent him. Eventually, Storm and I put the situation behind us, and Storm was welcomed back with open arms.

Soon after that event, I left the house. Christian stayed for a while and then left. At some point, so did Storm.

* * *

PERSONAL THOUGHTS: Even today, when I need straight talk, when I need answers from someone I trust, I call Storm. We exchange Christmas cards – his is always prompt, mine always last-minute.

I told you in this segment I need for Storm to be larger than life. I also shared with you Joey is probably alive today because Storm was there to protect him. Joey isn't the only person Storm has protected. Storm has, for a long time now, also protected me.

A friend of mine marvels that I have the personal phone number of an internationally famous gay porn star and can call him whenever I want. I see it differently. For me, having Storm's phone number is like having Superman's phone number or Batman's. When trouble comes, I know that I can call Storm and he will do whatever he can to comfort or protect me.

Being pressured to vacate my manager's position in Louisville and to take a $10,000-a-year pay cut – in part, I believe because of my involvement with Capital City Boys – I called Storm.

Storm, more than any of the boys who ever escorted for Capital City Boys, knows what it is like to deal with the real world after having been connected with the gay sex world. He, more than most, knows that some can never erase that stain.

Storm was not home but called me back around 3 a.m. Deeply troubled and very sleepy, I told Storm that I was so happy to hear his voice and that I had something really deep to discuss with him, something only he could help me with.

Not hesitating a second, Storm's reaction floored me but his reply was so off the wall that it was just the medicine I needed. The Backstreet Boys described Storm perfectly when, in "Larger Than Life," they sang about there being prices to fame and when they said:

Every time we're down,
you can make it right,
and that makes you larger than life.

Portion of conversation with Storm
on Feb. 27, 1999

Background: Storm was afraid someone had tapped his cell phone because he kept hearing clicks.

He also was worried because an escort from two other services had said he wanted to learn all he could about the companies and then disappeared. Storm thought the escort was a cop and would use what he had learned to bust the services. That never happened.

Andrew was a client who claimed to work for a high-ranking senator. I loved talking with him because of his personality.

At the time of this conversation, Andrew had written both Storm and Capital City Boys cold checks. We were both trying to collect.

Storm: I just don't want my cell phone number to be showing up anywhere and having my congressional phone numbers pulled when they pull my records or something. There's bigger people then me who have to worry if I get any fallout.

Mack: I understand.

Storm: So I have to protect all as responsibly as I can.

Storm: My head off in a dumpster wouldn't appeal to me right now, although I do have a splitting headache from all this nonsense.

Mack: Let's keep your head on your shoulders.

Storm: I'm going to stay overnight at my friends on the Hill. I'm gonna discuss it with them.

Mack: OH – you going to go see Andrew???

Storm: Andrew!!! What? Are you nuts !!! No, My congressman and his neighbor the senator. Please, I think Andrew cleaned toilets at the White House.

Mack: Maybe so.

Storm: Or at least he should have.

The Backstory

"**Larger Than Life**"" was the second single released from the 1999 Backstreet Boys album, "Millennium." The song topped out at #25. The song was written by Brian Littrell, Kristian Lundin and Martin Sandberg. It is published by B-Rok Publishing (ASCAP).

"Rescue Me"
Fontella Bass
A Top 10 hit in 1965

Escorting can be dangerous work. Most of the people I met in the escort business in Washington either knew or had heard of an escort who had been beaten, tied up or drugged by someone they visited. These attacks almost always took place in a private residence.

There was also a danger an escort might see or hear something a powerful person would not want revealed. This was the biggest risk Capital City Boys and The Agency faced.

"You learn and hear things from a lot of your important clients that you should not know," Storm says. "These people are not only hiring you for your services but also for your discretion and your silence."

Escorts working with a service knew the client had been pre-screened and, at that level, had been judged acceptable. Escorts were also told if the client had used the service before and, if so, if there had been any issues in the past.

Escorts working with a service had the comfort of knowing that someone at the service knew exactly whom they were with and where. Those represented by Capital City Boys and The Agency knew someone at the service was also keeping watch on the time and that the service would call the client if the escort did not call the service within a certain time frame.

Escorts working on their own generally had no such safety net.

Capital City Boys and The Agency were prepared to physically "rescue" any of the guys we represented should the need arise.

Clients in Washington had been known to sometimes drug an escort or, one way or another, hold them against their will. This includes by refusing to pay for the visit. Because escorts had been drugged, those who worked with Capital City Boys were warned never to accept any drink – even water – unless it was handed to them unopened.

The need for Capital City Boys to rescue someone physically occurred three times. The first happened soon after Capital City Boys opened, probably in early November 1998.

Sean had to be rescued from a house in the 1800 block of 16th Street NW. Sean's call was for one hour. The hour came and went. Sean did not call to say he was leaving the client's home, which was procedure. Calls to both Sean and the client went unanswered.

Jayme, Sean's roommate, happened to be doing a call at nearly the same time Sean was. When his session ended, Jayme and I went to Sean's client's home. Sean answered his phone as we rang the client's doorbell. It quickly became clear Sean was acting strange.

Sean attempted to convince me he was OK and was still in the house because he wanted to be. Having a limited amount of experience running an escort service and not knowing what kind of situation I was facing, I demanded Sean and the client open the door or I was going to call the police.

Reluctantly, the door was opened and Jayme and I were invited inside. It appeared that Sean was on something but equally clear he was safe and at ease with the client. That settled my nerves. The client was polite, and I realized he had not taken advantage of Sean. Whatever Sean had taken, if anything, he had taken it because he wanted it, not because the client had slipped it to him.

I was standing in the client's living room when my son called from Kentucky. Needing privacy, I walk into the foyer to talk. Getting off the phone, I notice the client, Sean, and Jayme have gone into the kitchen. As I walked in, I noticed dozens of small medicine bottles on the counter. All had been opened.

"Mack," Sean said to me, "look at all of the 'K' [the client] has cooked up." For the first and only time in my life, I stared at numerous platefuls of illegal drugs. I was stunned.

The client suggested Sean and Jayme help themselves to the drugs. The client then turned to me and said, "Take as much as you like." I declined his offer.

Sean later told me the client was a major wholesale-level drug dealer in Washington and New York City. Sean also said the client sold "K" to a drug dealer he and Jayme knew.

The second rescue happened when a deaf escort Capital City Boys represented went to visit a client on Corcoran Street.

The client had been told the escort was deaf, and because of that condition, additional precautions would be taken before a booking would be made. The extra safety measures were explained and the client agreed to them. The escort arrived and the client called us to report that the guy had arrived – just as had been arranged.

The hour went by and then an additional 10 minutes. Understanding no one expected the session to end promptly 60 minutes after it started, the service always waited 10 minutes before calling the client.

When Capital City Boys called, the client's answering machine answered. A message was left saying the hour was up and someone needed to call the service. The person handling bookings waited an additional five minutes then called back. Again, the answering machine took the call. A second message was left.

Capital City Boys called right back. The phone just rang. Storm was briefed and asked to go to the client's home. He was asked to beat on the client's door until the escort came out.

When the client finally answered his phone, he said: "Your boy was having so much fun he didn't want it to end. He told me not to answer the phone. He's leaving now."

Five minutes later, the escort called Capital City Boys to confirm he was out and safe. The escort reported the client had "made him stay and had unplugged the answering machine because (the service) had kept calling."

Storm was five minutes away from the client's house when he was called, told the escort was safe, and to abort the rescue.

I called the client and told him what the escort had told the service. The client laughed. He was told never to call Capital City Boys again. Other services in town were called and told the client had been blackballed. Services paid close attention when another service blackballed a client. No service took such action without good cause.

The Agency also had a list of blackballed clients. I found it among the files that came when I purchased the service. One of the names on the list was that of one of our best clients.

The third and final rescue happened around 3 a.m. one Saturday, a few months before I left Washington. The event played a role in my decision to leave.

Zack had gone on a call the previous afternoon. Charles and I had been shopping and were returning to the office when Zack called to say he was leaving the client's home and would pay his referral fee the following Monday. Zack had proved to be reliable and had earned that right.

Zack's boyfriend called an hour or so later, asking where Zack was. We relayed what Zack had told us.

The boyfriend called back later, saying Zack still had not come home. He wanted the name and phone number of the client Zack had seen earlier. I refused to give it to him but promised to call the client myself.

The client – a man named Aaron – told me Zack had left "hours ago." I relayed this news to Zack's boyfriend.

Somewhere around 2:30 a.m., Zack's boyfriend woke me with a call saying he had just received a phone call from Zack and Zack had said he was still at the client's home and "they were doing drugs together." I reminded the boyfriend I had called the client hours before and the client had assured me Zack was not there.

It became clear the client had lied when Zack's boyfriend told me the client's first and last name and his telephone number. That info had come up on the boyfriend's Caller ID when Zack had called him moments before.

I got out of bed, got dressed, went to the client's home in Northwest D.C. and banged on his basement apartment's door. The client and another man came into view, both naked and both yelling at me, wanting to know who I was and what I wanted.

We could hear one another clearly because one of the panes of glass in the door was missing. I identified myself and told them I needed to talk with Zack, to make sure he was OK. I told them I just wanted to make sure Zack was safe and he was there because he wanted to be.

Aaron again denied Zack was there. I told him Zack had called his boyfriend from there within the past hour. Walking into the yard, I called 911. Hearing me do so and sensing I might gain an upper hand, Aaron called 911 and reported someone was outside his door threatening him.

Two officers arrived a few minutes later.

Aaron, now dressed, joined me and the officers outside the apartment. Seeing him clearly, I realize this is not the first time he and I have met – he had interviewed once to be represented by The Agency. I had decided against representing him.

I told the officers I had reason to believe a friend of mine was being held inside, against his will. The police asked me questions then talked to Aaron.

The precision dance Aaron and I did in front of the officers was amazing. Both of us told our side of the story. Neither of us told the whole story. Both of us had a lot to lose. Neither of us mentioned that Zack had visited the client as an escort, nor did either of us bring up the possibility of drugs being involved.

I asked the police to go inside and see if my friend was there and, if so, to ask him if he was OK. The police turned and asked Aaron if they could.

Aaron said "No." Aaron said that he worked for a major law firm on Pennsylvania Avenue and it was his understanding police could not enter his home without a warrant. He added, in his opinion, the officers did not have enough to get one.

The officers asked me why I thought my friend was inside. I told them my friend's boyfriend had called me saying Zack had called him from inside the apartment. The officers asked me if I "knew for certain" my friend was being held against his will.

Standing there in the dark, with snow falling around me, I carefully reviewed what I do and do not know. Whatever I was about to tell the police had to be the absolute truth and nothing more, no matter what the outcome.

I knew that Zack was inside. I also knew Zack had done drugs in the past but never on a call. I knew Zack had told me he had left the house and was safe. He had either lied or had gone back on his own, or both. I also knew Zack had talked with his boyfriend from inside the home and the boyfriend never mentioned Zack was being held against his will. Finally, I also knew the client was smart enough not to harm Zack since the police had been called and there was a record of his involvement.

Considering all these facts, I looked up at the officers and truthfully whispered, "No."

"Then we can't go in," one of the officers said, and they walked back to their car.

Aaron and I stood there for a few seconds, both of us considering just how close to the edge we had danced. "Take damned good care of Zack," I told Aaron as I turned to leave. "He's safe," the client said.

Early the next day, Zack's boyfriend came to see me. He told me stories about Zack. All were designed to turn me against Zack. He need not have bothered. Blind acceptance requires I judge people by what I see and know, not by stories others tell.

I had already decided Capital City Boys could no longer represent Zack unless he had a convincing story about what had happened and why it would never happen again.

Aaron visited me that afternoon. He wanted to make sure "there were no hard feelings." Aaron explained he had been forced to resign from his job at the law firm the day before and had wanted to "party with someone" to "forget work altogether."

Writing out a check addressed to Mack, Aaron paid the referral fees Zack owed. "I promised him I would," he said. After Aaron left, I looked at the check and mused at what it said. On the check, next to the word "for," he had written: "My Holiday."

Zack and I talked later and agreed it was best he take a break from escorting. We both needed time to heal.

PERSONAL THOUGHTS: No one knew the purpose of running Capital City Boys was to gather information for this project. No one knew being around drugs and condoning their use threatened my assignment. I had to protect the integrity of my reporting. I also had to protect Mack's boys and clients.

Calling the police that night put everything at risk. It was a price I was prepared to pay. Since Capital City Boys had sent Zack there, I was obligated to do anything I could to make sure he was safe.

Photo by Danny

In what had to be the oddest coincidence while I was in Washington, Austin and Wes invited me to their "new" apartment. It was where Zack did his last call. Aaron showed up while I was there. If you look closely at the door, you'll see cardboard taped over the broken window Aaron and I had talked through six months before.

"Safety Dance"
Men Without Hats
Topped out at # 3 in 1983

The toughest challenge Capital City Boys had to deal with was when an escort would confide he was HIV-positive. Such news always had a major impact on future bookings.

Capital City Boys operated on the belief – legal and morally – that the client was paying for the escort's time – whatever happened during their time together was strictly between them.

Did Capital City Boys have a responsibility even though the service never promised or even knew if something sexual happened during a session? Capital City Boys was twice advised: "No." Two Washington-based attorneys said since clients had the opportunity to ask their own questions and to evaluate possible risks involved in meeting a stranger, the company could not be held responsible unless we represented that someone was healthy when we knew otherwise.

When a client would raise health issues – including AIDS – Capital City Boys always recommended he discuss those issues with the escort before deciding whether or not to meet.

Legally, Capital City Boys and I were protected but morally, I struggled with the question: "What if?" The situation was made even more difficult because the escort had been truthful and had confided in me, something I greatly respected. I always felt I owed the escort something for that.

With 35 million people suffering from AIDS worldwide – along with their families and friends – AIDS is a real concern.

Washington's Whitman-Walker Clinic is a non-profit, community-based health organization that provides high-quality, dependable, comprehensive and accessible health care to those infected with or affected by HIV/AIDS.

Whitman-Walker estimates one in every 20 adults in Washington is infected with HIV. The clinic says Washington has the highest rate of new AIDS cases per 100,000 people in the

United States – a rate that is 12 times the national average.

In Washington, blacks account for eight out of every 10 cases of AIDS.

Whitman-Walker says more than 15,000 people in the Washington metropolitan area are living with AIDS and that tens of thousands more are estimated to be infected with HIV.

Everyone represented by Capital City Boys was required to disclose any existing medical and physical conditions. They were also required to report any changes in their physical or mental health. Other services in Washington were not as concerned about an escort's health. Some services kept sending out escorts even though the owners and managers knew they were HIV-positive. This happened at both gay and female services.

* * *

There were 4,764 AIDS cases reported to Kentucky's Department for Public Health's HIV/AIDS Surveillance Program between 1982 and December 31, 2007. There were 201 new AIDS cases reported in Kentucky in 2007. There were 215 in 2006.

In Kentucky, 65% of reported AIDS cases involve whites, 31% black, and 3% Hispanic. The department's 2007 annual report shows that 55% of AIDS cases involve men having sex with other men. It also shows 13% of cases are related to injection drug use.

Kentucky ranks 37th in AIDS diagnosis while Washington, D.C., ranks first.

Lexington/Fayette County has had a total of 649 reported AIDS cases since 1982. The report says 410 of those 649 patients were living with AIDS at the end of 2007, meaning 239 had died.

Of the 4,764 reported cases of AIDS Kentucky has recorded between 1982 and the end of 2007, 4,027 were men and 737 were women. Of the 4,764 reported cases of AIDS in Kentucky, the state reports 2,802 as living with AIDS, meaning 1,962 – or 41% – have died.

The federal government says 900,000 people in the U.S. are currently living with HIV/AIDS and that an additional 300,000 people may not know they are HIV positive. It says that 70 percent of those infected are male. The report also says that 46 percent of those who have died due to AIDS are white (non-Hispanic), 35 percent are blacks, and that 17 percent are Latino. It says for males, men having sex with other men accounts for 47 percent of all cases while injected drug use caused 25 percent of the cases.

AIDS Volunteers, Inc.

AIDS Volunteers of Lexington

AIDS Volunteers of Lexington (AVOL) is a community based organization that provides HIV/AIDS education, prevention initiatives, service programs, and financial assistance to persons infected and affected by HIV disease. Founded in 1987, AVOL provides programs and services throughout Central and Eastern Kentucky.

"AVOL Project Life: Building on Our Legacy" commemorated the organization's 20th anniversary, with a goal to improve the quality of care for its clients and its level of outreach through prevention efforts.

AVOL is worthy of your support.
www.aidsvolunteers.org

"Money"
A million reasons to cash in, one to do otherwise
Pink Floyd, peaked at #13 in 1973
Barrett Strong's "Money (That's What I Want)" topped at #23 in 1959

If you knew a secret worth a million dollars, would you tell it? Say you knew half-a-dozen such secrets, would you come forward, tell what you know, collect your "reward," disappear and live a quiet life somewhere where nobody knows either you or your past?

What if you had that information – gathered through personal experiences, printed telephone logs, signed statements and audio recordings? What if you knew you could document your claims to anyone's satisfaction?

Would you tell what you know? Would you tell, knowing the information could wreck other people's lives, force some of them to give up their jobs and maybe break up families? Would you tell?

At what point in a person's life does one cash in big-time by selling out others? Does it come after losing the career you chose and cherished because some consider you morally and professionally unsuitable to continue that work?

These are questions – real questions – I have faced the past several months. And while I have resisted coming forward with what I know and cashing in, I find myself struggling to find an answer powerful enough to trump the recurring question that runs through my head: "Why Not?"

* * *

A lot of people have great distain for Larry Flynt, the publisher of *Hustler* magazine.

While society has the right to denounce the products his company sells, it should also applaud Flynt for certain other efforts and achievements.

Born in Magoffin County, Kentucky, on Nov. 1, 1942, Larry Claxton Flynt Jr. grew up in poverty. It is estimated that Flynt's net worth today is about $400 million.

Flynt has initiated several legal battles involving the First Amendment – cases that now protect your rights and mine, and those in the publishing world.

Flynt is paralyzed from the waist down, a result of injuries he suffered during a murder attempt in 1978. Many would have given up their fight and lived a quiet life. Flynt did not. He has continued to fight for what he thinks is right, no matter what others say or think.

During the 1998 impeachment proceedings against President Bill Clinton, Flynt offered $1 million for evidence about sexual affairs involving Republican lawmakers, saying "desperate times require desperate measures."

The Flynt Report, an 82-page magazine detailed what Flynt learned. Web sites give Flynt's investigation credit for forcing the resignation of incoming House Speaker Bob Livingston. One Web site credits Flynt's actions with keeping Clinton from being impeached.

In June 2007, Flynt ran an ad in *The Washington Post* offering $1 million for documented stories involving sex with current congressional members or high-ranking government officials.

$1 million.

Why shouldn't I come forward, collect some of that $1 million bounty, then move to South Carolina or Florida and live a quiet life where nobody but a few friends and my son know about my past?

The money would allow me to help my son buy his first house.

I could donate enough money to properly furnish the library at the Lexington Day Treatment Center (a city-run facility for at-risk students in Lexington, Kentucky) with new books – not ones with the word "DISCARD" stamped on them in large letters and other donated used books.

I could send current newspapers and magazines to the school's library, doing away with out-of-date publications bearing yellow stickers effectively saying "the only reason you're able to read this is because real owners could not be located."

Why care about this school for at-risk students? I very easily could have been one of them.

An employee at the school told me about a student who came to school one day after a major incident at her home. The student came to school that day, the teacher said, "because the school was the most stable part of her life and where she felt safest." I know how that student felt.

Many students at the center have experienced things they never should have faced, things often not of their own choosing. Generally speaking, life has not been kind to these kids. For many, the center is their last chance.

* * *

So what if my information might wreck other people's lives, force some of them to give up their jobs and maybe break up their families? All this happened to me, why not them? Are they any less "guilty" than I?

The answer, at least in part, can be found in the pages of a book I read as a teen – Jesse Stuart's *A Penny's Worth of Character* – and a poster I bought the summer I graduated from high school. The answer also lies in Flynt's own words when he faced a remarkably similar situation.

In Stuart's book, Shan is going to the store for his mother. With a dime, he can buy a chocolate bar and a lemon soda. Shan knows the storekeeper pays a penny each for good used paper sack returned.

There are ten sacks at home but Shan's mother tells him to take only nine, because the tenth has a hole in it. Shan disobeys his mother and takes the torn sack. He hides the torn one among the good sacks, hoping the busy storekeeper won't notice it. The storekeeper does not.

Eating the chocolate bar and drinking the lemon soda, Shan has second thoughts about cheating the storekeeper, about exchanging his character for that which he desperately wanted.

The poster had a simple, yet powerful message:

*"A man is what he's done, seen
and experienced. Through his hands,
we see his heart."*

Wanting to tell other people's stories is what drew me into journalism. And though journalism does not require a reporter to raise his or her hand and swear never to harm "innocent" people we report about, most journalists, including me, feel such an obligation.

Theresa Klisz, Washington editor for the Gannett News Service, told those attending Eastern Kentucky University's

Distinguished Speaker Series in October 2007 how important integrity and credibility are to a journalist.

Klisz and I attended Eastern at the same time. She and I also worked together at the *Herald-Leader*. She is an excellent journalist, a credit to the Gannett chain.

I sat there listening to what Klisz said, but my mind was also flooded with memories of days gone by, days she and I lived so long ago at Eastern. We were journalism majors, Klisz and I. We went through the same program, the same classes, though maybe at different times.

As students in the Department of Mass Communications, we were taught many things, lessons designed to make us better journalists. Faculty members including Dr. Glen Kleine, Carol Wright, Dr. Elizabeth Fraas and Dr. Ron Wolfe, taught us the importance of integrity and credibility.

My mentors at the *Herald-Leader* – people like Dottie Bean, Margaret Maxwell, Jim Green, Don Walker, Lou Tayloe, Henry Wright and Walter Dorsett (may he rest in peace) – reinforced all I had learned at Eastern and taught me more.

My first free-lance assignment for the *Herald-Leader* was to cover a music festival in a nearby town. The assignment completed, I drove to the paper, proudly presented two photos and my article to Mrs. Maxwell, smiled and left. Looking through the paper the next day, I found one of my photos but not the story.

I later asked Mrs. Maxwell why my article never ran. "It wasn't good enough for our readers," she said quickly and with authority. "Our readers expect quality. My job is to make sure they get it." Smiling, she said, "Your picture was good. That's why I ran it."

I have always held close the primary reporting lesson Mrs. Maxwell drilled into my head: "Never mind what you think," she told me, "what can you get on the record?"

This project is the product of such reporting. It is written to the strict standards Mrs. Maxwell and the others all demanded.

* * *

In church, I learned character "is doing what is right when no one else is watching." So far, I have not revealed what elected officials or high-ranking officials or media figures called Capital City Boys. I will not now, nor will I in the future.

While there are a million reasons to walk away from the promise I made so long ago, integrity prevents me from doing so.

I never promised a single person in Washington that I would protect their secrets, just myself.

Money, so they say
is the root of all evil today.
But if you ask for a (raise) it's no surprise
they're giving none away.
– MONEY
Artist: Pink Floyd
Songwriter: George Waters
Hampshire House Publishing (ASCAP)

It was widely reported in November 2003 that Flynt bought fully nude photographs of Private First Class Jessica Lynch from soldiers who took the pictures in an Army barracks. The world came to know about Lynch while she was a prisoner of war and when U.S. troops freed her from Iraqi captors. The price Flynt is said to have paid for the photos ranges as high as $750,000.

Flynt never released the photographs, saying Lynch was a "good kid" who became "a pawn for the government." In an interview with the Associated Press, Flynt said, "Some things are more important than money. You gotta do the right thing."

Hate Flynt's products if you choose but when you look at the whole man, maybe you will realize there is a different side of Flynt you might have overlooked, a mighty good one.

And while I sure could use $1 million – especially after publishing this project – I was taught long ago that doing "the right thing" is worth a lot more. I have to believe that a certain publisher/fellow Kentuckian and a "boy" named Shan agree with me. Do You?

"Names," they said.

"You need names, lots of names."

"To be newsworthy, to get your project on the front page of the *Washington Post,* your project needs to name names."

More than one person in the newspaper business whose opinions I respect told me this project had to announce publicly the names of senators, congressmen and high-ranking government officials whom Capital City Boys and The Agency sent escorts to meet in Washington.

"Can you name names?" one asked.

"Yes I can," I said. "Six for sure."

"Two or three would do. There has to be blood on the floor before anyone will take you seriously," one said.

"Is there some level at which you might be comfortable naming names?" another asked. "Some level, maybe of hypocrisy?"

The question was fair, especially since it came from a journalism expert trying to help. Names on a printed page. Blood on the floor. This is how one wins journalism awards.

Sen. Larry Craig. Rep. Mark Foley. Would anyone doubt me if I said both were clients? Would anyone doubt me if I said I could produce the escorts I sent to meet them?

Can I write that Sen. Craig and Rep. Foley were clients? Yes I can. Can I produce escorts who will say they met with Craig and Foley? Yes I can. These would be names on a printed page. There would be blood on the floor.

I could also research elected officials who were in Washington between 1998 and 2001 and find two or three men where rumors hint they might be gay. I could drop, say, two more names. With this project's credibility and since so much time has gone by, I have to think those I might name would have a difficult time proving their innocence. Sadly, the public probably would not listen anyways.

Proving they never met with a gay male escort would be difficult, especially when a tipped-off media happened to "locate" two or three of Mack's "live boys."

Naturally, the appearance of the "just located boys" would be extreme and oh so gay – young, effeminate, multicolored hair, tight, sleeveless tank tops and the like. There would not be a single masculine, straight-looking guy among them. Not in this lineup. After eye balling the boys I would produce, only few would look closely at the facts. And then, there are the stories the escorts would tell …

I can visualize cable news channels running "Breaking News" banners for days – TV crews wouldn't be able to find all the boys at once, you know.

Keith Olbermann might even assign a number to the story on his MSNBC show and maybe have the great Michael Musto on to comment.

I could do all of this and more, but all of it would be a lie. I do not know if Sen. Craig or Rep. Foley ever met anyone from Capital City Boys or The Agency. I do know, however, other senators and congressmen did.

I could give you real names and – in every case – tell you the names of the escorts who met with them. I could cash in big with Larry Flynt's offer and might even win recognition and awards from organizations I greatly admire. I could, but I couldn't live with myself if I did. Naming names and spilling blood on the floor are too high a price to pay for any recognition or awards that might come my way.

No one involved broke any laws that I am aware of, nor are they guilty of corruption or violating the public's trust. The people I sent escorts to meet – elected officials and plain folks – simply had an interest or curiosity, which in some people's opinion, makes them different from you.

This project deals with issues that can scar a person's life forever. I know that personally. I bear such a scar. I will not be the reason others do.

PREMISE #4

"If prostitution is the world's
oldest profession
then the john, or the trick,
is the world's
oldest consumer."

– HOOKERS & JOHNS:
Trick or Treat
(an HBO special)

They'd call us gypsies, tramps, and thieves
but every night all the men
would come around,
and lay their money down.
– GYPSIES TRAMPS AND THIEVES
Artist: Cher Songwriter: Robert Stone
Careers BMG Music Publishing (BMI)

"Tainted Love"
Soft Cell
Peaked at #8 in1981

Everyone has a secret he does not want anyone else to know. Calling a gay male escort referral service and hiring an escort certainly is one for most people. This is true for an elected official, a lawyer, a celebrity, a husband, and for most of the rest of us.

In most places, if someone finds out you hire escorts, it can be embarrassing. In Washington, the price can be death – death politically or death in terms of your career.

Randall Tobias, Secretary of State Condoleezza Rice's deputy responsible for U.S. foreign aid, resigned in April 2007, after he was asked about using an upscale female escort service in Washington. *The Washington Post* cited an ABC News report that said Tobias explained he had contacted the escort service "to have gals come over to the condo to give me a massage" and that there had been "no sex" involved.

The article appeared on Page One of the *Post*.

The death of someone's career for hiring an escort is not exclusive to Washington. The same is true elsewhere.

The Rev. Ted Haggard was the pastor of the 14,000-member New Life Church in Colorado Springs, Colorado. He was also the president of the influential National Association of Evangelicals, an umbrella group representing more than 45,000 churches with 30 million members.

Haggard was forced to leave those positions after Mike Jones, a gay escort Haggard had been seeing for three years, came forward and revealed the reverend's dirty little secret.

Ask former New York Gov. Eliot Spitzer – known as "Mr. Clean" until wiretaps surfaced linking him to Ashley Alexandra Dupré.

Despite these and other examples, men still call and pay to spend time with gay and female escorts.

Just who called Capital City might surprise you. Congressmen called. So did senators. So did other elected officials, mostly from outside the District.

Democrats called. So did Republicans. Congressional aides called. Lobbyists called. Bankers, professors, and print and TV news people all called. Businessmen in town testifying before Congress called. Lawyers called, lots of them – both those who worked in downtown Washington and those in town on business.

Marvin, the owner of Tops Referrals, says the same was true at Tops.

Why would someone pay to meet an escort? There are lots of answers, many of them practical, some as simple as the thrill of meeting someone special, someone he could only fantasize about otherwise.

I see them every night in tight blue jeans,
in the pages of a Blue Boy magazine.
Hey I've been thinking of a new sensation,
I'm picking up – good vibration
– SHE BOP
Artist: Cyndi Lauper
Songwriters: R.Chertoff/G. Corbett/C. Lauper/S. Lunt
Rella Music Corp. (BMI)

"Calling a service ... is just so convenient," Jeffery, who has hired Washington-area gay male escorts for 20 years, says. (You met Jeffery in an earlier segment.)

Another client, a man in his late 40s, explained his reasoning this way: "Why should I go out to the bars, meet someone, buy him drinks all night, and then lose him to a younger, nicer-looking guy right before closing time?" The client was smart. Every gay bar in Washington had guys working that routine.

Wayne, an escort who will share his experience with you in the upcoming "Will You Still Love Me Tomorrow" segment, says he once had a "hot" 23-year-old client pay him $600 for a two-hour visit. "I eventually asked him why he was paying to meet an escort since he was certainly hot enough to hook up on his own," Wayne said. "He told me that he just wasn't into the all the BS involved in going to the bars looking for someone."

Most who called Capital City Boys were white men in their late 30s or 40s or early 50s. Most were professionals.

Capital City Boys' youngest clients were 19-year-olds. There were two of them. One had never met with a guy before and had a list of things he wanted to "discuss" during his session. The other came with his parents to George W. Bush's inauguration. Capital City Boys checked both their IDs before going through with the calls.

Marvin says most of Tops' clients are in their 40s and 50s. "Some are in their late 30s. We also have a spattering in their 70s and 80s."

Capital City Boys' oldest client – at least as far as we knew – was in his late 70s. A repeat client with medical problems, escorts often referred to this client as the "crypt keeper."

Marvin says half of Tops' clients are married. "Twenty-five percent are in gay relationships and the other 25 percent are single gay men who do not want to play the game of going to a bar."

Marvin says 80 percent of his clients are regulars.

* * *

Very few high-profile clients ever used their real names. Still, you cannot appear on TV or have your picture appear in a newspaper or magazine and not run the risk of being recognized.

Capital City Boys once sent an escort to the Hyatt on Capitol Hill and when he returned, he bragged the client he had met was a certain congressman whom he recognized from having seen on TV earlier that week.

One businessman routinely entertained Capital City Boys escorts in his corner office downtown late at night. Several escorts who visited there said the client always started the session by showing them his collection of framed photos showing him with important, well-known people, including the then-pope.

While Capital City Boys handled calls from elected officials, lawyers, celebrities, and media personalities, it also handled calls from ordinary people like the bellhop who paid his booking fees mostly in $5's and $1's. He once paid the last $30 of his bill in quarters.

Most who called Capital City Boys were gay but the service also handled calls from "straight" married men who wanted to meet an escort – some times a transsexual or a drag queen – before going home to their families.

"What we deal with in this business is a lot different from that of a female service," Marvin says. "In a lot of cases, those are men who are cheating on their wives or girlfriends. If a married man hires from me, he's getting something he cannot get at home. It has nothing to do with loving his wife. The intimacy you get with a guy is different than with a woman. That (intimacy) is different than just not being happy with his wife."

Capital City Boys also handled a few calls from women wanting to meet a "straight" man. A couple of times, the service took calls from women wanting to meet another woman.

Marvin says Tops has a few female clients, a few male/female couples and one client who likes to hire a male and a female escort for a single call.

> **DENNY CRANE:** *When you go out with a young girl like Sarah, you have only one thing to offer -- money. She can have younger, better looking guys, better lovers, guys with more interests in common. What you have is power. I actually begin my dates by putting cash right on the table.*
> **ALAN SHORE:** *And that works?*
> **DENNY CRANE:** *With hookers.*
> **– BOSTON LEGAL**
> David E. Kelley Productions /Twentieth Century Fox Television

Capital City Boys catered mostly to out-of-towners but had a reasonable number of local clients. Tops Referral tended to cater mainly to a select group of Washington residents, though it too served out-of-towners.

Although most repeat clients had a "favorite" service, very few were exclusive. It was not uncommon to have a client call to see who was available then say "let me check my schedule and get back to you."

Those working the phones knew the client was actually saying, "Let me call Tops and see who's working before I commit." This was just part of the game – why settle for "hamburger" from one service when "steak" was available at the other?

Capital City Boys clients generally liked younger guys – usually boys 19 to 29. Capital City Boys never represented anyone under the age of 18 nor anyone over 35, though the service kept getting calls for guys in their 40s. Those calls were referred to Tops, who mostly represented guys in their mid-20s to late 40s.

Marvin twice told me he was happy to let Capital City Boys handle the twinks. "They are way too much trouble for me," Marvin said. "There's always drama of one kind or another." As always, Marvin was right. The fear of adding additional drama kept Capital City Boys from representing drag queens and transsexuals in a major way. Tops excelled in that market and Capital City Boys was happy to let them.

* * *

Because escorts often used stage names that might change or just their first names – clients did likewise – one could never be sure that the escort you met was going to be a complete stranger.

A client once hired an escort through Tops. The escort unexpectedly turned out to be someone the man had seen socially, when his son brought his roommate (the escort) home. "That call went through," Marvin says. "No one ever told the son."

Another such case happened when an escort, a guy in his late 20s, arrived for an appointment and unexpectedly found the client to be a former lover of his. The client had used a made-up name. "They had broken up a couple of years before," Marvin said. "That call also went through."

* * *

Capital City Boys had one client who was part of "The West Wing" TV show. For the record, it was not Rob Lowe. Lowe's character, Sam Seaborn, did spend a night with a "call girl," though he did not know she "did that kind of work."

The client also was not actor John Spencer. *The Globe,* in its January 9, 2006, issue had a two-page spread on Spencer headlined "West Wing Star Took Gay Secret to Grave."

I met Spencer in Washington once and spent a short amount of time with him. I happened to run into him seated at a table outside the Soho Tea and Coffee shop on P Street. He was there talking with a group of young hangers-on, males and females. Spencer seemed comfortable being there and seemed to enjoy talking with the group. I did not get the idea any of them knew Spencer from his roles on "The West Wing" or "L.A. Law." They just knew he was a celebrity and that was good enough for them to spend time with him.

Thirty minutes after I joined the hangers-on, Spencer left. He walked across the street with his driver and got in a black Lincoln Town Car, and they drove away.

I wondered that night if Spencer had come to Soho looking for a hookup. If you were gay and looking for a cute boy, Soho was a good place to go. There was no indication that was the reason Spencer was there.

If Spencer ever called Capital City Boys or met with one of our guys, I never knew it. And after meeting him that night, I listened for his distinctive voice – the one I first heard in "War Games" and later in "Presumed Innocent" and had admired hundreds of other times on TV.

Trust me when I say, if Spencer had been a client, I never would have mentioned him by name.

The Globe highlighted a quote reportedly from one of Spencer's friends. I do not know if the quote is true about Spencer since I do not know if he was gay, but I can tell you it is true about most of the people who call gay male escort services: "His worst fear until the day he died was that he'd be exposed."

> "His worst fear until the day he died was that he'd be exposed."
> – **THE GLOBE**
> (Jan. 9, 2006)

* * *

It was routine to check the Caller ID before answering a call. It was best to know – as much as possible – who was calling before answering. Capital City Boys had some clients who never mentioned their names unless asked. They expected the service would know who they were. Many times, we did, sometimes only because their names appeared on the Caller ID.

On one occasion, I looked and froze. The ID read "Ronald Reagan." Doubting the former president was calling, I answered the phone ready for just about anything. It was a client calling from Ronald Reagan National Airport. He and I shared a good laugh about the situation.

* * *

Although most clients worked hard to keep their identity a secret, we had others who could not have cared less who knew.

We once had a client call, asking all kinds of in-depth personal questions about various guys. From time to time, he would say something to someone near him. When I asked what was going on, he said, "I'm downtown being fitted for a new suit." One can only imagine what the person assisting him must have thought.

* * *

Once, Zack came out of an appointment at the Radisson Barcello Hotel and told me about the client he had just spent an hour with.

"He was a creepy old dude," Zack said. "Kept bragging that he was a (state) senator from Kentucky and was in town for hearings on the coal industry." Zack did not know I was from Kentucky or that his news would be of particular interest to me.

This self-confessed state senator was not the only Kentucky client Capital City encountered.

A guy from Lexington called once wanting to know "everything" about the guys Capital City Boys represented and its pricing. "I don't want to pay more than $50," he said. "It won't take more than 10 minutes. I shouldn't have to pay for a whole hour." It was suggested he might try one of the P Street hustlers. It was also suggested he put some money away to cover the cost of a doctor visit once he returned home.

I also took a call one day from someone at the *Louisville Courier-Journal.* I was apprehensive it might be a reporter calling saying he was doing a story about me and wanted me to confess my "sins."

Luckily, the man just wanted to know who might be available when he came to town. I often wondered who it was I talked with and if he was still at the *Courier-Journal* while I worked there.

* * *

For most clients, meeting an escort ensures you will meet someone, but the person who knocks on your door may not be the guy you were expecting.

Dreamboys, at one time considered Washington's second-most popular service, became very unreliable about who it would send out. The same was true of independents who often stretched their physical descriptions past the limit of reasonableness.

"My friend hired a guy from the *Blade* about a year ago who said he was 18, 5'10" and I think it was 160 pounds, blond hair and blue eyes," a client named Bob once told me. "I don't think he (the escort) had seen 18 for at least 18 years. Then they had another one who said he was a porn star. He might have been in the '50s but he sure wasn't in the '90s."

Sometimes, a client would explain that he was looking for a "really good-looking guy." As one client explained, "The term good-looking fits loosely to some of these businesses. My version of good-looking guy is not necessary the version of the good-looking guy I wind up with."

* * *

One repeat client was the key aide to a powerful Republican senator. Many would probably think this particular senator would denounce gays and the gay lifestyle based on his conservative stand on issues. The client, however, told a different story. The client told Ryan that the senator had come to learn he was gay and had remained supportive of him. "Never has the senator made my being a homosexual an issue even though it could embarrass him deeply if anyone ever found out," the client said.

* * *

When a client booked an overnight visit, Ryan and I would meet the client and the escort at one of the gay bars on P Street, usually the Fireplace. I would buy a couple of rounds of drinks. Sometime during the hour we were there, the escort would discreetly hand his fee over to me for safekeeping.

Everyone involved knew this was happening. My holding the money protected everyone – the client, in case the escort decided to bolt (that happened twice); the escort, so the client could not take the money back sometime during the night and bolt (though it never happened to one of our guys, it happened occasionally to others), and the company, so that it was protected from being messed over by one or both of them.

One escort who bolted after a couple of hours was paid by the escort who replaced him. How much, I do not know, just that he was not happy. I explained his abrupt departure left me few options, and since I just handled bookings, I had to leave the "who-gets-what" decision to the escort who replaced him.

* * *

One Capital City Boys client – a congressional aide – liked to have escorts dress in costumes with him. He once rented Batman and Robin outfits. Another time, the client and our escort dressed up as the Lone Ranger and Tonto.

Most escorts wanted to visit this client only once. The client was nice but possessive. Even those of us working the telephones felt that way. He was the only client who would call the service to say he would be calling back in 10 or 15 minutes. We never understood why. We would have understood if he asked us to see if a certain escort would be working that night. Such calls were common. Calling to alert us that he would be calling back never made any sense but then, he was a congressional aide.

* * *

One of the more unusual clients we had was a Middle Eastern-sounding man who would come to town a couple of times a year with his younger sister and stay at the Four Seasons Hotel. The man always arranged for an escort to meet with his sister. "She does not care to meet with a 'soft boy,'" he said.

The first time he called, red danger flags went up all over the place. Red flags went up when a client said something suspicious or something that might get Capital City Boys in trouble. The term "soft boy" certainly set off alarms. The man assured the service he was not into playing games, that he would not be in the room during the visit, and that he was setting up the call "as a favor" for his sister.

After the call, the escort reported the man had met him in the suite, introduced the escort to his sister, and then left, just as he had said he would. (I loved clients who kept their word.)

The escort also told me the man's sister was quite "lovely" and that they both enjoyed their time together. He did not have to tell me that part. The client had already called, saying that his sister had given him a similar report. "Your choice was excellent," the client said. "I will call you again when we return." He did.

The client had said he did not wish for me to send a "soft boy" meaning a gay man. Capital City Boys sent a guy who was bisexual and very straight-looking – exactly what the client was seeking. Understanding and providing what the client needed led to additional bookings. If Capital City Boys had sent just anyone who happened to be available, like some services, it is likely the client would not have called again.

* * *

Capital City Boys had a few clients who brought their families to Washington to do the sightseeing thing but who also wanted to meet one of the boys. Being classy enough not to send the wife and kids out for a couple of hours and have an escort come into their room, some clients booked a second room in the same hotel.

The extra room cost money but eliminated the chance of "Louise" and "little Johnny" coming back early for some reason, opening the door, and possibly finding Daddy doing something none would ever forget.

* * *

It did not happen often but occasionally an escort would show up for a call and have to pass through security men wearing black suits. It always helped calm nerves when the service was told this in advance. Knowing that the escort was going to encounter security ahead of time took the scare out of showing up and being surprised.

Ryan often told about the time the Secret Service came to The Agency's home on Ingraham Street NW and looked through the house in advance of one client's arrival. "Secret Service guys stood out in the yard and in the hallways while the client was there," Ryan said. "When the client was through, they left, thanking us for our cooperation."

* * *

David, who loved being called "bear," was another mysterious client. Though no stranger to Washington and to Washington's escort world, David lived and worked elsewhere. He came to Washington a couple of times a year "for a little fun and relaxation."

That statement was as misleading as someone saying that Hurricane Katrina breezed through New Orleans on its way up north. It was factual but nowhere near accurate.

David always booked an overnight stay. The sessions would begin around 4 p.m. at the Fireplace, a gay bar on P Street. They would end the next morning whenever the escort woke up and decided to go home. The routine was always the same: David and the escort would have dinner, then go out to one of the male strip bars in Southeast Washington.

David was generous to the escorts he met. He respected the escorts and often took them on shopping trips. Once, he took two of Capital City Boys' guys on a shopping trip in Georgetown. He spent nearly $500 on them.

David was the only client who was ever invited over to the house who was not seeing someone who lived there. He came as my guest and understood just how special this invitation was. The invite was special but then, so was David. I loved listening to his stories about how he worked as an independent contractor for the Pentagon.

David told about the time he got in a fight with someone at a gay bar and activated the "panic button" assigned to him. Guys in suits came running and "saved" him, he said. "They were not too happy, though."

I never knew whether David's stories were true or made up. As a trained journalist, they sounded credible to me.

Nothing David ever told contradicted something else he had said previously or even reasonable logic.

During one of our conversations, David suggested the two of us should go into business together. I welcomed the idea. "I'm not going to be in the escort business forever," I told him. "Eventually, I want to move on to something else."

We settled on buying or opening a bed-and-breakfast in Washington. Seeing a real chance to move on, I agreed to look into the possibility.

I found two – an existing bed-and-breakfast and a burned-out building on 17th Street. The bed-and-breakfast was for sale and would have bookings on the day we closed on the deal.

David was excited about both possibilities. He made a special trip to Washington to look at the two properties. By this time, I had included Ryan in the discussions because I trusted his judgment. Ryan would have been our assistant manager.

Liking what he saw and the plans Ryan and I outlined for him, David authorized me to proceed with trying to buy the bed-and-breakfast. When it came time to put in our bid, David called to say that he had overnighted me a package granting me legal rights to work on his behalf and a certified check for the good-faith deposit.

The package never materialized. Neither did our bid.

David eventually responded to my e-mails and phone calls. He e-mailed me saying that he had been sent to the Middle East (no doubt on a secret mission for the Pentagon) and that he would

Subj:	No Subject
Date:	Saturday, October 21, 2000 11:01:57 PM
From:	davi
To:	Capcboy

Mac,
   Sorry I haven't been able to talk to you but this is the best I can do for now I am in the Middle East can't explain further now. I will contact you ASAP.

explain everything later. That was the last I ever heard from David. It was also the last time I ever fully trusted a client.

> *It's the same old story everywhere I go,*
> *I get slandered, libeled,*
> *I hear words I never heard in the Bible.*
> *just trying to keep my customers satisfied.*
> **– KEEP THE CUSTOMER SATISFIED**
> Artist: Simon and Garfunkel
> Songwriter: Paul Simon
> Paul Simon Music (BMI)

Generally speaking, an escort decided when to quit the business. Clients, however, sometimes play a role in that decision.

"An escort can't work for years and years," Christian says. "It's not a job you retire from. It's a temporary thing for everyone, lasting a year or two, if that long. A lot of clients don't want to see the same escort over and over. I thought my personality would be enough to get me through, to keep me working. I was wrong. Eventually, the number of call for me faded. I guess clients see you on the Web site and pass over you, saying: 'Oh, he's been there forever.'"

The Backstory

Once, while traveling to or from D.C., I apparently joked to Danny that "Tainted Love" could be Capital City Boys' theme song. Whenever Danny heard the song on the radio, he'd call me. Not saying a word, he'd just let the song play. It was because of this that I came to love the song.

Capital City Boys' best client was a man in his early 60s named Tom. He first called soon after Capital City Boys opened and remained a client until just before I sold the service in 2001.

For most of that time, Tom called Capital City Boys every night. He probably averaged meeting someone five nights a week. Such clients were unheard of – few people had the time, even fewer had the money.

There were times when Tom would book two meetings a night. And though rare, there were nights – usually Saturdays – when he would book a third.

The opportunity to possibly be intimate with someone seemed to be secondary to Tom, or so those who went to see him often said. Much of the time escorts spent with him was devoted to sitting in the living room talking. "Tom just wants someone there," one escort once told me. "He's a lonely guy." A lot of our clients wore that same badge. A lot, like Tom, simply wanted a cute, younger guy to spend some time with them.

Tom was one of many clients who would meet an escort simply on Mack's recommendation. He complained only once, and then the complaint was made more out of confusion than out of disappointment.

Tom was one of the few clients I met. He was one of only two clients I ever had an in-person social relationship with. Tom invited me into his home, and we went out to eat a few times, usually with a cute boy in tow. I enjoyed socializing with him.

Because of his "Best Customer" status and because I knew the call would be simple, Tom routinely got to meet Capital City Boys' new escorts first. It was an arrangement that worked well for all – Tom, the service and the escort.

Tom always paid by check, which meant the escort had to come back to the service if he wanted the check cashed that night. All did. Cashing a client's check was a free service Capital City Boys offered the escorts it represented.

Tom worked Monday to Friday in a retail store. Most weekdays, Tom would get off work and then go to a nearby restaurant/bar where he sometimes would meet up with a couple of friends. Eventually, he would go home and call Capital City Boys to see who was available.

For a long time, our biggest fear with Tom was that he might pass out before the escort was able to grab a cab and get to his place. That happened a few times. When it did, the service always paid the escort's cab fare, there and back. The service ate the expense.

Tom was very close to one Capital City Boy escort, you know him as Christian. Tom and Christian would often go to dinner then go back to Tom's home. Capital City Boys rarely knew about these outings ahead of time. Tom made arrangements with Christian directly. After the session, one or both would call Capital City Boys and tell the person working the phones they had spent time together and that the escort would be coming by shortly with a check.

There was never any indication Tom and the escort cheated the service out of its referral fee. Capital City Boys completely trusted both. Neither ever gave a reason to do otherwise.

The same was not true of other escorts and clients. One repeat client, a lawyer from Texas, once called, saying he was in town and wanted to see someone that night and someone different the following two nights.

The client made arrangements for that night and the next. The first call went very well. The client failed to call the second night. Because Capital City Boys rarely sent any escort out on more than one call a night, the escort who was to see the lawyer that night did not work – at first, because we held him in reserve for the lawyer, later because it got so late there was not another opportunity for him.

On this particular night, Skyler, a cute 23-year-old escort, had called on wanting work. I promoted him to those who called the service that night. I found a call for Skyler but could not reach him on his cell phone. When I called the client saying I could not contact Skyler, the client decided to "try another time" and hung up.

Skyler cost Capital City Boys a referral fee of $60. A lost

booking fee was never a welcomed event. In most cases, like this one, Capital City Boys had completed most of the work it did to earn its referral fee. Having the escort lose the call, meant he cost the service money.

The lawyer called later, saying he had been to dinner with "a friend" at a high-end restaurant downtown. He apologized and set a time to see the escort he was to have seen that night.

A few minutes later, Skyler, who lived outside Washington, came by unexpectedly and paid a referral fee for a call he had gone on a night or two earlier. He apologized for not answering his phone earlier, saying he had gone out to dinner with "an old friend." The restaurant happened to be the same high-end place the lawyer had mentioned.

The lawyer had booked two sessions with Skyler the last time he had been in town. It does not take much of an imagination to jump to the conclusion that Skyler had met the lawyer outside the service, probably having given the lawyer his phone number during one of their previous meetings.

It became clear that Skyler had cost the service two calls that night – his and the one the other escort expected to have with the lawyer. That was $120.

Skyler was moved from "heavy" promotion status to "when needed." Experience showed once an escort went around the service, it was likely he would again in the future. This situation was not unique to Capital City Boys. The same is true at most escort referral services.

In fact, Marvin says the biggest problem Tops Referrals has faced over the years has been theft – escorts stealing clients or making their own deals. "Like other owners," Marvin says, "I have had my fair share of getting cheated out of commissions."

Marvin has also heard his fair share of stories from clients who had arranged to meet an independent escort, paid him upfront, showed him where the bathroom was and then later discovered that the escort had fled without the client knowing it and without entertaining.

Independent escorts know that the odds a client is going to call the police and report the "theft" is incredibly small. Would you call, if you found yourself in such a situation?

Marvin says some of the clients telling such tales were people who usually called Tops Referrals. "They'd call me up and say they only had $150 left in the house and ask me to cut my rate to the point I don't make anything. I ask them, 'why didn't you just call me in the first place?'"

* * *

Eventually, Tom came to have money problems. I came to know this when Tom's bank told me there were not enough funds in his account to cover the checks I had come to cash.

At first, Tom explained away the situation, saying he had to cover unexpected repairs to his mother's home. He said he was liquidating a money market account and assured me plenty of new funds would be available soon, and added, "Oh, by the way, who is available tonight?"

Capital City Boys continued to send escorts to Tom, who continued to write checks the bank often would not cash. The time it took to cash Tom's checks began to stretch out over a period of weeks. At $200 a pop, the amount added up to big money – money Capital City Boys did not want to lose, could not afford to lose.

Knowing when automatic deposits were made into Tom's account, I made sure I went to his bank on that day. At first, the money was there to cash the handful of checks I always had. As time went by, it became clear I needed to get to the bank earlier in the day, before the "new" money was gone. Eventually, even at 9 a.m. on auto-deposit days, there was no money to be had.

When it became clear there would be no big infusion of cash, Capital City Boys started cutting Tom back on appointments, saying the service just did not have the money to "lend" him.

Capital City Boys put Tom on "pay-cash-as-you-go" status. Tom later said he took this as an insult. "I had always paid you," he said.

Indeed he had, but the service's financial exposure was too large, and even from a distance, one could see Tom was reeling out of control.

Tom never called Capital City Boys after that night (until after I sold the service). Instead, he switched to Tops Referrals. When I found out, I called Marvin and warned him about Tom's checks.

Marvin told me he had an account at Tom's bank and that the

bank was honoring Tom's checks. "If the money's not there right now, I guess the bank knows it will be," Marvin said. "You know how banks are," Marvin said, "they'll get their money before letting anyone else get theirs."

I hated losing Capital City Boys' "best" client, but if Tom could not pay, then I had to let him go. Besides, like with any other business, a client is free to take his business elsewhere.

* * *

When it came time to sell Capital City Boys, Tom was one of the two people I called to ask if they would like to buy the business. Tom had once expressed such an interest.

Tom had the people skills needed to run an escort service successfully. To be successful, however, he would have needed to greatly cut back on his drinking and be able to keep his hands off the escorts he represented. Both, in my opinion, would have been difficult for Tom.

Tom said he was interested in buying the service. I shared appropriate business-related documents and information with him. I insisted Tom prove he had the money available to go through with the sale. "No problem, Mack," he said. Tom "disappeared" when it came time for him to produce his financial documents and to tender an offer.

In the end, both Capital City Boys and Tops Referrals ended up with cold checks bearing Tom's name.

* * *

PERSONAL THOUGHTS: If Tom somehow happened to call and say he was in my town, I would drop whatever I was doing and go see him, fully believing we would resume our friendship, right where we stopped off years ago.

Gay men in committed relationships also hire gay escorts. "This is very common with couples, so they can live out their fantasies," says Dr. Maurice J. Smith, a psychiatrist and member of the American Gay and Lesbian Psychiatrists Association. "They prefer the live version of porn movies as entertainment."

Dr. Smith says it is "an expensive hobby for those that can afford it." He also says that many times, hiring an escort often "covers what each cannot do to satisfy the other."

Marvin, the owner of Tops Referrals, agrees. "Couples, in my opinion, hire to bring some spice to their personal lives. Rather than accept a lackluster sex life, many find creative ways to keep things interesting."

Marvin says his experience has shown that a couple hiring an escort is a boon to most relationships.

Sometimes, only one member of the couple hires an escort. Dan is such a person. Dan is in a committed relationship with a man who does not know about this part of his life.

Dan sometimes hires three or four escorts a week. It is always an in-call and it is not unusual for him to see two escorts at a time.

Marvin says he used to send escorts to a now-former Republican congressman and his partner, just not at the same time. "Both were into seeing escorts from us," Marvin says, "but neither knew the other one was."

One night both men called independent of each another and both asked for meet with the same escort later that night. "One got to see him that night," Marvin says, "The other saw him on a different day."

While most of those who called Capital City Boys had "vanilla-type" interests, some had ones more toward the deeper end of the fantasy pool. Capital City Boys handled few of these types of calls, deciding since Tops Referrals already excelled in this area that we would concentrate our efforts elsewhere.

Marvin, owner of Tops Referrals, says most clients wanting "specialty services" are powerful men – judges, doctors, lawyers, etc. – who tell people what to do all day long. "They hire someone who will reverse that role, someone who will tell them what to do."

Specialty services, such as this, cost more. "These clients gladly pay," Marvin says.

* * *

"Foot-fetish Mike," a repeat client, carefully interviewed guys before inviting them to his home. Toward the end of the conversation, Mike always said something weird to see how the escort would react. If the escort handled the situation well enough, Mike would ask him if he would mind squeezing his neck with his legs and letting him play with his feet.

Capital City Boys finally figured out Mike's interview techniques after several guys failed his test. Once it was learned that Mike was looking for someone who would not be shocked by whatever he said, Capital City Boys coached its guys how to handle the call.

Despite all the strangeness on the phone, escorts reported Mike was a great host.

* * *

Christian and I still laugh about a conversation he once had with a prospective client named Bill.

The client had asked Christian if he enjoyed water sports. "I told him I sure did. I love scuba diving, swimming, and skiing,"

Christian said. "All the client said was, 'Oh.'"

Smiling broadly, I explained to Christian that the client did not mean diving, swimming, or skiing. Then I had to explain what he really meant (experiences involving urine). "That's OK, kid," I told Christian. "I learned about water sports not too long back myself. Someone had to explain it to me too."

* * *

Marvin says S&M (slave and master) and fetish scenes make up about 5 percent of the calls Tops Referrals books. He says the vast majority of clients wanting a foot-fetish encounter want to service the escort's feet.

Marvin says one client, a man named Jim who routinely hired transsexuals, found a unique way of justifying what he was doing was not morally wrong.

"In hiring a transsexual, I'm hiring a lady, so I am not gay," Marvin says the client explained. "Putting my hand up under her skirt, I find ... and say, 'What is this?' Oh, it's a guy, so I'm not cheating on my wife." Marvin says the man reasoned one event canceled out the other to the point that, at the end of the call, the man considered his time with the transsexual "as a non-event."

At one time or another, Marvin says Tops has represented four types of escorts: Males, females, transsexuals and female dominatrices. "You have to handle and market each one differently," Marvin says.

"By and large, those who are serviced by a female dominatrix are straight men," Marvin says. "Rarely is sex involved in these types of calls." When it is, Marvin says, it usually happens when the dominatrix introduces another guy into the scene.

Marvin says a good-looking female dominatrix in Washington can earn a minimum of $500 an hour. "With the top ones, the price goes through the roof."

"The gay community has not yet evolved much into the S&M world," Marvin says. "We are babies compared to the straight world."

* * *

The strangest call I ever heard about involved Austin and Wes. A client, staying in one of the finer hotels in downtown Washington, had Austin and Wes climb inside a cloth bag he provided and to "enjoy one another's company." The client watched them from outside the bag. We never figured that one out.

* * *

Jeffery has hired gay male escorts in the Washington area for the past 20 years. You met him earlier in a couple of different segments.

Jeffery is a longtime client of Tops Referrals. Calling an escort referral service "is just so convenient," he says, "especially considering the things I want." Jeffery enjoys taking part in slave/master situations. Jeffery is the "master," the escort is the "slave." "There are always going to be certain people who will always be in control," he says. "I am one."

Jeffery, who hires escorts twice a month, says he uses lots of oils during a session and says the encounter usually involves some form of bondage.

"Sometimes it's handcuffs behind the back, sometimes handcuffs behind the neck," he says. Jeffery says he sometimes ties escorts spread eagle on the bed. "They usually get paddled when that happens," he says.

Asked what makes a good escort, Jeffery quickly responds: "I don't like a smart ass, someone who is going to tell me what he isn't going to do. He (the escort) doesn't have an opinion in that respect."

Jeffery has some advice for anyone who routinely meets with escorts: "Hiring an escort is just like anything else in your life," he says. "You damn well better live within your budget or you'll go broke."

"Games People Play"
Joe South
Topped out at #12 in 1969; won Grammy Award for Song Of The Year

Like every service, Capital City Boys had its share of clients wanting to play games. Sometimes, we simply shrugged it off. Sometimes, Capital City Boys reacted – when it did, it was usually quick; it was almost always loud, and it was definitely always unpleasant for the person who had messed with the service.

One such incident involved a client named "Chris." He called and took a great deal of time asking questions about various guys. Chris settled on Drew.

Drew talked with the client, and arranged a meeting for later that night. Fifteen minutes after the scheduled appointment time, Drew called to say the client had not shown up. Drew also said he had called the number we had been given and that a fax machine kept picking up.

I tried the line and also got the fax machine. Knowing there might be a reasonable explanation for the client not to keep his appointment, I tried calling the following Monday and Tuesday but also kept getting the fax machine.

Deciding I was not going to reach a human and not wanting just to forget the matter, I wrote a few choice words, identified who I was and detailed why Chris had called us. I then faxed the letter to the number Chris had called from.

Another caller arranged to meet Austin at 10:30 one night. He strictly stated he did not want to meet if Austin would have already gone on another call that night. Austin, who sometimes would do two calls, agreed not to see anyone else and did not despite having a call coming in for him just before 7.

Austin knocked on the man's door at the Jefferson Hotel in downtown Washington promptly at 10:30. There was no answer. Austin waited a few minutes and knocked again. Still, no one opened the door. Austin left the Jefferson and called Capital City

Boys, saying, "Mack, the man was there because I could hear him breathing behind the door."

Knowing what Capital City Boys had gone through to book the call and that Austin and the service had both "lost" another booking for this client, I had Reece drive me to the Jefferson.

"Circle the block once, then wait for me, right here," I told him. "I won't be long but they'll know I was here."

Passing through the lobby, desk clerks smiled at me, probably thinking I was a guest. I waved. Up the elevator and down the hall, I followed the numbers until I came to the client's room.

Knocking on the door, I yelled to the client – a guy named Karl – identifying myself as the owner of the gay male escort service he had called and from whom had booked "the youngest-looking boy I had because you said you fantasized about 'doing it' with your 14-year-old nephew."

"Karl, I'm worried about you," I yelled. "I know how much you wanted to meet Austin and how you wanted him to pretend to be your nephew."

I then said some other choice things, making sure there was no way anyone in a neighboring room could miss hearing what I was saying or to whom I was saying it.

Karl had never mentioned a nephew nor anything about a 14-year-old. Not being into physical retribution, the only weapon escort services had to use against clients who messed with the company was to embarrass them into never calling again.

Checking my watch, I see that I've been in front of Karl's door for almost two minutes, long enough for someone to call the front desk. I imagine the time seemed much longer to Karl.

I knew I needed to leave and do so quickly. I remember looking down the hallway and starting to hear the wonderful sounds of the theme song to "Hawaii-Five-O" in my head. Why? I have no idea but there it was, that beautiful drum solo – you know the one.

The pounding starts as I turn to leave...

> *Shocka docka docka docka docka da dock*
> *Cha ch-ch-cha, ch-ch-cha*
> *Cha ch-ch-cha, ch-ch-cha*
> *Shocka docka docka docka docka da dock*

The full band kicks in as I pass by the second or third door ...

Da da da da daaa Da da da duh
Da da da da daaa Da da da duh
Da da da da da da Da da da da da da dum Dum
Da da da duh

I come to the turn. Looking down the hallway, I do not remember it being so long. The music keeps playing in my head as images from the show's intro flash before me. I have not seen the show since it went off the air on April 26, 1980, but the images are clear. There's Steve MaGarrett and Danno and that wonderful wave and the beautiful woman brushing back her long hair ...

Da da da da daaa Da da da duh
Da da da da daaa Da da da duh
Da da da da da da Da da da da da da dum
dum dum da da dum duh

The elevator's doors open as I get to them. One of the desk clerks bolted out and headed in the direction of Karl's room.

"Some guy was yelling down that way," I told him. "Thanks," he said, racing off. The elevator doors closed, and I headed to the lobby hoping that Reece and his car were both outside ...

One Mississippi.

Two Mississippi.

Three Mississippi.

I remember counting as the elevator descended, taking what seemed to be an eternity, all while the Ventures continued to play inside my head ...

Da da da da daaa Da da da duh
Da da da da daaa Da da da duh

Four Mississippi.

Five ...

Finally, the doors open and I sprint out. The desk clerks looked at me as I breezed through the lobby. Smiling and not stopping to chat, I bid them a good night. I pushed open the door and breathed "free" air. Reece was waiting for me, just as he was supposed to be. I always did like that kid ...

Mack And The Boys

Da da da da da Da da da da da da dum dum
Da da dum duh da da dum duh

Not waiting until I closed the door and could get settled, I said, "Get us the hell out of here." Reece, not sure what was happening, complied. (big finish here) ...

Da da duh da da duh da da duh
Da da duh da da duh da da duh dum dum duh

Once we were away and safe, I told Reece what I had done and how I imagined poor Karl had reacted. We shared a long laugh on the ride home. "Mack, if I ever get on your s**t list, let me know so I can make things up to you before you come after me," Reece said, laughing.

Karl never called us again. I suspect he thought long and hard before calling anyone.

* * *

Sometimes an escort and a client would become personally involved – the client wanted a lover, the escort usually started off just wanting a call. Somewhere along the way, the escort was persuaded to cross the line between being an occasional visitor and a lover.

When an escort and client became involved, everyone got screwed. The service got messed over because it lost a good escort; the escort, because he usually burned his bridges with the service, thinking he had found someone who would take care of him and buy things for him; and the client, because the service would not send anyone else to him.

One such case involved Reece. He went to see a client and ended up moving in with him. Reece got to drive the guy's Mercedes occasionally. He and the man soon parted ways, Reece said, because the man was "very domineering."

Reece was allowed to return to Capital City Boys because the client had a reputation for luring young guys into his home by promising them far more than he could or would deliver. It also helped that Reece had proved he was willing to help the service by doing things like driving me to that hotel.

* * *

On three different occasions, someone paged a Metropolitan

police officer and keyed in Capital City Boy's phone number.

The officers called, identified themselves and then was a puzzled as I was when I gently explained that they had called a gay male escort referral service. I never found out if the someone was playing a trick on them or on us.

"Will You Still Love Me Tomorrow?"
The Shirelles
A #1 hit in 1961

Author's note: Sometimes, it is easier to trust a stranger than those one sees on a daily basis. That was the case with Wayne and me. Wayne arrived in Washington as I was leaving. During the one month we were both in Washington, our paths never crossed. He came to work at Capital City Boys soon after I left town. Our deep friendship was developed through countless telephone calls.

Questions I asked about what happened at Capital City Boys after I left prompted Wayne to ask me directly why I was asking. I explained my project to him and then sent him a copy of what I had written.

Wayne told me how much the report and some of the songs meant to him. He told me the songs brought back memories of his time in Washington. I asked him to share his thoughts with you.

* * *

When I read the draft of *Mack And The Boys,* I was really drawn into it. The story is true, I know it is. I was an escort in D.C. and while I worked for Capital City Boys and The Agency, I worked for them after Mack sold them and had left Washington.

Mack and I formed a bond when I started to manage the services for the new owner. Mack had to be consulted on many things dealing with the company.

I not only came to trust him during that time but to respect him. That trust and respect still hold strong today. I was thrilled when I was asked to preview a draft of his research. It was there that I came across the lyrics to a song titled "Summer Sand." I wasn't ready for the imagery the song instilled in my mind. As an escort, I saw many clients and the imagery in the lyrics of "Summer Sand" triggered lots of memories.

For me, the lyrics *"Tonight I'm yours and you are mine now,"* painted a picture in my mind of me spending time with a client.

When I would see a client, for that time, I was the client's. He had my undivided attention. Everything that was important to him in the time, was important to me.

There were no pretenses what we had for that short time was love – it was business. While I came to be friends with most of my clients, I never fell in love with any but that didn't make what we had anything less special for us.

I would never say that nothing ever happened between me and my clients but when it did it was purely our choice and had nothing to do with money. It also was not because we were in love but because we both had needs we wanted to take care of. We would wrap ourselves in each other's arms for the time we were together and share something that the money I was being paid for my time could never buy.

> *"There were no pretenses what we had for that short time was love – it was business. While I came to be friends with most of my clients, I never fell in love with any but that didn't make what we had anything less special for us."*

We would never talk of "next time" or the future. We didn't want to waste time talking about something that meant nothing. The next day the client would go back to his life, maybe his job or his wife and children, whatever it was, it had nothing to do with that night, with that time. If ever the client wanted to see me again, he knew he could. After all, I was always only a phone call away.

Elsewhere, we readers come across the following passage: "Couldn't you visualize sand slipping through the someone's hands? Sure you could." While you, the reader, may not visualize sand slipping through someone's hands, you will see something in the eye of your mind.

I thank you, fellow readers, for letting me tell you what it was like for me. And thank you Malcolm, for writing this and telling your story ... our story.

– Wayne

"House of the Rising Sun"
The Animals
Was #1 for three weeks in 1964

I first heard the Animals' haunting ballad "House of the Rising Sun" while listening to WAKY on my transistor radio.

The song was dark and way too deep for me to understand fully. Yet it was that darkness and the way the song painted a picture in my mind that drew me to it – just as the need to tell the story about gay male escorts in the nation's capital would years later.

There is a house in New Orleans
they call the "Rising Sun."
And it's been the ruin of many a poor boy
and, God, I know I'm one.

What imagery. What storytelling. There was Eric Burdon's wonderful, raspy voice and the simple, almost church-sounding organ music that came with it.

Who didn't feel compelled to listen to the story? Who wouldn't want to hear what had "been the ruin of many a poor boy" from someone who had personally suffered that fate? And then, as if that were not enough, there was the storyteller's even-more-haunting declaration:

Oh, Mother tell your children
not to do what I have done

I did not fully understand the song but then – as I found out while researching "House of the Rising Sun" – a lot other people did not understand it either.

The song was originally sung from the point of view of a young woman who had worked at the House of the Rising Sun. I was shocked to learn the song had first been recorded by Georgia

Turner, then a young woman living in Eastern Kentucky.

I was shocked, though I should not have been. When I worked at the *Lexington Herald-Leader,* I was amazed how many major national stories had some sort of a Kentucky connection.

The millions of us who know the lyrics of "House of the Rising Sun" by heart may not fully understand the song but we are enticed by it. Go online and you can find hundreds of stories about the song.

One I found was by Associated Press writer Ted Anthony. Anthony's article tells how Alan Lomax, traveling the mountains of Eastern Kentucky recording people singing their favorite songs, came to meet 16-year-old Georgia Turner in Middlesboro.

Anthony tells about Georgia's performing her favorite song, "a twangy lament" called "Rising Sun Blues." He recounts how Lomax took the song back to the folk-music scene in New York City and how it eventually became the song we all know.

Chuck Berry and Jerry Lee Lewis were touring Britain in 1964 along with Eric Burdon and The Animals. Knowing he could not "out rock" Berry and Lewis, Anthony writes Burdon decided to rewrite "House of the Rising Sun."

"Their version began with Hilton Valentine's now-famous guitar riff. Then Burdon's ragged voice began spitting out lyrics almost resentfully before the organ music kicked in. It was a throbbing, uniquely 1960s anthem."

On September 5, 1964, the Animals' version of Georgia Turner's favorite song climbed into the #1 spot on the chart.

* * *

Washington has also had a colorful history of houses of prostitution, many reportedly having once been in the Logan Circle area.

So, where in Washington was Capital City Boys' House of the Rising Sun? Actually, there were two of them. Oddly enough, both near Logan Circle.

The first was located in the 600 block of P Street in Northwest Washington. It should have been in a beautiful three-story house somewhere in the 900 block of S Street. That location fell through when the landlord, looking at my application, asked one last question: where my "additional" income was coming from.

Everything went quiet. Chase, Danny, and Sean stood still, all wondering what I might say, all knowing – no matter what was at stake – I would not lie. I did not.

I was explaining to the man that I owned and operated a legally licensed gay-male escort referral service when he cut me off abruptly – "not in my house you won't. Get the hell out of here." He was not the least bit interested in hearing me say clients would never visit there.

Sean, Danny, and Chase jumped me as we got back in my car. "Why didn't you just say you had a trust fund?" Sean asked. At that second in time, knowing I had just lost us a great house, it sounded like a good idea. Me and the truth. Two peas in a pod. Again, I had told the truth, and again, I paid a heavy price for it. So much for "The truth will set you free."

* * *

The first time I passed through the 600 block of P Street I remember thinking I really would not want to live there. A couple of months later, when I rented a house there, I remember being happy that we had finally found a place. A few weeks later, we could not wait to leave.

The house was nice enough but had problems right from the beginning. Our landlords reportedly owned much of the block. They lived next door to us. Even with all its problems, our house may have been the nicest on the block.

Sean, Chase, and I moved into the house in early November. Before the month ended, Austin and Reece, both from Richmond, Virginia, joined us.

We quickly found out the house's single heating/cooling system did a poor job of heating the two-level home. Downstairs, we froze. We could see our breaths when we talked despite burning gas fireplace logs and using electric heaters. Upstairs, we had to prop the windows open because it was so hot. Looking back, I don't know why we didn't just turn the heat off.

* * *

An amazing thing happened while living in Northwest D.C. Somehow living with so many people, I became able to once again sleep soundly, even though there was noise being made in the house. This had not happened since I had to cope with my stepfather's threats.

I was even able to sleep through the occasional sound of gunfire in the alley behind our home. I slept through the gunfire knowing I was on the second floor of a brick home and the chances a bullet would find me were remote. I remember reasoning gunfire was a lot like thunder – if you hear it, you probably had nothing to fear.

* * *

There were always people – neighbors and others – out on the street in front of Capital City Boys' home and those on each side of ours. Few things that happened on the street went unnoticed.

I am sure it did not take the neighbors long to figure out just who we were or what we were doing. I am certain there was absolutely no doubt in their minds that a crazy bunch of gay white boys had moved in, especially when, on that first Saturday night, when Chase – heading out to one of the clubs – walked out of the house wearing nothing but a bra, a pair of panties, a blond wig, and a half-pound of makeup.

The crowd out on the street erupted with laughter. I am sure they had seen a lot of things but never anything quite like Chase. He was anything but ordinary.

"Mack, these people are making fun of me," Chase whined, dead serious about the matter.

"It's called fair comment, kid, and it's protected by federal law," I yelled back. "If go you out dressed like that, you have to expect people to react." The crowd roared again, in total agreement with my response.

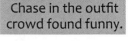
Chase in the outfit crowd found funny.

The situation had not been planned but I have long believed Chase's whining and my defending the crowd's reaction went a long way toward my quickly being accepted as just another neighbor.

The truth is, I had a good relationship with many of them.

When walking to the nearby Giant grocery store, I would sometimes stop by an elderly woman's house to see if she needed groceries. At first, the woman was quite confused why a stranger would ask such a question. She probably thought I wanted money from her.

The second time I asked, the woman again said "No" but smiled and thanked me. I sensed she now understood my offer came from friendship, not from wanting something from her. She smiled even more broadly when, a few minutes later, I knocked on her door again and presented her with a container of ripe strawberries and a small tub of Cool Whip.

Without giving her time to speak, I explained a similar

package of strawberries had called out to me as I passed through the produce section, pleading with me to take them home.

"I would invite you down to my house to have some of my strawberries," I said, winking, "but you know how people on this street talk and a lady like yourself must protect her reputation. So, we'll both dine on strawberries in our own homes tonight, and the neighbors will never be any wiser." The elderly woman smiled. That was all the payment I wanted.

Then there was the law student. I would catch her out on the street from time to time when I needed a quick legal opinion. She always reminded me that her advice was worth what I was paying for it – a smile here, a "hello, how ya doing" there. Her advice was always sound.

I counted the elderly woman and law student as friends but I was closest with Ed and Stanley.

You could always find Ed sitting out in his front yard unless there was a heavy downpour. Ed would often go out to the street to converse with the drivers of cars that would stop in front of his house. Ed and the driver would talk for a minute or two then the car would leave and Ed would return to his chair.

Sometimes, when returning home, Ed would call me over and with his back to the crowd on the sidewalk, whisper to me about who had been by or if he had seen anything the least bit suspicious. He whispered so no one else would hear. In those days, in the 600 block of P Street, someone was always watching, someone was always listening.

Stanley took a more direct approach. He would knock on my door bearing some whopper of a story about how he just needed $20 or $40 to pay this bill or that one and that he was sorry to have to ask but that he had sent "way too much money" to his kids in Georgia or South Carolina or somewhere down South.

Stanley did not ask for money too many times. I do not remember ever turning him down. I once helped him file paperwork with the government for veteran's benefits. Stanley said he was going to use the money to leave Washington. Once the claim was paid, Stanley never asked for money again.

Unlike Ed, who once borrowed $40 and repaid me $10 at a time and in quick order, Stanley never repaid a dime. That was OK. Stanley "ran" the block. Everyone who lived there knew him and followed his instructions. Stanley told those who lived on the block and who visited to leave us alone. They did.

I knew – for my own protection and that of the boys – that Mack had to come across like the movie character Shaft had been described – as "a bad mother—."

Once, when a guy who worked for the service walked from the Giant store to Capital City Boys' home, a man approached him and tried to get money. The escort told me what had happened. I immediately went flying out onto the street in search of this man. I found him a block away. I shared with him – in no uncertain terms – he was not to approach any of my friends at any time and that the next time he threatened one of my friends, I would do more than just warn him.

I do not know who told Stanley what had happened but he appeared at my door 20 minutes later saying he too had talked to man and had given him a similar sermon. Stanley apologized and promised it would never happen again. It never did.

* * *

During the 12 months Capital City Boys was on P Street, lots of guys stayed there. Sean, Chase, Jesse, Jonathan, Austin, Reece, Brett, Ryan, Michael, and I all lived there. Others, like Zack, Christian and Bryce, stayed a night or two when they had no other safe place to go.

Everyone who worked with Capital City Boys knew they were welcome to stay if they had the need. All knew that nothing other than being available to work was ever required or expected.

What they did not know was the backstory behind that policy. I have never told anyone, out of shame. Earlier in this report I told you my mother, my sisters, my brother and I twice had to flee our home to avoid my stepfather's abuse when he was drinking.

My mother's friends took us in and saw to it that we were comforted, fed, and had a warm, safe place to sleep. To this day, when I open my home to a friend in need, I do it to help my friend but also in tribute to those who did the same for my family so long ago. Demanding sex or money from a friend in his or her time of need would dishonor those who opened their home to my family with no such demands.

* * *

I do not handle the task of moving very well. I never have. I have a habit of deciding it is better to toss personal belongings I have not used in a while rather than move them. Having converted much of my music collection to CDs, I tossed out most of my LP collection. Stanley immediately laid claim to them. I

One of Capital City Boys' houses was on P Street

remember watching him sort through them, picking out the best ones. Stanley was not foolish; there was no need to carry away any LPs he did not want. He ended up taking several.

* * *

Capital City Boys' second location was on Wallach Place, a short one-way street between 13th and 14th, one block off U Street.

The real estate broker handling the rental knew who I was and that I owned Capital City Boys. He knew because he was active in Washington's gay community and had seen our ads in the *Washington Blade* and the *Metro Weekly.*

The broker, concerned about his responsibility to the homeowner, consulted with an attorney about leasing the property to an escort service. The lawyer told him that as long as the city had licensed us, he could not legally deny Capital City Boys' application. Documents showing Capital City Boys was registered with the District and with the IRS were provided and we moved in a few days later.

Clients rarely came to the two houses, probably fewer than 10 in two years. When they did, it was to "visit" Ryan, or someone who was living there. Unlike other services in Washington, Capital City Boys did not open its house to clients. This was my home, and I did not want visits conducted there. I made other arrangements for clients but never invited them into Capital City Boys' home.

Boys, on the other hand, were another matter. There was

One of Capital City Boys' houses was on Wallach Place.

always a steady stream of handsome men between the ages of 19 and 35 knocking on our door. I loved the company. So did Max the Wonder Dog, aka "Killer." The parade of friends in and out of our house was the best part about being in Washington, the best part of being Mack and "Killer."

* * *

One night, a few months before Capital City Boys moved away from P Street, Ed got into an argument with a man in front of the landlord's house. The man taunted Ed and encouraged him to defend his honor. We know this because the crowd saw and heard the exchange.

Ed took the challenge. He went to his basement apartment, returned a minute later, and shot the man dead there on the sidewalk.

We know this because the crowd saw and heard this exchange too. Then they fled. The crowd – ever present up to now – was nowhere to be found when police flooded the street with patrol cars, lights flashing.

I did not witness the exchange and shooting. Ryan and his boyfriend did. Sitting on a bench outside Capital City Boys' house, Ryan and Michael saw and heard everything.

Ed was sitting in his chair in his front yard when I arrived on the scene. He looked very scared. He had good reason to be. Questioned by police, Ryan had told them what he and Michael had seen and heard and that Ed still had the gun on him. Ed was arrested and charged in the man's death. I later read in the

Washington Post where he pleaded guilty.

* * *

PERSONAL THOUGHTS: One of the few unanswered questions I still have about my time in Washington is this: Would I have told the police about Ed's involvement, as Ryan did, or would I have simply gone into the house and locked the door?

A good citizen would have told police what they knew. A good friend, even one like me who thinks the truth must always be told, might have found justification for doing otherwise that night. You see, I personally know how quickly the dead man could anger someone. The man had angered me the week before, while working on the basement in Capital City Boy's home.

The man taunted me too. Like with Ed, the man challenged me to take extreme measures. I went and got my landlord. Ed went and got his gun. Killing the man was wrong but, unlike most, I know how Ed may have been pushed to that point.

Despite the fact this question still nags at me, I have never pressed myself for an answer, fearing I might decide I would have been a better friend that night than citizen.

* * *

I never saw Stanley after we moved away. I heard from the crowd on the street that he moved away soon after we did.

Sometimes, late at night, I reminisce about the people I met in Washington, about my friends – escorts and clients alike – about the elderly neighbor and those strawberries, about legal questions and the law student – and about unusual friends like Ed and Stanley.

I like to think that Ed is somehow better off today, living a better life than the one where he sat in his yard and talked with motorists who circled our block.

I also like to think that Stanley took his settlement and moved closer to his kids, wherever they lived. It is my hope that from time to time, Stanley wipes the dust off one of those LPs, plays a cut, and thinks of me. I like to imagine him toasting me, saying, "Mack, I don't know where in the hell you are man but here's to ya. You sure were one crazy mother—."

The Backstory

The Animal's version of **"House Of The Rising Sun"** was written by Alan Price. It was published by Beechwood Music (BMI). It was the first #1 song that was more than 4 minutes long.

A gay male escort service is not your typical social club but it is a club – a club complete with members and membership requirements. And, in this club, membership does have its rewards, for escorts and clients alike.

Despite the success of Capital City Boys and its guys, it never re-created the attitude and social status that The Agency seemed to have had under Troy, its original owner.

> *"Other guys imitate us,*
> *but the original is still the greatest."*

It was as if The Agency's boys knew all about Dobie Gray's classic hit, "The 'In' Crowd" and had made it their anthem. It is as if they lived the song every day. Written by Billy Page, "The 'In' Crowd" oozes pure confidence and elitism. Agency boys – at least in 1998 when I first encountered them – were like that.

There was Jonathan, Christian, Hunter, Brad, Matthew, and Charlie. All of them were Agency boys. All of them were a part of the "in" crowd.

Charlie was one of the few "original" Agency boys who worked with me. Charlie became Ryan while represented by Capital City Boys/The Agency. And though he was not one of the most-popular guys on our escort list, those who met Charlie/Ryan almost always wanted to see him again.

* * *

Repeat clients that were part of Capital City Boys' own "in" crowd got perks first-time clients did not. The one-hour rule was relaxed a bit for repeat clients. Escorts could stay an extra 15 or 20 minutes and no one cared, we knew they were safe. This often generated a bigger tip for the escort. "In-crowd" clients were also allowed to take an escort to dinner without charge as long as the client picked up the tab and there was a booking afterward.

* * *

Being part of the "in-crowd" meant escorts had a safe haven if they needed one. Even after an escort left us, he knew he could call or knock on the door at any hour and be welcomed inside.

On Thanksgivings, there were turkey dinners. On Christmas, there was a steak-and-egg breakfast. In between holidays, escorts were invited over for a home-cooked dinner or invited to go out to dinner. Since business was conducted during these dinners, the service paid the check.

It was not widely known but when a guy needed to see a doctor and did not have the money to pay, Capital City Boys quietly paid the bill. When someone needed a prescription filled and did not have money, the service stepped up to the window and paid that bill too. And if a guy needed clothes, he got them – usually from Target or Marshall's or TJ Maxx and not the Gap – but he got them. Nothing was ever expected in return.

* * *

Several times late at night, a small, "outted" group of Capital City Boys associates would go to Annie's on 17th Street for a late-night dinner or snack and to socialize. It was not unusual for someone to walk into Annie's at 2 in the morning on a weekend and see two large tables with cute guys eating. One would have been the Capital City Boys/Agency group; the other would have been strippers from Wet or LaCage.

* * *

Another perk of being one of the "in-crowd" was – when the need arose – an escort could get a loan from Capital City Boys. The loan was never a lot, almost always under $200. Sometimes the loan was repaid; sometimes it was not. I did not really care. I knew, before I lent the money, the escort really needed it. And since the money had already been reported as income and I was the sole Capital City Boys stockholder, no one else, including the government, would be harmed by a loan that went unpaid.

* * *

Escorts who had come to Washington from outside the region were encouraged to come over and use one of the company's phones to call home. The escort's family knew he was OK and a connection had been renewed. Twice, the escort decide to go home. I never minded losing an escort this way.

In one case, the guy's parents wired him the money for a bus ticket. In the other, Capital City Boys paid for it.

* * *

Once, when Corey, a new escort, and his boyfriend got caught living at Gallaudet University without the school's knowledge, Capital City Boys paid for them to stay in a Washington motel for two days. It also provided them money for food.

A frantic Corey called at 2:30 one morning, saying university police had found them and was throwing them off campus. Saying they had no place to go, Corey asked if I could help. Two hours later, the boys were safe and asleep in a motel.

Corey had completed two calls for the company when this happened. He never did another. Instead, he and his boyfriend went home at Capital City Boys' expense. Though Corey was a member of the "in-crowd" for only a short time, he was one of Mack's boys, and that meant he was cared for.

I paid for six similar rescues after I sold Capital City Boys and moved back to Kentucky. In all, 14 escorts and Corey's boyfriend benefited from Mack's rescue program. No one ever paid a penny back. No one was ever asked nor expected to do so.

* * *

PERSONAL THOUGHTS: I told the people at the *Herald-Leader* conducting my inquisition about Corey and his boyfriend. My notes from that session show one of them remarked I had crossed over the line of being a journalist "and became a social worker."

When I taught photojournalism at Eastern Kentucky University, I spent at least one class each semester discussing the role of a photojournalist at a news event.

"Say you are shooting photos of a burning building," I would tell my students. "You get there before fire officials do. While shooting, you hear someone inside the building shouting for help. "Do you put your camera down and rescue the person or do you continue to shoot, since that is your job?"

Students expressed opinions supporting both sides. The same is true in the real world of journalism. Even today, there is great debate about this situation in the journalism world. When is it right for a journalist – reporter or photographer – to cross that line and become involved with people they encounter while covering a story/event? I am not sure anyone really knows.

* * *

After rescuing them, Corey and his boyfriend sent me an

electronic thank-you card. I showed the card to my bosses at the *Herald-Leader.* "Is this the face of evil?" I asked. "Is this the heart of wickedness? Is this the handiwork of someone just out to make money? No," I said. "Ironically, I think this is the face, heart, and handiwork of someone with a great deal of integrity."

* * *

There were a few times when my roommates and I would go to Wet or LaCage, male strip clubs. The company would buy the first round of drinks and, every once in a while, would buy a drink for everyone who worked with us or anyone who had ever worked with us.

Once, at Wet, the bill was almost $90. What the hell, I thought, asking the bartender for a receipt. When Ryan made fun of me for being "such a Republican," I tore the receipt in half amid cheers and laughter. I knew Mack's boys very well. There were times – like this one – when they seemed to know me pretty well too.

"And if I had the choice,
yeah, I'd always wanna be there.
Those were the best days of my life."
– SUMMER OF '69
Artist: Bryan Adams
Songwriters: B. Adams/J. Vallance
Irving Music (BMI)

The Backstory

"The 'In' Crowd" was written by Billy Page and published by Unichappell Music (BMI). It was in the Top 20 for three months in 1965. It peaked at #13.

"Only The Lonely"

Martha Davis and The Motels – Peaked at #9 in 1982
Roy Orbison – Topped out at #2 in 1960

It may seem odd but there were lots of Saturday nights, especially busy ones, when I felt like the loneliest person in Washington.

Clients called and made arrangements for a visit. Escorts would stop by to drop off their referral fees and would tell what a great time they were about to have with friends. I always smiled, even though many times my heart ached. It was a pain I knew only too well.

I cannot remember anyone other than my roommates and Drew ever asking if I wanted to join them. The reason was simple: most who worked for Capital City Boys did not want their friends to know they escorted.

While I was not widely known in Washington's gay community, I was not a total stranger either. To be seen with me would be a good indication that you escorted or were considering starting.

I had friends in Washington, friends who had once worked at the *Herald-Leader* and had moved on to Washington as their careers advanced. They worked for Washington-based Knight Ridder and Gannett bureaus and other journalism-related organizations.

It would have been good to go to dinner with these friends, to talk about journalistic matters. I never called a single one, knowing I would have to explain what I was doing in Washington or lie to them. No one in Washington was to know about this project – no one. Besides, at times, I was not sure if there was even going to be a project.

I also never figured out how to make my "Man Behind the Curtain" title and job duties sound as important as the ones they had. So, on Saturday nights, I stood in the doorway, telling the escorts goodnight and to be careful. I smiled even though my heart ached. What else could I do?

* * *

Saturday nights, after the phones died down or after the available inventory of boys had run out, Max the Wonder Dog and I would escape into a world of make-believe via my music collection. When the journey was over, I would turn out the lights, and Max and I would go upstairs to bed.

Outside, I would often hear strangers walking by, coming from the clubs on U Street. They laughed and talked. They enjoyed each other's company.

A couple of times, I stared out the window, watching the happy people below, and felt very alone. Twice I cried because I was alone, far from home, working on a blasted project that had spun out of control and had cost me so much of what I had once held dear. What else could one in my place do but cry?

Your heart may be broken tonight
but tomorrow in the morning light,
don't let the sun catch you cryin'.
– DON'T LET THE SUN
CATCH YOU CRYING
Artist: Gerry and the Pacemakers
Songwriters: L. Chadwick/L. Maguire/
F. Marsden/G. Marsden
Universal Songs of Polygram (BMI)

Most people would never imagine that the owner of an escort service could be lonely. They are wrong. At least in my case and others I know about, they are.

Marvin, the owner of Tops Referrals, thinks that this segment will surprise you, the reader, the most.

"While everything you've written is the truth, most people think those of us who own escort services have non-stop sex," Marvin says. "The truth is, there (are) a lot of lonely nights. No disrespect intended," he says to me, answering my question, "but it's a Saturday night, you're here, and I'll be sleeping alone, again."

Marvin says he rarely hires one of his own escorts, not because of quality issues but "It's a complicated experience and usually not worth the trouble." Some escorts find time spent with the owner no different than with any other client. Others, however, view such a call completely different. Some even become offended by being approached about doing such a call, a few to the point of leaving the service.

"It's often awkward to meet with someone who works with your service," Marvin says. "A lot of people have a problem being with the boss." Instead, Marvin often times hires an independent escort. "I tell them who I am and, if they are good, make a pitch for them to work with me."

* * *

An escort referral service is much like any other business – run it professionally and you have a shot at doing well; run it poorly and it will crash and burn.

Washington has had its share of both types of gay escort referral services. Owners who respected and took care of their guys far outlasted those who started a service as a way of having easy hookups.

Generally speaking, there are five main ways an escort referral service owner hooks up:

(1) Be young and "hot" enough to hook up with almost anyone anyway.

(2) Demand encounters as a condition of working.

(3) "Pay" for it in money, drugs, or some other means.

(4) Require or take advantage of a "free" session during the interview process.

(5) Take advantage of a current escort who might "offer" a session free for one reason or another. Such times are generally rare and almost never involve a service's top talent.

With the record selection
and the mirror's reflection,
I'm a-dancing with myself.
– DANCING WITH MYSELF
Artist: Billy Idol
Songwriters: W. Broad/A. James
Chrysalis Music (ASCAP)

It is dangerous for the owner of a service to become involved with one of his escorts. Word quickly gets around and, whether true or not, the perception and talk is that the owner is favoring his boyfriend over everyone else.

* * *

PERSONAL THOUGHTS: It was difficult not to have someone special in my life but on the other hand, it was not anything new for me. I was lonely long before I came to Washington and long after I left.

I learned to keep my hands off people I supervised and how to keep my desires in check long before going to Washington. Having taught at a state university for six years, I knew I could not be both instructor and become involved with a student for any reason.

I never allowed myself to become involved with any student, and although I cannot say the same about my time in Washington, when it happened, it was always a private, professional situation. I never took advantage of anyone.

My ex-wife once told me I would live a lonely life and die alone. At the time, I thought she was speaking from bitterness. As time goes by, I think maybe she was right.

Maybe I was meant to be alone. Many of my role models have been loners too: Robert McCall, TV's "The Equalizer"; Dr. Samuel Beckett of "Quantum Leap"; Steve McGarrett of "Hawaii-Five-O"; Thomas Magnum of "Magnum P.I."; Lilly Rush of "Cold Case"; author Robert Parker's Jesse Stone.

They are all loners. They are also survivors. So am I.

The Backstory

Martha Davis wrote The Motels' 1982 version of **"Only the Lonely."** The song was published by Dimensional Songs of the Knoll. (BMI).

Roy Orbison co-wrote the second version of **"Only the Lonely"** with Joe Melson. It was Orbison's first major hit. Released by Monument Records in 1960, "Only the Lonely" topped out at #2 on the Billboard pop music charts.

Orbison suffered a fatal heart attack and died on Dec. 6, 1988. He was 52.

* * *

Playing **"Don't Let the Sun Catch You Crying"** was the way that WWKY – the only radio station I ever worked at – signed off at dusk. At the time (1974), I thought it silly. Today, I can't think of a more appropriate song. Way to go (program director) Tim Earl.

PREMISE #5

"If a man does not keep pace
with his companions,
perhaps it is because
he hears a different drummer.
Let him step to the music
he hears, however
measured or far away"

– HENRY DAVID THOREAU

"Don't Let Me Be Misunderstood"
The Animals
Peaked at #15 in 1965

"Have you been fired yet?" my attorney asked when I returned her call.

"No," I replied.

"Well get ready," she said. "You're about to be."

I'm just a soul who's intentions are good,
Oh, Lord, please don't let me
be misunderstood.
– DON'T LET ME BE MISUNDERSTOOD
Artist: The Animals
Songwriters:
B. Benjamin/G. Caldwell/S. Marcus
Benjamin Bennie Music (ASCAP)

The next morning – after 25 years of faithful service – my employment with the Lexington Herald-Leader Co. and Knight Ridder Newspapers came to an abrupt end.

"In early May, we investigated your involvement in an outside business (male escort service) and found your conduct to be in violation of Company policy and business ethics. As a longtime manager in the newsroom and New Media, we believe you fully understood the intent of our policies...

"We are sorry we were unable to reach a settlement

agreement, since there has been no formal response to our final offer, you and your attorney have left us no choice except to terminate your employment..."

While not unexpected, the termination hurt. Hurt deeply.

* * *

There were two daily newspapers in Lexington when I worked my first free-lance assignment – the *Lexington Herald* and the *Lexington Leader.*

The morning *Herald* covered Lexington as well as Central and Eastern Kentucky. The *Leader* – the afternoon paper – covered Lexington and Central Kentucky.

I started free-lancing for the *Herald* in November 1974. I came along soon after Knight Newspapers merged with Ridder Publications and formed Knight Ridder Newspapers. I was later hired as a full-time employee.

Both papers greatly improved when Creed Black, who had worked at the *Philadelphia Inquirer*, became publisher. Black led the transformation of the *Herald* from a so-so community newspaper into one that earned national recognition.

Black hired John S. Carroll to be the *Herald's* editor. Carroll had played a major role in the *Philadelphia Inquirer's* coverage of the Three Mile Island nuclear power plant disaster. Carroll would later become editor at the *Baltimore Sun* and the *Los Angeles Times.*

It was under Carroll's leadership that the *Herald-Leader* began doing serious investigative reporting. Under Carroll, the *Herald-Leader* won national awards for its reporting and public service. Such reporting led to the paper's winning two Pulitzer Prizes – one for its reporting about a University of Kentucky basketball scandal and one for a series of editorials about spousal abuse. The paper would later win a third Pulitzer for editorial cartooning.

I played a supporting role in the first two projects. I handled layout/design/ production duties on both.

The basketball project won a Pulitzer but was not well-received locally. Basketball is sacred in Kentucky. When the *Herald-Leader* reported certain UK basketball players were taking $50 handshakes from boosters and the NCAA was going to investigate the program, someone shot out or broke windows at the newspaper's building.

The incident got the newsroom's attention but what really

demonstrated the power of investigative reporting to me was that on both days we ran the report on the basketball team, I saw UK's newly hired basketball coach out in the paper's back parking lot reading first-edition papers. I saw him as I was leaving work, sometime after midnight.

Some people, when they know a load of bricks is going to fall on them in the morning, like to size up what the load looks like the night before. I imagine that is what Coach Eddie Sutton was doing.

* * *

When I decided to work this project, I knew it was possible I would be fired. I had seen others who had crossed the publisher pay a price. I knew I would not be treated any differently.

I felt the publisher, Tim Kelly, would not welcome news about my project. I feared no matter how hard I tried to sell the merits of this project, Kelly would reject it outright.

I also suspected my bosses would be shocked – not by the fact I was working on a project outside the *Herald-Leader,* I had done that before – but because my project involved gay male escorts.

What I did not know is the *Herald-Leader* had already been told I owned and was operating Capital City Boys. Tristian, working on the Dreamboys owner's behalf, called the paper's Human Resources department and – in an attempt to shut the service down – told them I owned and was running Capital City Boys.

I was later surprised to hear two *Herald-Leader* employees had spent "a considerable amount of time" looking for Capital City Boys' Web site. Somehow, they did not find it though it was called capitalcityboys.com. They also apparently failed to follow up on the lead with anyone else in the building, including me.

* * *

Having completed as much research as I could from a distance. I needed to be in Washington to witness things personally and to meet people.

It was my request for a leave of absence in April 1999 that opened the door to my leaving the *Herald-Leader.* My leave request was simple yet dangerous because I knew it would likely force me to expose the nature of my project and face whatever consequences that might follow.

My request came in the form of a seven-page letter to my boss, David Reed, and the New Media director, Mary Epple-Ekhoff, on

April 21, 1999. The letter detailed how I had come to the *Herald-Leader* in November 1974 as "a young, skinny, long-haired college student." I told them about the thrill of seeing my photograph published in the next morning's paper.

"The experience left the kid wanting more," I wrote. "Having something of his printed for others to see and enjoy satisfied a hunger he had felt for a long time."

The letter also recounted some of my achievements at the paper:

– That I had shot the first color breaking-news picture that appeared in the *Herald-Leader* (at least while I was there and that I am aware of).

– That a photograph and article of mine ran on Page One of the *Herald-Leader's* last hot-type edition. That page is enshrined in the paper's lobby.

– That the Page One covering the Beverly Hills Supper Club Fire disaster hanging in the fourth-floor lobby has two articles bearing my byline. The fire, at the Northern Kentucky club on May 28, 1977, killed 165 people.

– That two of the front pages hanging in the fourth-floor lobby are ones I designed.

– That I mentored three designers who went on to larger papers and became successful presentation editors.

My request explained, "Today is the day I take that big step and let the two of you know more about my interest in D.C. and why I have such strong ties there."

I told Reed and Epple-Ekhoff how I am fascinated by people and their lives – who they are today and how they became that person. Then I told them about Sean, just not *everything.*

"I met a guy in Washington who told me this incredible story about himself and his life. I was fascinated by what I heard." He told me "about his life in the shadows on the streets of D.C.

"He told me about how he and others make a living doing things many of us could never really imagine. The stories he told me moved me. Some made me laugh. Others frightened me. His is a world I knew almost nothing about and yet the more he told me, the more intrigued I became and the more I wanted to know. I am convinced others will feel the same way."

I told my bosses I had started a yearlong personal reporting project the previous summer. I told them my project would center on Sean's life and his experiences.

I told them the project would be told in Sean's own words. "I hope to share what the lives of those who live and work in the shadows are like: the excitement, the dangers, the joys; and the disappointments."

I pointed out others had taken leaves for personal and professional enrichment. I stressed how I would benefit from working my project.

My leave request took my bosses by surprise. They were even more shocked when, checking on the company's policy with Human Resources, they were informed about the phone call telling the *Herald-Leader* that I owned Capital City Boys.

I had already prepared a full accounting of my project for my bosses. Lying was never an option and withdrawing my request would not stop the firestorm that was coming.

On May 4, I was told that my bosses and I would meet with Paula Anderson of Human Resources the next day.

When I arrived at work the next morning, I was handed a Post-It Note telling me, "They've found your Web site and they are not happy." I took the note to mean my bosses had found Capital City Boys' Web site – the one showing a semi-naked guy on the cover and pictures and/or descriptions of all the guys we represented. Descriptions included endowment sizes for those who were curious about such things.

Capitalcityboys.com was never obscene; just nothing you wanted to show your bosses, your mother, or your minister.

I quickly typed a coversheet for my project outline, put the coversheet and outline in envelopes marked "For Your Eyes Only," and slid them under my bosses' doors. I also left one for Anderson. All would know I had fully disclosed the nature of my project before the showdown.

Anderson led the meeting. She, Reed and Epple-Ekhoff complimented me for being so forthright in discussing my project with them. The Human Resources person talked about the leave-of-absence policy, but I do not think any of us were seriously considering that issue anymore.

My outline confirmed I owned a gay male escort referral service in Washington. I told them I feared what the paper's reaction might be to that news.

Having been told management had found my Web site, I freely spoke about capitalcityboys.com and its contents.

Surprise #1: Anderson, Reed and Epple-Ekhoff did not know

anything about Capital City Boys' Web site. Instead, they found dcboys.com, a second Web site I owned. Dcboys.com is where I originally planned to publish this report. Nothing was on dcboys.com but a notice saying the site was under development.

Then, it was my turn to surprise them. I explained that Capital City Boys was a legally licensed company – a legally licensed escort referral service.

One of them – I do not remember which one – gasped when I passed out copies of the Business License granted to me by the District of Columbia and a document showing I was also properly registered with the Internal Revenue Service.

All three of them had looks of disbelief. The documents proved I had met all the requirements necessary to run this business – legally and openly. I got the impression all three had thought I was running Capital City Boys in the shadows, running it illegally – no doubt on a street corner. Such operations did exist.

While the process of licensing Capital City Boys had been embarrassing, seeing the shock on the three people's faces made short-lived pain worthwhile. There was no way anyone could argue what I was doing was illegal. The government-issued documents proved otherwise.

Stunned and grasping for something to support her position, Anderson said the paper could not condone my project because something might go wrong and the *Herald-Leader* "could be embarrassed."

Anderson offered this scenario: What if a senator hired "an escort from your service [and he] was found dead the next morning in a hotel room with your [service's] phone number in his pocket? What if someone traced that number and found that it was an escort agency's number and that you were the owner and they found out that you worked for the *Herald-Leader?*"

Stunned by Anderson's question, I paused, then replied: "That is a mighty huge 'what if.'"

I pointed out the *Herald-Leader* accepted advertising from massage parlors, strip clubs, and escorts alike. I reminded them the paper took in more than $1 million a year from such clients and pointed out the hypocrisy of the paper saying it was wrong for me to take money from some of these same people.

Unfolding a copy of a recent day's paper, I pointed out ads I suspected were from escorts. No one disputed my claim. They were too smart to challenge me on that point. For all they knew, I

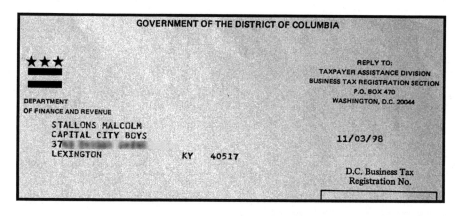

had already called those who had placed the ads.

They also were smart enough to know, if challenged, I would not hesitate to call every ad. My bosses knew this because they knew the paper had done a excellent job of teaching me how to document a story properly.

I also showed them an Ann Landers column that had run in the *Herald-Leader*. The headline: "Prostitution should be legalized." Had I known it at the time, I would have also pointed out the federal government once ran a brothel in Nevada and that Eleanor Roosevelt advocated legalizing prostitution.

* * *

I casually mentioned I had discussed my project in detail with someone in the *Herald-Leader's* newsroom. My comment – meant to show at least one other journalist thought the project was interesting and worth researching – hijacked the investigation.

Those questioning me immediately demanded to know whom I had told. I had misjudged the effect my casual statement would have. It became clear to me my friend would undergo a similar interrogation and possibly also face disciplinary action for not bringing my project to management's attention.

I refused to tell them. Whatever they were going to do to me had already been set in motion and would not be any worse by my protecting the person I had told. My refusal set off a witch hunt for my accomplice. I had given no clue to identify this person and quickly warned the individual to deny any involvement, if asked. I had seen witch hunts before. None ever ended well.

I also decided not to tell my interrogators that – on three separate occasions – I had discussed working on a project in

Washington with Reed. That information would have been misleading. Accurate, but misleading.

Each time I went to Washington, I gave Reed a telephone number where I could be reached (Sean's home number). Three times, Reed and I talked about my trips to the District. Each of the conversations ended with me telling Reed that, when the time was right, I would tell him what I was doing in Washington and why I kept going there.

Maybe Reed should have asked me to explain. He did not. For both the good and the bad, that was not Reed's style.

I could have thrown Reed under the bus. I could have told the panel interviewing me that I had told my supervisor I was working a project in Washington three times and he had done nothing about it, effectively blessing my efforts. I could have, but doing so is not my style.

My project was about to draw blood and I decided all of it would be mine and mine alone. Reed and the other person were both sideline players. Neither deserved to be harmed.

Repeatedly, the panel demanded to know whom I had talked to about my project. Repeatedly I refused to tell them. The panel made it clear it would conduct its own full investigation, strongly implying it would interview everyone I interacted with.

Through my attorney, I threatened to sue the *Herald-Leader* on behalf of Capital City Boys and each of the 30-some men it represented – if the company conducted its search. I also threatened to bring a van-load of escorts from Washington to picket the *Herald-Leader* building, knowing this was the last thing the company would want. Management knew I was serious. If I said I was going to do something, they knew I would. I had a 25-year history of doing so.

Storm, my friend the porn star, would have coordinated the protest and certainly would have led local TV and radio coverage of the event. Storm's appearance and message would have been something Lexington would have long remembered.

The *Herald-Leader* blinked. I am guessing no one was ever asked about my project. It was to the paper's benefit that no one know. It was also in my project's best interest.

Management would have gone ballistic if it had known the person I had confided in about *Mack And The Boys* was an "insider" and the person who tipped me off with that Post-It Note.

* * *

At the beginning of my second interview, Jim Green, the *Herald-Leader's* Human Resources director, went over a long list of conditions and terms for the session. I was told I could not tape the session. This made me wonder if my being able to quote the Human Resources person so directly in legal papers sent to the paper by my attorney had caused management to suspect I had taped the first session or if it was part of a shopping list of terms and conditions set forth by the company's attorney.

I was also told I could not have an attorney present to assist me. I found this condition odd and a bit confusing. My attorney was not in the room nor was she anywhere inside the building. I took the statement to reinforce the notion I was there all on my own, not a friend anywhere.

It was as if someone wanted me to feel like the *Herald-Leader's* 500-some employees and all of Knight Ridder was standing on one side of this issue and me – all by myself – on the other. What management did not know was that I was used to such things. Loners and "damaged" people are.

I do not remember what Green said that made me ask but I came to think that someone outside the room was listening in on our conversation – probably via Green's speaker phone.

When I asked if anyone outside the room was listening in on the conversation, the room got quiet and Green said "that is possible." I decided it really did not matter who might be listening, they were not there to protect my rights or to assist me. Let them listen, let them hear what I would say. They would one day, anyway.

I came prepared to tell my story and I did. I brought books of documentation, transcripts of conversations, dozens of audio tapes, and copies of e-mails.

I talked for what seemed to be hours. I answered every question asked except those dealing with Capital City Boys' finances. I knew – from my time as a reporter and editor – the *Herald-Leader* wanted to gauge how strong Capital City Boys was financially. By doing so, the paper could gauge how much of a legal challenge to the company I could pose. I knew if I did not tell them, they could not guess, not with any degree of certainty.

I feared some investigating my case might be homophobic and their feelings about gays might influence their actions and decisions. I based my belief on having worked with them at the *Herald-Leader* and having personally heard two of them talk about people they thought or knew to be gay.

While one can paste various labels on Publisher Tim Kelly, homophobic is not one of them. I remember hearing he played a role in shaping Knight Ridder's diversity policy to include sexual orientation.

Kelly has treated me politely since first learning about my project. He also treated my mother with great respect when she – without my knowledge – called him and begged him to let me stay at the paper.

While I disagree with the decision that forced me to leave the *Herald-Leader,* I have always believed Kelly's actions stemmed from working to protect the paper, not from prejudice.

I knew my time at the *Herald-Leader* was over. I just did not know when the end would come or how it would happen.

Time to resign from the human race,
wipe those tears from your lovely face.
Baby, wave to the man in the ol' red caboose
before all hell breaks loose.
– BEFORE ALL HELL BREAKS LOOSE
Singer/Songwriter: Kinky Friedman

The *Herald-Leader* said I "was no longer worthy of being a manager because I might not be sensitive enough to recognize a threat to the company."

Mack And The Boys was a personal project done completely on my own time and at my own expense. It was also done outside of Kentucky, 554 miles from the *Herald-Leader's* building.

Against my lawyer's advice, I wrote two letters to Kelly, telling him my side of the story. He and I never talked about my project. I never had an opportunity to explain my actions.

"In order to research my story I opened a legally licensed business. I have made sure the business is run properly and legally. No one disputes this," I wrote.

"The *Herald-Leader*, however, is offended that an employee who was trained and served as a reporter and then as an editor, finds a story he wants to write about. The *Herald-Leader* is offended this properly trained journalist takes his own time and his own money to research (that) story.

"The *Herald-Leader* is so deeply offended that it is prepared to fire a well-respected editor. That employee is also offended. He is offended the company he worked for and looked up to has lied to him, has tossed aside promises conveyed to him."

I was told the *Herald-Leader* thought I was ashamed of my involvement in this project. The company tried to use that position against me. "I assure you if I was timid or afraid that someone might find out, I would not have survived the first 30 days in the D.C. market," I wrote.

"It may be painful to admit but when you really get down to the core, there's not a lot of difference between the service the *Herald-Leader* provides its customers and what Capital City Boys provides its clients," I said.

"Neither of us promise anything nor force anyone to do anything. We simply make it possible for two interested parties to get together. Whatever happens, if anything, is between them.

"That is why the District of Columbia allows escort businesses to exist there. That is why the [Lexington-Fayette] Urban County Government allows such businesses to exist here.

"Is it appropriate to dismiss a long-term employee because he owns a business some might find distasteful? Is it appropriate to dismiss a long-term employee because he dares to dream a dream different than those of others or to follow a different drummer?"

The letter did not make a difference. The call inviting me back never came. Instead, when our lawyers talked, they talked about a dismissal settlement.

* * *

I did not want to leave the paper. I loved being a part of the *Herald-Leader*. I loved being a part of a newsroom that stretched beyond what it should have for a paper its size and one that – for a while – touched greatness. I was fortunate to be a part of that greatness.

I did not want to leave even though much greatness had passed when people like Henry Wright, Walter Dorsett, Keith Hollar, Ray Walker, Theresa Klisz, Joedy Isert, Fred Povey, Keith King, Philip Kearney, Dottie Bean, Jerry Wakefield, Jim Jennings, and a host of other newsroom professionals left the paper in search of opportunities elsewhere.

For the record, others who played a part in making the *Herald-Leader* great are still working there.

I knew staying or going was not going to be my choice. It was just a matter of time before this chapter of my life would end.

* * *

The company suspended me with pay while it investigated whether I had used *Herald-Leader* equipment – computers, software, telephones – in the production of the Capital City Boys Web site and in running the company. The paper's investigation confirmed what I already knew – I had not.

I was escorted out of the *Herald-Leader* building and told to wait for instructions about what would happen next.

I waited and waited and waited. Finally, I decided to go to Washington – at least there, I could work – and if the call came telling me to come to the paper to answer more questions, I could be back in Lexington in 10 hours.

I was back home in Lexington when the fateful call came.

"Have you been fired yet?" my attorney asked.

"No," I replied.

"Well, get ready," she said. "You're about to be."

The next morning, FedEx delivered a letter saying my employment had been terminated.

My attorney faxed the Knight Ridder attorney handling my case a copy of the lawsuit she had already drafted on my behalf and was prepared to file. The suit demanded $2 million in compensation and asked for punitive damages.

A short time later, my attorney was informed the firing had

been rescinded. I was a *Herald-Leader* employee again. We both laughed when she congratulated me.

I was still barred from entering the building or talking with anyone there other than my supervisors but I was an employee again – at least for a few more days.

Against my lawyer's wishes, I wrote a second letter to the publisher. This one much more personal in nature.

"Some have questioned the worthiness of my project. They have that right. But they have that right only if they allow me the same right – the right to decide for myself if I was right or if I missed the mark.

"I ask you, as one journalist to another, if I was right in judging the importance and outcome of the Buddy Holly story and shooting that video [of basketball fans celebrating UK's victory over Utah in 1998's NCAA's championship game] when others frowned, is it not possible that I am right about the importance or interest in *Mack And The Boys?*

"Isn't it possible I have seen something here of value that others, later on, will see?

"Dr. Martin Luther King Jr. told us about his incredible dream. Some laughed at him, some thought he was crazy but, oh what a dream it was. The American public listened and the world was changed.

"Columbus also had a dream. Some laughed at him, some thought he was crazy. One person believed in his dream and the world was forever changed.

"Someone had the vision of writing and filming a fake documentary called "The Blair Witch Project." It cost $50,000 to make, has no stars and no special effects and is now expected to gross more than $100 million.

"Isn't it possible that my dream, while nowhere near as important or life-changing as Dr. King's or Columbus' or as successful as "The Blair Witch Project," has merit? I think it does."

I sent that letter on May 29, 1999. I am still waiting for an answer.

* * *

It was becoming clear that running Capital City Boys was going to become my full-time job. It was not what I wanted.

Changes had to be made. I put my house up for sale and sold it for less than market value. I knew I had to tell my mother what

Part of the contract between Herald-Leader and me. My contention is that the Herald-Leader "broke" the contract when one Herald-Leader employee told another about Capital City Boys. That person then told my boss at the Courier-Journal. (You will read about that later.) Because the leak came from within the Herald-Leader, I feel that I can discuss this matter with you without breaking my word.

was going on. She had no clue. I knew the experience would not be pleasant.

I believed I had a good legal action against the *Herald-Leader*. So did my attorney's law firm – one of the largest and best in Lexington. It offered to handle my case on a contingency basis.

Pursuing the case was tempting. In my opinion and in my attorney's, I had been harmed. Damages were due.

I might have won and cashed in big if I had pursued the case, but it would have come at a high price. My son would have had to answer for me with his grandfather; my mother would have been embarrassed, thinking neighbors and friends would blame her for who I am; and this project would have been made public and shut down.

Eventually, the *Herald-Leader* and I settled. They paid me somewhere in the neighborhood of six months' salary, including the time I was suspended with pay.

I was told that if I ever revealed the terms of our settlement, the *Herald-Leader* would officially change my status from having resigned to having been fired. They put that threat in writing. I have included it (above) for you to see.

Unlike management feared, I was never arrested or had run-ins with the D.C. police or any other law enforcement agency. The Lexington-Fayette Urban County Government has run three criminal background check on me since I returned from "working" in Washington. All have come back "clean."

* * *

No client – senator or otherwise – was found dead with

Capital City Boys' phone number in his pocket. The Human Resources person's point, however, turned out not to be as crazy as I originally thought.

One guy who had briefly worked with us was charged in connection with a murder that captured international attention.

A *Washington Post* reporter called, asking me to confirm if a certain guy worked for Capital City Boys. This was the only time while in Washington I was truly afraid.

It was company policy never to confirm if someone did or did not work with us. But this was the *Washington Post* calling. To a journalist, the *Post* calling is like God calling. A good journalist knows not to lie to either one.

Technically, no one worked for Capital City Boys – it worked for them. This is a fine point but an important one.

I asked the reporter for the guy's name again, remembering it only too well but stalling for time to think. Knowing I was telling the truth but also knowing I was splitting the finest hair doing it – I answered, "No, he doesn't."

Without breathing, I asked, "What has he done?" "He and three others are accused of killing a woman in..."

I stood in my bedroom, shaken by the call. The freaking *Washington Post* had called. How did it know the man had a connection to Capital City Boys? Why did it suspect he worked with the service?

I had answered the reporter's question accurately. The guy did not work for us. He had worked before leaving on the trip but we had already parted ways.

Someone claiming to be a friend later called me from inside the guy's apartment in Washington. The caller told me the former escort wanted to talk to me but would have to do so through faxes since he could not just come to the phone whenever I called. I never called, I never faxed, fearing it was the police who was calling. There was nothing I could do to help him. I was afraid if I confirmed the guy worked as an escort the information would be used against him.

The man and two others were released after a trial. One was convicted. Sometime after returning to Kentucky, I watched with great interest an hourlong news report on this case.

Pulling the guy's file, I came across notes from our first conversation. The information was pretty standard – age, height and weight, etc. He had a smooth chest and hairy legs. The notes show he liked the "Teddy bear" type of client. The notes also stressed he had good, boyish looks.

A quote written at the bottom of the page made me smile as it prompted memories of the times he and I had met and the couple of dinners and then long walks around downtown Washington we enjoyed. The quote proved to be revealing and was backed up by a comment about his looks during the news report:

"If flawless was worth a penny,
I would be worth a $100 bill."

Yes he was. And if the woman had not been killed, the guy might have become a legend in D.C.'s escort community. In my expert opinion, he had what it took.

* * *

I was suspended in May 1999 for my involvement in the *Mack And The Boys* project. I would have been allowed to stay at the *Herald-Leader,* just not the news editor's job I held if:

— I sold Capital City Boys and never had anything to do with escort companies and escorts I had come to know and care about in Washington;

— I agreed never to write this project or anything about the escort business;

— I agreed not to suggest to anyone at any publication (newspaper or magazine) or online organization that they write about the escort business.

I refused to accept those terms. The journalist in me could not accept selling out that way.

What right does a newspaper have to tell a journalist he or she cannot report a story on their own time and at their own expense? Three attorneys have advised me they do not.

In an odd twist of fate, a Washington-area mortgage banker offered to buy Capital City Boys on June 14, 1999, for $34,000 — "$10,000 cash upfront and $2,000 a month for twelve (12) months in the form of a 'consulting fee.'"

If my goal was just to make money, I would have accepted the deal and kept whatever job the *Herald-Leader* found for me. How many times might I have been asked to "consult" anyways and how would the *Herald-Leader* have ever known if I had?

Accepting both deals would have been wrong. And though the *Herald-Leader* considered me unworthy of being a manager, integrity prevented me from benefiting by lying to them.

Even the best fall down sometimes,
even the wrong words seem to rhyme.
Out of the doubt that fills my mind,
I somehow find, you and I collide
– COLLIDE
Artist: Howie Day
Songwriters: H. Day/K. Griffin
HDK Music (BMI)

* * *

PERSONAL THOUGHTS: Looking back, I have come to believe – in the worst of all cases – I needed to be rescued by the *Herald-Leader,* not terminated; I needed to be helped, not punished. The *Herald-Leader* made it clear what it thought of someone who owned or operated an escort company, yet by pushing me out the door, forced me into becoming the very thing it found so perverted.

Would the *Herald-Leader* have granted me a three-month leave of absence to research and write a project on the Amish who live in Kentucky or those who live in poverty in Appalachia? I think it would have. I also think it would have seriously considered co-publishing my report in some form.

So why did *Herald-Leader* management work to shutter my project by saying the company would fire me if I did not walk away? Why did the *Herald-Leader* threaten further harm to me – a threat they "renewed" in December 2007 – if I ever told you about my project?

Why is the *Herald-Leader* still so terrified by a participatory observation project that took place in a gay community 554 miles away from Lexington years ago?

You, dear reader, know the truth to that secret.

* * *

I understand why the paper did not want to publish my project. That was certainly its right. Well-meaning people can disagree about the project's merits.

What I do not understand is how a once-great newspaper – one that had won multiple national awards for writing stories that powerful interests wanted kept secret – tried to kill this project by threatening to terminate my employment if I didn't.

Even if I had walked away from this project, the *Herald-Leader* would still have punished me by stripping me from my news editor's position and in other ways.

How is that possible? How is that right? How is this threat any different from those the *Herald-Leader* once stood up against from other powerful organizations and influences and won national awards for doing so?

The dirty truth is, there is no difference. I believe the *Herald-Leader* and Knight Ridder secretly tried to silence me because it was in their own self-interest to do so.

Finally, how could anyone not be changed by such an experience? How could any journalist not come away feeling betrayed by the once-great paper he used to work for? The truth is he could not. Trying hard to convince myself otherwise, I finally discovered I couldn't either.

No more Mister Nice Guy,
no more Mister Clean.
No more Mister Nice Guy,
they say he's sick, he's obscene.
– NO MORE MR. NICE GUY
Artist: Alice Cooper
Songwriters: M. Bruce/A. Cooper
Ezra Music (BMI)

Imagine my surprise, while reading the *Herald-Leader* on Friday, January 26, 2007, I came across this statement in a staff-written editorial:

"In a free society, people are allowed
to make money in legal ways
that others find distasteful."

Capital City Boys was a legally licensed business – recognized by both the District of Columbia and the Internal Revenue Service – recognized by everyone but the *Herald-Leader*.

Has the *Herald-Leader* had a change of heart? Has it come to see what I saw back in 1999?

Only it can answer those questions.

Herald-Leader's Response

The *Lexington Herald-Leader's* publisher was offered the opportunity to read *Mack And The Boys* in advance of it being published and to comment on the report. He was also asked to consider the possibility of the paper co-publishing the project.

The *Herald-Leader* declined my offer. It did take the opportunity to suggest I uphold our agreement from long ago:

"We also remind you of your obligations under the contract between you and the Lexington Herald-Leader dated August 10, 1999 and expect that you will continue to abide by the terms of that contract."

My guess is the publisher/paper does not know *Herald-Leader* employees violated that agreement in October/November of 2002.

The publisher was also asked to present the *Herald-Leader's* side of this story. His response will be added as soon as he makes it available. I suggest you look for a response in the *Herald-Leader* or on kentucky.com.

Society Of Professional Journalists' Code of Ethics

Members of the Society of Professional Journalists believe that public enlightenment is the forerunner of justice and the foundation of democracy. The SPJ Code of Ethics is voluntarily embraced by thousands of journalists and is widely used in newsrooms and classrooms as a guide for ethical behavior.

Included in the Code are the following goals:

– To tell the story of the diversity and magnitude of the human experience boldly, even when it is unpopular to do so.

– To support the open exchange of views, even views (some) find repugnant.

– To give voice to the voiceless.

– To encourage the public to voice grievances against the news media.

– To admit mistakes and correct them promptly.

– To expose unethical practices of journalists and the news media.

Read the SPJ's Code of Ethics:
www.spj.org/ethicscode.asp

Was My "Mistake" Worse
Than Paper's Actions?

Part of the role of a journalist is to give voice to those who otherwise would have none.

Through its actions, the *Herald-Leader* tried to take away my voice, tried to take away Sean's and Jeremy's and the voices of all whose stories are told in *Mack And The Boys.*

In my opinion, the *Herald-Leader* violated my First Amendment right to tell you our story when it demanded I walk away from this project in order to keep my job.

Freedom of speech – the right for anyone to say or write anything as long as it is true – is the Holy Grail of journalism. The men and women who died serving our country in the military – maybe your son or daughter, husband or wife – made the ultimate sacrifice so ordinary citizens would have this right.

I believe the *Herald-Leader* also violated my constitutional Right of Association. This right grants each of us the freedom to associate with anyone or any group in order to advance a belief or idea. This right is a part of the liberty assured by the 14th Amendment. Freedom of association grew out of court cases in the 1950s and 1960s after certain states tried to curb the activities of the National Association for the Advancement of Colored People.

If one possible mistake in judgment – my decision to report *Mack And The Boys* – was proper grounds for my dismissal, one has to ask: Was not the *Herald-Leader's* effort to take away my constitutional rights an equal or even bigger mistake in judgment?

All publishers have an obligation to protect their papers. They also have an obligation to protect the people who work for them. In this case, the *Herald-Leader's* publisher could have done both.

Growing up, I watched the old "Superman" series on TV. I remember the announcer, his voice booming, saying: "Faster than a speeding bullet, more powerful than a locomotive, able to leap tall buildings in a single bound."

Remember that? If you do, you likely remember the intro ended with the words: "The never ending battle for truth, justice, and the American way." I believed in truth, justice, and the American way. It was my path to having a better life, having a level playing field with others despite my humble beginings.

I am not Superman. I am just a journalist who was taught that the truth should always be told, that a voice should be given to those who have none. I was also taught, that as a journalist, I have an obligation to bring to light violations of the public's trust.

I went to Washington to research the secret world of gay male escorts. I came to know the names of powerful men who met such people. The greatest violation of the public's trust I found was not carried out by elected or high-ranking government officials in Washington, but rather in the most unlikely of all places – in Lexington by the *Herald-Leader's* management.

Protecting the First Amendment is a public trust given to newspapers. In my opinion, the *Herald-Leader* and Knight Ridder Newspapers violated that sacred trust. I also think they violated several parts of the Society of Professional Journalists' Code of Ethics. What do you think?

Actual document listing conditions of my being able to remain a *Herald-Leader* employee

We have taken into account your long-term employment and are prepared to offer you the following options:

1, You can take an unpaid leave of absence of four weeks during which time you will permanently divest yourself of the escort service in Washington and the associated web sites. During the term of that leave, you will have no authority to hold yourself out or represent to anyone that you are employed by the Lexington Herald-Leader or Knight Ridder, Further, you must provide evidence that you have no financial interest, direct or indirect in Capital City Boys or any related entity and, further, that you have no connection whatsoever in the business including, but not limited to owning the associated web sites, handling referral calls, finances or participating in the business as a worker, adviser or shareholder or consultant. You will also:

    a. Agree not to own or operate or become involved in any capacity with any web site without prior approval of the Herald-Leader's management as long as you are an employee with this company.

    b. Sign documents agreeing not to pursue this story about escort services in Washington D.C. or elsewhere; not to write about the same subject for anyone else and not to promote the idea of a story to any other publication or on-line organization.

    c. Receive a letter of reprimand for policy violations and critical lack of judgment, which will be placed in your permanent personnel file and will be a factor in your performance evaluation.

    d. Be placed on probation for six months and your performance will be reviewed at three-month intervals.

    e. Inform the Herald-Leader of any other outside business interests now and in the future.

    f. Be suspended without pay for one week.

    g. Be reassigned to a position that does not include managerial responsibilities.

    h. Agree to hold the Lexington Herald-Leader harmless from any and all damage claims, expenses or attorneys fees should any claim be asserted against the Lexington Herald-Leader or Knight Ridder.

2. You may resign your position with the Lexington Herald-Leader, freeing yourself to pursue whatever business interests you choose.

PREMISE #6

"I ask myself, 'what more I could have done?'
And all I can think is, what kind of world is it
when it's more viable to kill yourself
than to be who you are?"

– John Fleck, as Louis Heinsbergen
MURDER ONE
Season One – Chapter Nine
Steven Bochco Productions

Chantuse (a drag queen who has been beaten and hospitalized): "Those boys wanted to kill me just for being who I am. If it weren't for the man who stopped them, I'd be dead. I'd like to thank him."
Det. Mike Logan: *"Too late. He's the one who is dead."*
– Law and Order Criminal Intent
Episode: Maltese Cross
Wolf Films/Universal

"It's My Life"
Bon Jovi: Reached #33 in 2000
The Animals: Topped out at #23 in 1965

When Max The Wonder Dog and I left Lexington, I promised him we would stay in Washington just long enough to figure out what to do next. It was a bold promise, one that took almost two years to keep.

I had lost my job. I had sold our house. I had left my son, my friends and almost everything I held dear. I was deeply bruised. The only thing I had left was Max and this project and, at times, I lost both of them.

I was supposed to have been only a small part of this report. Being forced to give up my job had either made me a major part of the story or had killed it. When Max and I moved to Washington in August 1999, I was not sure which one was true.

How could I accurately report *Mack And The Boys* and not have it revolve around me? This is a position no journalist is ever supposed to find himself in.

I continued gathering information, continued working the project but with a dampened spirit.

Leaving Lexington and everything I held dear except this project, took a heavy toll on me. It was only with the friendship and encouragement of Mack's boys – people like Storm, Danny,

Sean, Magenta, Dave, Chase, and others outside that world, like Toby and friends I knew from Soho that got me through the rough first few months in Washington.

Getting my head and act together was not an easy task; on the other hand, the only other choice I had was to give up, and that just is not in me.

* * *

Rarely have I ever done anything halfway. If I promise you something, I will deliver it and on time or tell you in advance why I cannot. If I am going to start a business, then count me in for the long haul. I do not cut and run because things get tough or do not go according to plan.

That is just who I am. Having been let down by others who failed to keep their promises, I work twice as hard at keeping the ones I make. My dedication to this project should come as no surprise to those who know me. Neither should the dedication and serious way I ran Capital City Boys and The Agency. I did not want my companies to reflect poorly on me, regardless of the nature of the business.

Both services steered clear of selling drugs even though they could have easily doubled the amount of money they made by doing so. Some joked Capital City Boys was one of the few escort referral services in Washington that never sold drugs of one kind or another. I heard too many stories from too many sources not to think there might be some truth to that statement.

Accessing drugs would have been easy. Several escorts I came to know used drugs on a regular basis. It would have been easy enough to ask to be introduced to their dealers. I also knew former escorts who went into dealing. A phone call or two and I could have easily obtained any drug I wanted to market.

That did not happen. It also did not happen when, while living in Louisville, I repeatedly was asked to front money for drug buys in Washington by a trusted friend. The requests always came with the promise I could double my money within 48 hours.

* * *

So, why did I choose to leave Lexington and go to Washington? Let me ask you: Why did Columbus set off looking for a new world? Why did the Wright brothers take to the air when others had tried and failed? Why did you once try doing something that logic or your mother told you was ridiculous? Yeah, I went to Washington for that very reason.

Baby the rain must fall,
baby the wind must blow.
Wherever my heart leads me,
baby I must go
– BABY THE RAIN MUST FALL
Singer: Glenn Yarbrough
Songwriters: E. Bernstein/E. Sheldon
Colgems EMI Music (ASCAP)

For whatever reason – fate, planets aligning or totally by chance – I had come across a story I felt needed to be told, felt called to tell.

Because of my past, because I was "different," I felt oddly qualified to tell the story of *Mack And The Boys* even though, at the time, I had no idea what that story was or that it would span 10 years from its start in Washington to its conclusion one special morning in Lexington.

I have always thought this project was something I was supposed to do, not for myself, but for a greater purpose. Some will say this is just wishful thinking, an excuse for doing what I did. It is not. I am responsible for doing the things I did, for making the choices that led me to Washington.

I have an advantage when it comes to assessing the full merits of this project. I know the truth, I know the whole story. I know what the people involved – escorts and clients alike – were really like, what motivated many of them.

I met people whom society considered "damaged" because they were a part of Washington's gay male escort world. Researching this project, I found them to be otherwise. I also stayed because I felt I owed something to those who had invested their trust in me, guys who had left other services to work with Capital City Boys or had ignored opportunities to switch to a competitor.

I felt an obligation even though I knew at one time or another each of the escorts working with Capital City Boys would likely leave and most likely at an inopportune time.

My research showed most guys escorted for about six months and then quit. I had no reason to think the guys at Capital City Boys would be any different. Time proved most were not.

* * *

You now know how a mild-mannered, Republican, church-going journalist from Kentucky came to be the man behind the curtain in Washington's gay male escort community.

In Washington, I traded my pica stick (ruler) and *Associated Press Stylebook* for a list of guys who would entertain clients. I no longer had to worry about things like checking facts and libeling someone. In Washington, I dealt with exaggerated claims of endowments and fulfilling fantasies of all kinds for all kinds of clients.

* * *

PERSONAL THOUGHTS: I was wrong to believe that everyone who worked for Capital City Boys when I made my choice would eventually desert me. Storm, Sean, Jesse and Christian were with me when I left the *Herald-Leader.* And though only Sean was a part of Capital City Boys when I left Washington, all remain close friends today.

I have known all along it is possible only a handful of people would ever read this project. I am OK with that. If nothing else, *Mack And The Boys* will be a heck of a journal about my life I will share with my son and a few special friends. And while *Mack And The Boys* will not answer all the questions a son might have about his father, it will tell him a lot more about me than I ever knew about mine.

Researching and writing this project, I repeatedly looked to find answers to questions I had about myself – questions like who I am and what is really important to me. My time in Washington gave me the opportunity to find those answers.

I'm only a man in a silly red sheet,
digging for kryptonite on this one-way street.
Only a man in a funny red sheet,
looking for special things inside of me.
– SUPERMAN
(It's Not Easy)
Artist: Five for Fighting
Songwriter: John Ondrasik
EMI Blackwood Music Inc. (BMI)

PREMISE #7

And the parents of the nameless
darers and dreamers,
they too said to their sons,
"Why you,
why now,
why there?"

– SONS
Florence B. Freedman

"Mama Told Me (Not To Come)"
Three Dog Night
A #1 hit in 1970

When it became clear I would not be returning to the *Herald-Leader* and other major changes were about to happen in my life, I went to see my mother in Western Kentucky.

I really do not remember how I started the conversation, just that it went downhill very quickly. I told her I owned a gay male escort service, that I was bisexual, and that I would be moving to Washington to run Capital City Boys. The news was a lot for anyone to take in, especially one's mother.

> *Mama told me not to come.*
> *She said, "That ain't the way*
> *to have fun, son.*
> *That ain't the way to have fun."*
> **– MAMA TOLD ME (Not to Come)**
> Artist: Three Dog Night
> Songwriter: Randy Newman
> Unichappell Music Inc. (BMI)

As others had and others would, my mother asked what I meant by the word "boys" in the company's name. "You're not dealing in under-aged boys, are you?" she asked, probably terrified of the possibility. "No, absolutely not," I said. "I'd never do that." My assurance came as little comfort to her.

During our conversation, my mother kept referring to gay men as *"those people."* Finally, I asked her point blank – "Who the hell do you think *those people* are?"

"They're queers," she said to which I replied, "So am I."

"You didn't used to be that way," she said, grasping for something to knock some sense into me.

"Yes, I did," I said. "You just didn't know it. I am no different than the son you've been proud of for years."

Then came the questions.

"Does (my son) know?"

"Yes," I said.

"Do the people at work know?"

"No," I said, "They are too afraid to ask but I have to imagine they're wondering and whispering about it."

Then she asked the question – the one that parent or parents of most gay sons or daughters eventually ask: "Did I do something, when you were growing up, that made you *that way?*"

"No, Mother," I said. "You didn't do anything wrong. You didn't make me *that way.*"

I left my mother's house about 2 a.m. I was not tired, and I had no desire to sleep there that night.

* * *

I continued to call my mother after moving to Washington but not nearly as often as I had when I lived in Kentucky. I wanted her to know I was all right. She wanted to convince me what I was doing was morally wrong and I should come home right away.

This routine continued for three months, until I told her I was tired of hearing I was the scum of the earth and had been stupid for not taking whatever deal the paper had offered me. I told her if she was going to continue "beating up" on me that I just would not call her anymore. The "beatings" stopped.

Mama always told me
not to look into the eyes of the sun,
but mama, that's where the fun is.
– BLINDED BY THE LIGHT
Artist: Manfred Mann's Earth Band
Writer/publisher: Bruce Springsteen (ASCAP)

My mother never became comfortable with my being in Washington. Neither did my son. Both were sure someone would knock me in the head or shoot me.

I think the only thing I ever did in Washington that pleased my mother – other than leaving – was to go to the vice president's home during the election debacle in 2000. I joined crowds there waving signs and chanting for Gore to "Get out of Cheney's house," as absurd as that was.

Calling her from deep inside the chanting crowd, my mother

Protesters waved signs and chanted at vice president's home just after 2000 election.

told me she was watching the event live on MSNBC. It thrilled her to hear the chanting over the phone, to see the event on her TV, and to know I was there, doing something noble. OK, "noble" is a strong word but I can tell when my mother is beaming with pride. Maybe it is correct to say she was proud I was doing something so Republican-like.

* * *

Sometime after I returned to Kentucky, probably responding to something I said about one of my Washington friends, my mother said, "Well, you, better than anyone, should know how *those people* are."

"Those people are my friends," I said. "And I do not appreciate you talking like that about my friends."

"*Those people* are no good," she said. "*Those people* sell their bodies. All escorts are going to go to hell."

I resisted using the easy slam comeback: "Well, if escorts are all going to hell, what does that say about me? After all, I ran the whole f**king show." Instead, I simply hung up the phone without saying another word. A good son does that occasionally.

* * *

PERSONAL THOUGHTS: Jeremy's life changed the day his

mother walked into his room and found him with his friend. Mine changed the day I told my mother about my secrets. Her reaction and attitude toward gays and escorts – my friends – created a rift between us.

While still loving her very much, I could not get past the hurtful words she used: *"Those people."*

"Those people." I am one of *"Those people."*

While we remained close, our relationship was never the same. While I continued to call my mother two or three times a week after I moved back to Kentucky, I rarely traveled to visit her. Time and distance were a factor but the greater truth is I never felt comfortable being in her home, pretending to be someone other than who I am.

I have interviewed hundreds of people and have asked thousands of questions since becoming a journalist. I have interviewed governors and other high-ranking elected officials. I have interviewed noted celebrities and a man some said was "very connected" to "organized" crime.

I once interviewed astronaut Jim Lovell, Jr., commander of Apollo 13, which suffered an explosion on its way to the moon and whom Tom Hanks portrayed in the movie by that name.

My toughest interview was with a father who had buried his teenage daughter earlier that afternoon. She and her boyfriend had died of carbon monoxide poisoning one cold night while snuggling in his parked car. The car's tailpipe had become buried in a snow pile. The man had been kind enough to walk down his long gravel driveway to meet me, far from the rest of his grieving family. My questions were very respectful of his situation. So was the article I wrote.

As a reporter, I have asked routine questions, silly questions and questions that made important people sweat for a second or two.

Asking questions come easy for me. That said, I never asked my mother what she meant by the phrase *"those people."* I did not have the courage to ask. I also never asked because I was too afraid to ask the natural follow-up question: "Do you think of me *that way?"* You see, sometimes, even a veteran question-asker thinks it is best not to have some answers.

* * *

My mother died on November 14, 2007, three days after I made what I thought would be the final editing changes to *Mack*

And The Boys.

Like my two sisters and my brother, I have always had a great deal of admiration and love for our mother. She gave so much of herself for us. She gave us life, sacrificed for us, and protected us.

Mother was an avid reader. When I started out as a free-lance writer, she often helped me write leads on my news stories. She was also a great story teller. It is from listening to my mother that I came to enjoy hearing stories about other people. It is possible, because of my mother's storytelling, that I developed my passion to tell other people's stories.

That is why I felt the need to eulogize our mother at her funeral. The woman who loved hearing and telling stories deserved to be remembered that same way, not with well-meant but "cold" words from a stranger. Who better to tell a mother's story than the son who had made telling stories his life's work, especially if she had given him that desire and helped develop his talent?

I cannot say with certainty what my mother would have thought about this project. I know she would have been pleased I had completed something that meant so much to me. I also know she would have been embarrassed when the report first became public, afraid the neighbors would think she had failed as a mother. That said, I have little doubt but that she would have been there to defend me after the first attack.

When I was a little boy,
my mama said to me:
"Any man can be a fool,
a man is hard to be."
– ANY MAN CAN BE A FOOL
Artist: Rare Earth
Songwriter: John Persh
Original Publisher: Jobete

"Losing My Religion"

R.E.M.
Topped out at #4 in 1991

As once mentioned in an episode of "Desperate Housewives," there is a widely read book that says each of us is a sinner. I am a textbook example.

My ex-wife's third husband, a lawyer, once called me "pure and polished evil." I am the first to admit I am not a saint but I won't go that far. One can only imagine what he might be thinking about me now.

> *Nobody knows, nobody sees,*
> *till the light of life stops burning,*
> *till another soul goes free.*
> **– NOBODY KNOWS**
> (from the movie Vanishing Point)
> Artist: Kim Carnes
> Songwriter: Mike Settle
> Warner-Tamerlane Publishing (BMI)

I believe in God. I am a born-again Christian. I have been since I walked down a church aisle when I was 12. I felt God's conviction; I felt the need to profess my belief in God.

I know God exists. I know because I have seen his wonders, I have felt his presence in my life, I have experienced his grace and forgiveness. I have not always seen and felt that same grace and forgiveness from those who speak in His name and claim to be Christians.

The pastor and his wife and the wonderful people at the church had a profound effect on my life. While some I went to high school with experimented with drugs and alcohol, I strengthened my belief by attending Bible studies and participated in church-sponsored youth activities.

When, in the spring of 1970, Vietnam War protesters marched

from the University of Kentucky campus to Main Street a night or two after the ROTC Armory was burned, I was praying with others at Calvary Baptist Church. We heard protesters chanting as they marched beside the church.

* * *

I became a journalist – at least in part – because of something that happened once at church. One Sunday morning the picture of a cute girl who went to the same church as I did appeared in the *Herald-Leader*. I could not wait to let her know I had seen it and impress her. Instead of showing appreciation, all the girl could talk about was the cute *Herald-Leader* photojournalist who had taken the picture. I later told David Perry that the girl's comments about him had convinced me to become a photojournalist myself.

* * *

I attended Southeastern Christian College in Winchester, Kentucky. Many of the students were Church of Christ members and had known one another for years. For them, SCC was a clique gone wild.

I was an outsider who went there because the college was church-based. I quickly made friends, and when the freshman class president had to give up his office because of poor grades, I was elected to the post.

Insiders who got in trouble were able to use their families' influence to make situations "go away." Outsiders, on the other hand, were often forced to leave. This difference did not sit well with those of us who could not have our fathers call, threatening to tell our church to hold back contributions.

When some students got caught smoking pot, the outsiders were dismissed while the insiders were told not to "get caught" again. As freshman class president, I spoke out against this injustice. I was eventually told to shut up or "you too might just find yourself in trouble."

Weighing the options, I sold out – I shut up. It was one of those decisions you look back on and wish you had handled differently, one that changes how you react to similar situations later in life, like being told to walk away from a reporting project.

At the end of the school year, I was elected student body president.

One night the next year, half of the residents in the men's dorm and a good number of those living in the women's dorm got drunk. It's more accurate to say they got s**t-faced drunk.

As resident adviser, I came to know what was going on midway through the event. I made sure those who had taken part in the night's activities stayed in their rooms and were quiet. I also turned out the hallway lights so those going to the bathroom could not be seen staggering about by anyone outside the dorm. I also did not allow anyone to leave the building.

I protected "my boys," but word about what had happened leaked out from the women's dorm. Seeking cover, someone there promptly told what they knew had happened in the men's dorm.

Knowing they could not expel this many students, the administration decided to punish one – David, a California resident who had been a thorn in its side.

When it came time to take David to the airport for his trip home, I made sure David went in style. I organized a 14-car motorcade to escort him from campus. Naturally, horns had to be tested as we made our way past the administration/classroom building.

Chapel was nearly empty that day. The only ones there were teachers, administrators, a handful of insiders, and a few, carefully chosen outsiders who had strategically been left behind to keep asking "What is going on" and "Where is everyone?"

We arrived at the airport in about the manner we had left SCC's campus – loud but orderly. Just as everyone in Winchester knew we had left, it quickly became evident airport personnel knew we had arrived. They did not know who or what we were doing, just that we had arrived.

Dressed in gray slacks, a red-and-white shirt, and a tie wide enough to be a table napkin – looking every bit the conservative Republican I was – I asked to meet with the airport's director. That did not happen but I did meet with someone who listened to me and then granted my request and, in fact, went a step further. When David walked out to get on the plane, he walked down a bright-red carpet normally reserved for visiting dignitaries. He also carried an official proclamation marking the "historic" occasion.

When I returned to campus I learned our horn-honking motorcade and "Where is everybody campaign?" had worked even better than I had hoped. It was especially sweet to hear the president's neck and face had turned beet red when he heard about the red-carpet treatment.

Me, at left, and David, at right, holding proclamation marking his departure. Even then, I stood up against "wrong-doing."

My experiences at Southeastern Christian College took its toll on my religion but not on my faith.

I cherish my time at Southeastern and experiences with many people there, including Nell Westbrook, Cecil Garrett, and Pat Flannery. All played a key role in my becoming a journalist. Westbrook encouraged me to go into journalism after taking the time to get to know me and learn what was important to me. Flannery taught me how to write and, more important, encouraged me not to be afraid to write about what I experienced and felt. Garrett taught me the basics of photography and how to put a newspaper together.

This project, in part, is dedicated to these three for talents they gave me. I will be forever grateful to these three and many others at SCC.

* * *

PTL came into my life during my divorce, a process that took two years. I became a Jim and Tammy Bakker fan.

Tammy Faye's message was simple: "God loves you. He really, really does." Jim told us no one was perfect – himself included. These messages were exactly what I needed to hear. It took me back to my early church days, when things were simple. Faith is simple. It is religion that's complicated.

I knew that others made fun of Jim and Tammy. That did not matter to me. I had experienced having people make fun of my religious beliefs lots of times since I was in high school.

Getting off work from the *Herald-Leader* at 1 or 1:30 a.m. I got home in time to watch Jim and Tammy at 2 a.m.

Jim repeatedly explained why PTL needed money for various projects and for a new hotel or a new, bigger, state-of-the-art broadcast/worship complex.

Having visited my wife's brother in Charlotte, N.C., a few times and having seen the *Charlotte Observer's* coverage of PTL, I knew it was a matter of time before Jim and Tammy would get run over by the *Observer.* That did not keep me from supporting PTL. My wife and I bought one of the $1,000 memberships. This entitled us to stay four days and three nights at the PTL Hotel and to enjoy the water park.

My son and I traveled to the PTL complex and had a great experience.

When the PTL scandal broke, I remained loyal. I had given my money to God, and if Jim and Tammy had misused it, well, they would have to answer to Him.

The good Rev. Jerry Falwell came to save PTL from "those who would do it harm." Again, I gave money. PTL was worth saving.

Entitled to a second stay, my son and I traveled back to PTL to see what was going on. All hell was breaking loose. It had become pretty clear Falwell was not going to just run PTL until Jim and Tammy could rehabilitate themselves or the PTL board could appoint a new leader.

My son and I joined a Jim and Tammy support group and stuffed envelopes seeking help from PTL members. The next day, we attended a private gathering of Jim and Tammy supporters. There, for the first and only time, I got to meet and shake Jim Bakker's hand and got a hug from Tammy Faye. For the record, he was humble and she was beautiful.

* * *

Jim and Tammy never returned to PTL. Falwell sold the complex and TV operation to another evangelist who promised he would keep the complex open. As I remember it, the new evangelist held a telethon, raised money and then shut the place down and auctioned off the parts.

PTL Partners gave to PTL because they shared Jim's dream and vision. However misdirected, however bad his actions, Bakker gave us the opportunity to take part in something special. The complex I visited honored God and welcomed believers from all faiths. I am a better Christian because of Jim and Tammy

Bakker.

While other Christians demonized the gay community, Tammy Faye preached that God loved all his children – gays and straights alike.

In 1996, Tammy joined Jim J. Bullock, an openly homosexual comedian, as co-host of a short-lived talk program, "The Jim J. & Tammy Faye Show."

"I never thought of him as gay," Tammy Faye was once quoted as saying about Bullock. "I thought of him as another human being I loved." This is a perfect example of blind acceptance. Bullock was quoted as saying Tammy "gave me the freedom to be who I am."

* * *

Having survived my divorce and the demise of PTL and having left the church that my son, ex-wife, and I attended after she started bringing her boyfriend there, I found a new place to worship – Victory Baptist Church. It was a new church, so new in fact that we met Sunday mornings for a couple of years at an ice rink complex.

Eventually, Victory built a lovely facility not too far from my home. Being a member, I was asked to be an usher from time to time. I did so with pride. One Sunday morning, while I was serving as an usher, the pastor decided to decry the evils of being gay and the gay lifestyle. It was easy to think the pastor would not approve of the secret life I was leading. I finished my duties there that morning and never went back. I am many things, a hypocrite is not one of them.

> *Go ahead and hate your neighbor,*
> *go ahead and cheat a friend.*
> *Do it in the name of Heaven,*
> *you can justify it in the end.*
> **– ONE TIN SOLDIER**
> **(The Legend of Billy Jack)**
> Artist: The Original Caste
> Songwriters: D. Lambert/B. Potter
> Songs of Universal (BMI)

* * *

PERSONAL THOUGHTS: In spring 2007, two men who offer themselves up as men of God, the Rev. Al Sharpton and the Rev.

Jesse Jackson, led a religious attack that eventually cost radio/TV entertainer Don Imus his program on CBS Radio and on MSNBC.

The attack came after Imus uttered a horrible phrase to describe the Rutgers women's basketball team. Imus took full blame for his actions.

Those of us who watched Imus, had seen him come close to crossing over the line of good taste thousands of times. We also know his heart. We know how he has dedicated his life to lifting up others.

A few days before making the comments, we heard Imus tell us about flying to Atlanta to pick up a child with eye cancer and bringing the child to New York. It was after the firestorm, that Imus' friend, Bo Dietl, told us the child was black. Imus never felt the need to mention the child's race because race was not important to him. That is the real Don Imus.

When residents of New Orleans were struggling to survive after Hurricane Katrina, no one condemned the federal and state governments' lack of response to help the black community there more than Imus.

With blood in the water and one trying to outdo the other, the two good reverends tore into Imus and came at MSNBC and CBS with threats of boycotts and pickets.

Sponsors ran. Imus was suspended by MSNBC then CBS. The next day, MSNBC fired Imus. The day after that, midway through a two-day telethon to raise money for sick children, CBS fired him.

The reverends appeared in front of every camera they could find. They all but stood over Imus' dead body, one foot each on the corpse, like hunters who had bagged a legendary buck.

Imus was wrong but the "hunters" came with dirty hands. When Jackson uttered a tasteless racial slur about New York City, he asked for forgiveness. The community he had slurred forgave Jackson and he was able to continue his work. When Sharpton made mistakes associated with the Tawana Brawley case and others, the public forgave him.

When Imus "sinned" and asked for forgiveness, Jackson and Sharpton refused to even consider such a Christian act. Instead of leading the public in healing, as real reverends do, Jackson and Sharpton led a hate attack.

Instead of working to educate the public about hateful

language, Jackson and Sharpton threatened to bring more.

People claiming to be men of God and working in His cause forced Jim and Tammy out of PTL. Jackson and Sharpton forced Imus' firing. In both cases, wrongs were committed by the principals but the biggest wrongs were committed by those claiming to be doing the Lord's work.

And let's not forget that the Rev. Falwell blamed gays and lesbians for the attacks in New York and Washington on 9-11-2001.

* * *

The Associated Press reported that a mega-church in Arlington, Texas, canceled a memorial service for a Navy veteran in August 2007, after it found out the dead man was gay.

The man's sister told the AP the nondenominational High Point Church called off the service after his obituary listed his life partner as one of his survivors. "It's a slap in the face. It's like, 'Oh, we're sorry he died but he's gay so we can't help you,'" she said.

The AP reported the church's pastor said no one at the church knew the man was gay until the day before the service, when staff members putting together his video tribute saw pictures of men "engaging in clear affection, kissing and embracing."

The pastor said the 5,000-member church believes homosexuality is a sin, and it would have appeared to endorse that lifestyle if the service had been held there.

I know I've got religion,
and I ain't ashamed,
let your light from the lighthouse shine on me.
Angels in up heaven, done wrote down my name,
let your light from the lighthouse shine on me
– SHINE ON ME
From the movie "The Ladykillers"
The Venice Four With Rose Stone
And The Abbot Kinney Lighthouse Choir
Traditional/Arranged by
B. Maxwell/ H. Burnett

Throughout these experiences I have shared with you, my faith in God has remained intact. I have never allowed anyone to shake that core belief. Some may say that I am a poor ambassador for God, one He would be embarrassed to be associated with. They may be right. The Bible I read, however, is full of stories where "damaged" people worked for God's good.

* * *

Love, including tolerance and compassion for others, was Christ's principle message. The same was true with Jim and Tammy Bakker.

God bless you, Jim and Tammy. While others tried to shake my faith in God, you preached that God loves and forgives everyone – including a sinner like me.

God has forgiven me for the wrong I have done. Society has not been nearly as kind.

* * *

With the rapid expansion of mega-churches with swimming pools, gyms, and movie theaters, a water park for Christians does not seem that farfetched anymore, now does it?

The Backstory

"Leap Of Faith" is one of my favorite movies and Steve Martin one of my favorite actors.

Is there a correlation between Jack Newton, aka the Rev. Jonas Nightengale (Martin's character), and Mack? Both were someone other than who they publicly professed to be; both were troubled by the truth of their past; both refused to "cash in" by selling out others; and both eventually got a chance to escape.

"Leap Of Faith" is worthy of being on the top-shelf of your DVD collection.

Considered eccentric by many, a talented artist by some, and a "brilliant" poet by Tennessee Williams, my thoughts about noted Lexington, Kentucky, celebrity Henry Faulkner are a bit more personal. Though we met only once, Faulkner forever changed my life.

Faulkner molested me in July or August of 1967, soon after I turned 14. He touched my genitals through my jeans, undid my pants, slid them and my underwear down around my ankles, and performed oral sex on me while I stood motionless. Faulkner did this while pleasuring himself.

How will they hear?
When will they learn?
How will they know?
– LIVE TO TELL
Artist: Madonna
Songwriters: M. Ciccone/P. Leonard
EMI Blackwood Music (BMI)

This experience occurred in his small white home on Arlington Avenue in Lexington. The house was on the right, the one closest to Maxwell Street.

It was a bright summer day and I was going door to door selling tomatoes grown in my family's 2-acre garden when I knocked on the door at 252 Arlington Avenue.

A somewhat dirty and disheveled-looking man opened the door and listened to my sales pitch about how fresh and tasty the tomatoes were. "Sold," he said, looking at the selection carefully laid out in the wagon I had pulled up to his porch.

After he selected a few and I weighed them, I gave him a price, and he invited me inside while he got his money. I followed him inside and came to stand in the middle of the living room.

Faulkner continued chatting about this and that while looking for the $2 he owed. Eventually, he ended up in front of me and, without warning, rubbed his hand up and down my crotch. I remember being shocked that he touched me there – no one had before – and equally shocked that I did not react. Confused, all I could do was to somewhat listen to whatever it was he was softly saying.

"How old are you?" I remember him asking as he undid my pants. "Fifteen," I said, hoping he would think me older than I actually was and better able to resist him. The talking stopped a few seconds later as I began to receive my first oral experience.

Eventually the session ended, and I pulled my clothes back up.

Faulkner then went down the street a few houses to borrow $2 from someone to pay for the tomatoes. While he was gone, I stood in the room, taking in all that had happened and all the animals that were roaming through the house, including a small black/gray goat. I had never seen a goat before.

Faulkner returned a few minutes later with dollar bills in his hand. "I have the money for the tomatoes," he said, smiling. Putting the bills in his shirt pocket, Faulkner once again dropped to his knees and once again undid my pants and repeated what had happened earlier.

I remember thinking, "I have to get the money. (Deleted) gonna want it."

Eventually Faulkner handed me the $2, and I left. Faulkner was still talking to me but I was not listening. I had the $2, and I was free.

Pulling the wagon still half-loaded with tomatoes, I went directly to my grandmother's home. When I got there, she remarked I had not sold many. "Yeah," I remember saying, "I guess I just don't have the knack today." I never told her what had happened. I was too confused to tell her or my mother when she came to get me.

I did tell one of my eighth-grade teachers that fall about having met this strange man who had farm animals in his house. I stopped short of telling her the man had also molested me. At that time, I did not know what to call what had happened that afternoon.

I also thought, for a long time, that I was somehow guilty of letting it happen; guilty for not running away; guilty for needing to stay and collect the $2 for the tomatoes.

* * *

It was sometime after the encounter, while reading the *Lexington Leader,* that I came across a photo of the man who had molested me that afternoon. I learned he was a local celebrity. Faulkner had a knack for getting his picture in the paper.

There was a third reason I never told anyone – a reason that forever changed whom I have been intimate with. I was embarrassed to tell anyone that I had been with someone that strange-looking. I feared some would judge me on what Faulkner looked like.

To this day – because of that day – I have never messed around with anyone I did not want to be seen with on TV or in a photo in the next day's paper. OK, there was one person ...

* * *

As a free-lance photographer in the mid-'70s, I sold several of my pictures to a local artist who bought some of my pictures and, with my permission, painted them.

Faulkner with one of his well-known paintings. Faulkner's paintings are prized possessions in Lexington. For example, while writing this report, I found a copy of this painting hanging in the Lexington-Fayette Urban County Government Center.

Once, while dropping photos off at his house on Third Street, the man happened to mention his neighbor and fellow painter, Henry Faulkner. I told the man I had once met Faulkner and his animals at his house on Arlington Avenue. "Yep, that was Henry all right," the man said. "Now the farm's over here." We both laughed.

* * *

From time to time, for reasons I never figured out, I found myself driving past the house on Arlington Avenue – always alone. I would never stop but would go past the house very slowly, as if I might see an unsuspecting 14-year-old standing at the porch with a wagon of tomatoes. I was always prepared to stop and willing to buy all the tomatoes he might have, even at a premium cost, if necessary.

* * *

Late on Saturday, December 5, 1981, while watching over a mostly deserted newsroom, word came across the police scanner that there had been a serious traffic accident on North Broadway near Third Street.

Unofficially, we were told Faulkner had been killed in the wreck. Confirmation would come too late to get the news in the next morning's paper. I left an extensive note for the next day's city editor, saying Faulkner had been killed and that this was big news.

I remember sitting at my desk, numbed by the news. Memories of my chance encounter with Faulkner came flooding back.

Days later, at Faulkner's funeral, local drag queen Bradley Picklesimer, dressed in black as a grieving widow, stole the show at the funeral. *Herald-Leader* photographer John C. Wyatt captured the moment.

As lead Page One designer, it was my responsibility to crop and order the art and to handle the story. I did it professionally. I also did it quietly. While others in the newsroom laughed at the picture and swapped stories about the "flamboyant" Faulkner, I remained silent, sharing my memory with no one. No one in the newsroom noticed. Why would they?

* * *

Others remember Faulkner in different, more positive ways. I do not mind that.

Kentucky Theater manager Fred Mills told the *Kentucky Kernel* that a patron once came up to the concession counter during a movie, complaining about a crying baby. Checking on the complaint, Mills entered the theater and sat down. Following the whimper all the way to the front row, Mills looked down the aisle to discover Faulkner holding a baby goat.

Lexington artist David Minton, a friend of Faulkner's, is compiling an oral history about the artist's life for the University of Kentucky's Oral History Program. Keren Henderson wrote in the *Kernel* that Minton wants to keep Faulkner from being forgotten or misrepresented.

"There are as many points of view about Henry as there are

Artist Henry Faulkner dies in car crash

Faulkner was loved for free spirit

Friends gather, eulogize Faulkner

people talking about him," Minton said in the article. "There are a bunch of contradictions. Considering how Faulkner lived, even outrageous stories are hard to deny. His life was a theater. He dressed in drag and sang blues at local bars or while riding his bike down Third Street. Paintings sometimes moved him to emotional convulsions. He filled up on salad bars without paying.

"Then there's a side to him not at all like the image that's out there," Minton told the *Kernel*. "He could show up and be a totally normal guy."

Charles House wrote the book *The Outrageous Life of Henry Faulkner.* House's publisher describes the book as being an absorbing account that traces Faulkner's life from his traumatic childhood in rural Kentucky to a flamboyant bohemian existence in New York, Los Angeles, Key West, and Sicily.

* * *

PERSONAL THOUGHTS: I realize the 14-year-old who stood in that room that day was not guilty of anything, had not asked to be molested, nor had much power to end it.

The house on Arlington Avenue and Faulkner are gone – the house was torn down and replaced by an apartment building – but the memories of what happened there that one summer day will remain with me forever.

There will be those who think Faulkner's action caused me to be gay and explains why I chose to work this project. I am not an expert on such things but I do not think so. That answer would be way too easy.

Being very candid, I was already doing "show me yours and I'll show you mine" scenes with other boys my own age in a dusty tobacco barn near our homes. I did the same with girls in the neighborhood in a basement across the street from my house. I do wonder, however, how much the encounter with Faulkner had on me and in my forming certain desires and attractions.

Old dogs care about you
even when you make mistakes.
God bless little children
while they're still too young to hate.
– OLD DOGS AND CHILDREN
AND WATERMELON WINE
Singer/songwriter: Tom T. Hall
SONY/ATV Acuff Rose Music (BMI)

"Old Dogs and Children and Watermelon Wine"

Tom T. Hall
A #1 hit (Country) in 1972, also Country Song Of The Year

"Max likes to do things his own way," the woman said, explaining why she was returning him to the animal shelter. She then went on to say he was housebroken and would make someone a great pet, just not her.

Seconds later, as if reacting to what the woman had just said, Max took two or three steps forward and wet all over the floor. Instantly, my son and I knew Max was the dog for us. It was clear Max had an independent mind and would fit in perfectly with our family. We also believed Max would carry his own weight and play an important role in our family. He did, for almost 16 years.

* * *

Monday, March 8, 2004, was the most difficult day of my life. That is the day that I had to put Max "down." It is no exaggeration to say my best friend died that day.

Max was ready, I was not. To this day, my heart tells me I had no right to decide to end his life but my mind tells me it was the right thing to do.

Max hurt severely from arthritis. Our walks had become shorter and shorter because of the pain he felt. He had lost his last tooth and was probably almost blind. Max suffered a major seizure of some kind the night before I put him down. Lying next to him on the floor and feeling him jerk with intense pain, I knew it was time to be merciful to my friend.

I also knew my life was about to change, and not for the better.

Max was my best friend. No matter what I did, no matter how stupid my choices were, Max still loved me. "Max held on for you," my mother told me. "He knew how much you needed him."

*　*　*

Max survived Washington pretty well. Call me silly but Max always seemed to smile when I mentioned that he had adjusted well to being a big-city dog.

Max's arrival in Washington almost did not happen. In fact, it took a miracle. The day we arrived in Northern Virginia to store my furniture, Danny drove Max to his sister's house, a couple of miles away so that Max could play and relax. Danny put Max inside his sister's fenced-in backyard.

The furniture in storage and the moving truck returned, Danny and I arrived to get Max. He was not there. A search of the neighborhood produced nothing. No one we asked had seen him.

I stood there, in shock. I had been forced to give up my job, to sell my home, to leave my family, and now Max was gone. What a welcome to my new life! Incapable of feeling anything, I stood in the street, praying for a miracle, knowing that was the only way we would ever find him.

Eventually I heard a noise and then saw Danny running toward me, holding Max by his collar. All we – Danny, Max, and I – could do at that time was to hug one another and thank God for the miracle He had provided.

Not knowing what else to do, where else to look, Danny had walked in the direction of the storage facility. He later confessed that walking anywhere was easier than facing me.

I believe Max mistakenly thought Danny was trying to separate the two of us and that Max was trying to find me. Call it what you want. I see Max's breaking free as fierce loyalty. Loyalty is something I have cherished and rewarded since I was a kid. It is also something I have freely given away, especially to my employers.

*　*　*

Our neighbors on P Street and on Wallach Place knew Max by his Washington name – "Killer." Max was the sweetest dog one could ever meet but the Shepherd in him provided a threatening bark.

To enter our house on P Street, you had to open an old steel security gate. Max always responded with intense barking. Soon after moving in, as a joke, I hollered "Don't bite me, Killer, it's Pops. Don't bite me." Neighbors and the crowd on the street heard me and thought Max's name was Killer. The name stuck.

* * *

Max was an excellent judge of who would make a good escort. If Max liked a guy, clients usually did too. He did not care much for guys who were too busy to pay attention to him. My guess is guys who paid attention to Max also paid attention to clients they met. Likewise, those who brushed Max off probably treated clients the same way.

* * *

I have long believed God sent Max to me, knowing I would love and cherish something I considered to be a "beautiful creature of God" whereas I would probably screw up a relationship with a person and chase them off. God is smart that way.

* * *

My son said several times that I loved "that dog" more than I did him. I repeatedly assured him that was not true but then would often add that I was seriously considering moving Max up closer to the beginning of my will. That way, Max would be sure to get his part before my money ran out. My son, knowing me as well as he does, always took my comments seriously. He is smart that way.

* * *

Max and I had several conversations about his advancing age and his failing health before the time to act finally came. I promised him I would be strong after he was gone and that I would always love and remember him.

I worried the end would come while I was at work and Max would die alone. I did not want it to happen that way. He did not deserve to die that way. No one does.

The seizure happened as I was cooking our supper. Max was at the end of the kitchen, watching me cook, as he often would. He yelped, in pain, and then started running through the house, shaking like I had never seen him do before. He then kept wandering into walls and the furniture.

I made the necessary arrangements the next day and then called my mother and then my son to tell them what was about to happen. Both knew something serious was up for me to call in the middle of a workday and because I kept choking on my words.

Max and I went for a walk and then for a long drive. Max loved to ride. When I opened the SUV's rear door at the vet's, Max looked right into my eyes as if he knew exactly where we were and why we were there. I could not speak.

Lifting Max onto the exam table hurt him. He cried out in pain. I stumbled over the words but once again I managed to promise my beautiful friend I would be strong and I would always love him.

When the vets came in, they examined Max and told me about his condition. They then gave me the option of staying or waiting outside. I mumbled I would stay.

Max loved for me to massage him under his chin. He would always close his eyes until I finished. And so it was that I held Max's head, kissed him, and massaged his chin one last time as the vet injected morphine into him.

"He's gone," the vet eventually whispered.

All I could do was nod. "Gone" was my best friend and full partner in *Mack And The Boys*. "Gone" was the one soul in the world who loved me unconditionally. I stayed with Max for a while, gently stroking him, knowing my "special gift" was gone.

I had Max cremated. I knew I would be leaving Louisville soon, and I did not want to leave him there in a place neither of us really considered home. I had planned on releasing Max's ashes on a hillside in Lexington, the one where he loved to explore once we returned from Washington.

I explained my plans to Danny. Danny had lived with Max and me for a while. "Mack, don't do that," Danny said. "The place Max loved the most was with you." He was right. So, Max remains with me today. He always will.

I cry myself to sleep each night
wishing I could hold you tight,
life seems so empty since you went away.
The pillow where you'd lay your head
now holds my lonely tears instead,
and it keeps right on a-hurtin'

since you're gone.
– IT KEEPS RIGHT ON A-HURTIN'
Singer/songwriter: Johnny Tillotson
Ridge Music Corp. (BMI)

PERSONAL THOUGHTS: My mother had a picture hanging in her living room my entire life, up to her death. The image is from a calendar for the year I was born.

The picture shows a young dog and a young boy lying on a hillside in the sunshine, underneath a tree. That picture is my idea of what Heaven will be like – a young, healthy Max, no longer wracked by arthritis, and a young boy – me – no longer burdened by life's choices and the prejudices of unaccepting people.

Thanks to my sister's generosity, the picture now hangs in my home.

If fate should ever,
bring us back together,
maybe we can follow through,
same old me, same old you.
– LOVE WILL NEVER BE THE SAME
(from the movie "Savannah Smiles")
Singer: Dave Gardner
Songwriter: Ken Sutherland
Savannah Smiles Music (ASCAP)

PREMISE #8

Exchange between homophobic
Sheriff Dollard and a man walking by:

*Dollard: "Look at 'em. Perverts. I tell you one thing,
when the founding fathers wrote the Declaration
of Independence and the Constitution
and what have you – liberty and justice for all –
they didn't mean them [gay men/drag queens]."
Man: "Well, I can tell you one thing
about them founding fathers of America."
Dollard: "What's that?"
Man: "They sure had fabulous wigs."*

**– TO WONG FOO, THANKS FOR EVERYTHING!
JULIE NEWMAR**
Universal Studios

"Heroes"
Marc Bonilla and Font 48 (written by David Bowie)
From the movie "The Replacements"

They were just two "ordinary" people until they happen to cross paths with history and were forever thrust into the public spotlight.

Oliver "Billy" Sipple was a decorated Marine and Vietnam War veteran. He saved the life of then-President Gerald Ford during an assassination attempt in San Francisco on Sept. 22,1975.

Mark Bingham was a 31-year-old public relations executive and rugby player. He is credited with helping to bring down the hijacked United Flight 93 over Pennsylvania on Sept. 11, 2001.

Both were gay.

* * *

Sipple was part of a crowd of about 3,000 who had gathered, hoping to catch a glimpse of the president. Sipple was standing next to Sara Jane Moore when she pulled a .38 caliber revolver from her purse and aimed it at the president. Seeing the gun, Sipple lunged and knocked it away just as Moore fired. The bullet went wild. The president was whisked away, safely.

Sipple told his friends "anyone would have done the same thing. It was no big deal," the L.A. Times noted in its February 1989 obit on Sipple.

Clearly, saving the president's life made Sipple news. It also led to his being outed. Though Sipple was known to be gay in San Francisco's gay community, he had not made his sexual orientation public. It was a secret he kept from his family and his employer.

Sipple's story is often talked about in journalism schools during discussions about the right to privacy and newspaper ethics. In the movie, "Absence of Malice", Sally Field portrays a reporter who writes a story that so embarrasses the subject that she (the subject) commits suicide. Field's editor tries to console her by telling about Sipple, describing him as "the guy in the crowd" who saved the president's life. "Turned out he was also gay. That's news, right? Now the whole country knows that too," the editor says.

The L.A. Times wrote that in 1975, "Harvey Milk, a long-time friend of Sipple's, was making a name for himself by making a serious run for the Board of Supervisors, trying to organize gays and urging that they emerge from their closets."

"Harvey's whole attitude was to show people that not everyone who was gay runs around with lipstick, high heels and a dress," the L.A. Times quoted Bob Ross, publisher of a gay newspaper as saying. Sipple, the ex-Marine, seemed the perfect one to break down the myths. Randy Shilts, in his book, *The Mayor of Castro Street: The Life and Times of Harvey Milk,* quoted Milk as saying, "for once we can show that gays do heroic things, not just all that ca-ca about molesting children and hanging out in bathrooms."

Sipple filed a $15 million lawsuit against seven major newspapers who had reported he was gay, alleging invasion of privacy. His lawsuit was dismissed after a five-year battle, the court saying he had become a newsmaker and therefore his sexual orientation was also news.

* * *

Bingham's sexual orientation was widely talked about in the days following Sept. 11, 2001. Many publications mentioned that Bingham had helped form the San Francisco Fog, a gay rugby club. Outsports.com reported that "tributes to (Bingham) sprang up on the Internet, and there was no shame or embarrassment in the disclosure, only pride."

Outsports.com went on to say "Bingham's sexual orientation (was) important, especially in light of the comments by Jerry Falwell and Pat Robertson, where they blamed gays, among other groups, as having had some responsibility for bringing the attacks on America. Falwell and Robertson are to Christianity what the Taliban are to Islam. Americans need to know that gay people, which included the pilot of one of the planes, suffered as much as their fellow citizens.

"When our country, and its symbols were attacked, Oliver (Sipple) and Mark (Bingham) got busy to save our citizens. Falwell and Robertson got busy assigning blame to our citizens. To some in this world, villains are heroes and heroes are villains. We know the difference. Oliver and Mark are heroes."

Girls will be boys and boys will be girls,
it's a mixed-up, muddled-up,
shook-up world, except for Lola.
– LOLA
Artist: The Kinks
Songwriter: Ray Davies
Abkco Music (BMI)

"Girls Just Want To Have Fun"
Cyndi Lauper
Peaked at #2 in 1983

Toby had a flare for the dramatic. He leaped out of the closet by singing "Can't Stop Loving That Man of Mine" at his high school talent show. His parents were in the audience.

You cannot be around Toby and not have fun. OK, maybe if you are dead but know this: If Toby comes to the funeral home to see you, everyone will be laughing before he leaves. You might even crack a smile, especially if he greets you with his infamous "How are ya, doll?" (He holds the "l's" in doll about four times longer than most.)

*   *   *

Toby once told Christian and I about a strange but remarkable dream he had the night before. Christian and I were staying at his home at the time. Always energized when telling a story, Toby had a knack for coming across as an actor on a stage.

Toby had dreamt he was on a train headed north out of Washington when this tall, bearded man sat down across from him. "He was so tall, and dressed in a striking black suit, that you could not help but notice him," Toby said. The man began writing something "and you could tell he was struggling with it, so I offered my help."

Toby took the man's paper and began radically marking up what the man had written. "This is way too long," Toby told the man, and "this doesn't make any sense at all. Let's say it this way, why don't we?" Toby said, seeking the man's approval but not waiting for it.

Finished, Toby handed the stranger the marked-up piece of paper and said, "This is a lot shorter, and reads a lot cleaner."

The man thanked Toby for his help and promised to read the speech just as Toby had rewritten it. The man then got off the train at the next stop, which happened to be in rural Pennsylvania.

The man was President Abraham Lincoln, and the speech Toby wrote for him is what we know as the Gettysburg Address. "Lincoln's first draft was a mess," Toby said. "I'm just glad I was there and able to help him." And, as if he were an actor who was due off stage, Toby bolted out of the room. Christian and I looked at each other and then erupted into laughter.

* * *

One way the boys and I had fun was to go shopping in Northern Virginia. A group of us would load into my Xterra and go to Target or Costco or the mall. Though we would arrive together and leave together, while there, everyone generally went his own way.

If a guy was buying clothes or food and came up a little short on money, I helped him out but if he came up short buying makeup or something I did not deem essential, he'd get a look that said, "You're asking me to buy you that?"

Buying habits changed. The boys learned to buy beauty products and other "non-essentials" first and to stick them in a plain sack or have someone else hold them when they approached me about covering the cost of a pair of jeans or shirt they just had to have.

I knew this practice was going on and privately was OK with it. I once happened to catch a guy in the middle of pulling this routine, coming up behind him as he was handing off his "non-essentials" to a friend.

"Here, hold this," he told the friend. "I'm seven dollars short of what I need to buy this shirt, and I'm gonna go find Mack and hit him up for the difference. He'll never know I got this other stuff." The friend and I just stood there, both of us smiling, both of us knowing something the other guy didn't – that I had heard the entire exchange.

It did not take long for the escort to realize he had been caught. Slowly, he turned to face me. "I think you said you were

Admirer takes a photo of a carload of "ladies" during
Lexington's 2007 Fourth of July parade

seven dollars short," I said. "Here's $10. Pay me back when you can." And then I walked away, smiling.

* * *

Some guys escorted to finance their social lives. It was not uncommon for a guy to handle a call and then spend all he had made before the end of the night out on the town. We had guys who drove up from Richmond, Virginia, on Saturdays to work just so they could pay their way into Nations nightclub.

* * *

Not all of the guys I was seen with were gay or even worked for Capital City Boys. There were a few who I always thought wanted to work with us but, for one reason or another, never had the courage or a pressing need to do so.

One was a cute blond boy whom clients would have loved meeting. He had a great personality. He repeatedly asked me about Capital City Boys and about what working with a service was like. I would answer his questions and then add, "If you ever decide you want to try it, let me know."

We talked several times over drinks – Snapples – at Soho. I never pressured him to escort – that was not my style. It was not my place. Even after he took a job at Starbucks in Dupont Circle, the boy would see me out on the street or in Starbucks and always start a conversation. That was his style, and I liked him for it.

* * *

Christian and I went to a dance bar once to meet a guy, and we watched – OK, stared at – Jason, a cute bartender at JR's, dance in tight jeans and white wife-beater T-shirt. If you would like to know how much change Jason had in his front pockets, just ask Christian. He looked so hard for so long he's bound to know exactly how many quarters, dimes, and nickels the boy had.

* * *

From time to time in Washington, I would catch a "drag" show. I went when someone connected to the service was performing. I had come to appreciate drag queens via the movie "To Wong Foo, Thanks for Everything! Julie Newmar" and at shows I had seen at Connections in Louisville with friends from Lexington's AOL chat room.

In the movie, three New York drag queens are on their way to Hollywood for a beauty pageant. Their car breaks down in a small Midwestern town, stranding the flamboyant trio for the weekend. Waiting on parts for their Cadillac to arrive, the "ladies" show the locals that appearing to be different does not mean people are not the same.

* * *

PERSONAL THOUGHTS: "To Wong Foo" also addressed the issue of blind acceptance. After getting to know the "ladies, the community "rescues" them from the homophobic sheriff. We see there has been a change when Carol Ann says to one of the "ladies:"

"Vida, I don't think of you
as a man. And I don't think of you
as a woman. I think of you as an angel."

A lot of people – escorts and non escorts alike – have waited to hear words of acceptance like those too, maybe from you. They're not all drag queens, they're not all gay, they're not all of a different race from you. They are just people who happen to be "different" from you in one small way or another. Or, as Albert in "The Birdcage," corrected himself, "Well, not that tiny."

"The Crying Game"
Boy George
Peaked at #15 in 1992

I had a lot of fun being Mack, but there were also times when my heart broke. More than once, I shared an escort's birthday with him because he had no one else to spend it with. The same was true my last Christmas in Washington when a former escort called and asked if he could stay at the house because he "didn't have anywhere else to be."

Escorts were always welcome. I understood their pain. I understood only too well just how cold and lonely a place Washington can be when you are alone, even when you own an escort service.

One day soon, I'm gonna tell the moon
about the crying game.
And if he knows, maybe he'll explain
why there are heartaches,
why there are tears.

My heart also broke when I would see a former escort I had cared about but who had fallen on hard times after leaving Capital City Boys.

Chase was such a case. After being tossed out by the recruiter boyfriend, Chase found himself sleeping in Dupont Circle and the homes of those who often times took advantage of his situation.

Some might say I too had taken advantage of Chase when I rescued him off the streets, cleaned him up, and gave him free shelter. I am willing to accept some responsibility but I also know I helped him and others far more than I "used" them.

After he left Capital City Boys, I would buy Chase dinner or give him money for food when I saw him out on the street and knew he was hungry.

Prone to drinking too much, Chase, more than once, got into

serious trouble with police for public drunkenness and more serious charges such as assault.

Someone from Washington's court system once called me, wanting to verify Chase worked for Capital City Boys. I told the woman I knew Chase, that he had worked with Capital City Boys in the past but I had not seen him for some time. The woman seemed to understand the awkwardness I was conveying.

Twice, people from some kind of social program in San Francisco called me on Chase's behalf. When I returned the calls, the person told me that Chase had been jailed and, once again, had listed me as a reference.

I was asked questions about Chase's past and the likelihood of him appearing in court if let out on his own recognizance. Though it pained me, because I knew it would not entirely help Chase's chances, I answered honestly.

Will you tell the folks back home
I nearly made it?
Had offers but didn't know which one to take.
Please don't tell 'em how you found me.
– IT NEVER RAINS IN SOUTHERN CALIFORNIA
Artist: Albert Hammond
Songwriters: A. Hammond/M. Hazelwood
EMI April Music (ASCAP)

Chase once called me from Hollywood, California, saying he had a casting call the next day to be in a gay video.

"Mack," he said, "you remember how cute I was, don't you?" "Certainly, kid. Of course I do," I said. "Well, they've told me they really don't care how cute I am; they just want me to have a cute ass. I'm going to be a bottom for someone," Chase said. "He's the one that has to have the cute face this time."

Chase's words took my breath away. Stunned, I did not know how to respond. Then, as if his words were not enough to tear out my heart, Chase said to me, "Hold on a minute, Mack," then started talking to someone else nearby. It quickly became apparent Chase was talking to someone who had pulled up next to him on the street.

After agreeing on what was expected of both parties, Chase came back on the phone. "Mack, I have to go, darlin'," Chase said. "Some man in a beautiful Mustang wants to spend some time with me, and I'm going."

Don't want no more of the crying game.

I never passed by Arlington Cemetery without being deeply moved by the graves and the sacrifices those buried there had made.

I have never taken for granted the liberty and freedom that the men and women buried there have given us. They paid the ultimate price for us – you and me. They stood and fell in our place. These heroes gave their lives for my right to make my own decisions, for you to make yours.

While I lost a lot doing *Mack And The Boys,* it does not begin to compare with what my freedom, what your freedom, cost them.

I was draftable during the Vietnam War. I went through my draftable year with no deferments. Doing so was a crapshoot. Lots of guys my age were being drafted and sent to Vietnam. Had I been drafted, I would have gone, I would have served.

My brother-in-law went to Vietnam. Thankfully, he returned, unharmed, as far as I know. He never talked much about his time there, still, you can tell the experience is very much a part of him.

A guy I somewhat knew at church also went to Vietnam. He too returned home – in a box. I was never privy to the exact details about what happened to him, most at church were not. Whatever happened required a closed-casket funeral.

Experiencing the loss my church and those who knew him suffered made a strong impression on me. I saw the cost of freedom firsthand, and the price was huge.

Stunned. Shocked. That's how I felt the night Mrs. Landingham was killed on TV's "The West Wing." I ran this ad to honor her. The actress who played Mrs. Landingham later e-mailed me, asking for a copy. I sent it to her.

The memory of that loss remains with me today. I hope I never forget it.

I understood only too well, when I registered for the draft, why the clerk asked me if I had any distinguishing marks on my body. The scar on my left elbow, obtained in a bicycle wreck, was listed on my draft card. Having heard whispers about what had happened to the guy at church, I knew someday the information about my scar might prove important to sending me home.

In Lexington, my former employer had been so ashamed of this project it pushed me out the door. My own mother was so troubled by my being in Washington with *those people* that she cried, begging me to come home.

Yet the men and women buried in Arlington Cemetery and places like it – people I never met, people who never once heard

my name, died giving me the freedom to make my own decisions – no matter how right or wrong, no matter how smart or dumb.

* * *

PERSONAL THOUGHTS:
Passing by Arlington National Cemetery while driving into Northern Virginia, I often wanted to pull to the shoulder of the off-ramp, walk over to the chain link fence and pay my respects. With no safe place to pull off, I always just turned the car's radio off, stared at those white headstones as I rounded the curve and whispered a word or two of thanks. Someday, I will go in the front gates and pay my respects more properly.

Having written so much about the sacrifices others made on my behalf, I attended the 2008 Memorial Day Observance at the Lexington National Cemetery.

I found comfort in the speaker's message: that each of us, "must honor our fallen heroes by reaffirming their faith in an America that stands for liberty, justice and equality."

The speaker, his voice filled with conviction, told those gathered: "That we must not only defend these freedoms and values, but we must also cherish and *exercise* the American

Headstone of Kentucky soldier killed in Vietnam in 1969. The grave is in the Lexington National Cemetery.

dream."

I have never thought one had to pick up a gun and stand post for our country in order to be a patriot. I believe the families of those serving in the military and those who work for the government are often times patriots.

The same is true for farmers and factory workers, teachers and students, saints and sinners – in other words, ordinary people who step forward when called or the need arises to take on missions that make this nation a better place for all of us.

While most patriots are called to handle ordinary and necessary missions, I believe some are called to handle unusual ones – missions that seem strange even to the dreamer assigned the task – causes such as *Mack And The Boys.*

* * *

Want to feel democracy in action? Call your local newspaper and make arrangements to stand in its pressroom while it is printing its next edition. You will likely feel the shaking that comes from a press printing a newspaper. It is a magical experience. The shaking and the roar from the running presses are a reminder of the precious freedom we as Americans have –

the ability for anyone to say or to report anything without fear of reprisal, as long as it is truthful.

That freedom has come at a high price and should never be taken for granted by any of us. That freedom came through the sacrifices of the dead and wounded soldiers and journalists from all of America's wars and conflicts – those who stood and fell so each of us can live our lives however we choose – so we can be who we want to be and, sometimes, who we really are.

Love your country and live with pride
and don't forget those who died.
Think of all your liberties and recall,
some gave all.
– SOME GAVE ALL
Artist: Billy Ray Cyrus
Songwriters: B. Cyrus/C. Cyrus
Sly Dog Publishing (BMI)

When I owned Capital City Boys and The Agency, only the offer to buy or sell sex was illegal under D.C. law – not the act itself. There was a $500 fine and up to 90 days in jail for someone's first solicitation conviction. The fine increased to $750 and up to 135 days in jail for a second offense.

Luckily, we never had a problem with Washington's Metropolitan Police Department or any law enforcement agency.

Tops Referrals was shut down for a while soon after Capital City Boys opened in 1998 when officials seized its computers and investigated the company. Tops was closed after a female escort, temporarily renting a room from Marvin, got busted during a call because she reportedly provided her client, an undercover police officer, with a small amount of drugs.

"Everything went to hell," Marvin recalls. "Friends and clients fled to the four winds."

Tops reopened after officials determined Marvin and his service had no connection to the drugs or any other criminal activity.

Marvin observes that "police don't want to get in your (business), but if complaints are filed, well, then they have to do something." Complaints sometimes include matters not directly related to the escort business itself.

A neighbor once called police to complain that one of Marvin's associates repeatedly threw her cigarette butts into her flower box. The associate, Marvin says, happened to be a female dominatrix, who would, in full dress, step outside Marvin's home for a smoke break, before or after a session with a male client.

"I have always believed the police would warn me if there was a problem," Marvin says. "I've told them several times, if you have a problem with what I do just tell me and I will change my operation.

"It's no secret I'm here," Marvin says. "If, one day I am arrested for doing the same thing I've done for years, well, f**k them."

Hiring an escort is not illegal in Washington. That is how an escort referral service can become a legally licensed business. Escorts get in trouble, at least in the District, when they perform a sexual act for money or provide drugs. Clients can get in trouble if they offer money for sex. That is why referral services stress that a client is paying for the time spent with an escort, not for what might or might not happen during that time.

"A prosecutor once told me that the worst mistake someone wanting to hire an escort makes is to ask: 'Are you a policeman or working with any law enforcement agency,'" Marvin says. "Right away, he (the prosecutor) said, the person demonstrates he thinks what he is doing is wrong or illegal. It is best just to ask and act as if what you are doing is legal."

* * *

Cute men in Washington were routinely offered "free" drugs in exchange for sex.

Several interviewed for this project told about waking up in a stranger's bed on a Sunday morning, finding themselves naked and seeing evidence of having had sex, though they did not remember doing so. Many said they had gone to a gay club the night before and had gone home with someone who promised them drugs.

Several times, the guy remembered the guest's name and that he had an unusual occupation. Sean once told me about going to an after party at the man's house.

I saw the man once at a strip bar called LaCage. He was large, wore a black suit and white shirt – not the type of person who would normally attract a flock of cute guys, yet the time I saw and observed him, several of the dancers were giving him a lot of attention between and during their sets. Normally, the man would have to be passing out money to garner that kind of attention.

I was also repeatedly told that a certain major drug dealer at the time enticed guys to his Logan Circle home with the promise of "free" drugs. The man was the dealer for whom Sean's client reportedly wholesaled drugs. Others I met told similar stories, some about their own experiences with the dealer. Most involved entertaining the man in one way or another in exchange for "E" (ecstasy).

* * *

I always thought if I got arrested while researching this project I would speak to the highest-ranking officials possible and come completely clean the nature of my project.

I would also make it clear that I wanted to make a deal – I would leave town within 30 days and never mention what I had learned in Washington or I would walk outside and start calling the media to set up interviews to tell everything I learned.

Had I been arrested, police would have found in my wallet, the phone numbers to all local TV stations, the news desks at Washington-based network operations, *The Washington Post*, the *New York Times*, the *LA Times* and D.C.'s two gay newspapers – the *Washington Blade* and the *Metro Weekly.*

A former escort I trusted "kept" four packages for me with instructions if I was ever arrested to hand-deliver the ones marked "A" to Bob Woodward at *The Washington Post* and to Bob Schieffer at CBS News. The packages contained enough information to document my project and research to prove my credibility.

UNIVERSAL
Luckily, I never had to bail any of the boys out of jail like Dan Aykroyd is seen doing here in "Doctor Detroit." Not knowing what situations I might face, I kept $7,500 in cash at the house in case one or more of Mack's boys were arrested.

The package also held the tease that much more detail was still to come. A second set of packages would have been overnighted to the *New York Times* and Don Imus three days later.

I was certain interested parties would discreetly come to my aid.

I had to rethink the success that plan might have had in light of what Deborah Jeane Palfrey went through. Palfrey publically threatened to make her client list public unless the case was dropped. The case was not dropped and eventually she released the list on her own.

* * *

PERSONAL THOUGHTS: Like many, I watched the "20/20"

Montgomery Blair Sibley, Deborah Jeane Palfrey and Carol
Joynt at Nathan's Q&A Cafe in Georgetown.
www.caroljoynt.com

special where ABC had promised to reveal the names of noted
people who had called Palfrey's service. Commentators on
MSNBC said ABC must have decided not to reveal names
because the list included major names from the media, possibly
even ABC.

I cannot say with certainty that Palfrey's phone logs and so-
called client list contained such names. I can tell you with
absolute certainty that Capital City Boys and The Agency phone
logs and client lists did.

Credibility.

With it, you can bring down a president, senator or chief executive officer. Without it, any investigation can be dead before it gets started.

One of the things I learned working at the *Herald-Leader* was that if you taped what someone told you it would be impossible for them to challenge successfully what you report. Having someone on tape might not keep them from denying what you write but once you go public with the tape, you gain the upper hand as your credibility grows and theirs diminishes.

Richard Nixon was not all wrong: Tapes are an excellent way to reference things later and to cover your behind.

Kentucky and the District of Columbia are two places where one party can legally record a conversation without the other's knowledge or approval.

* * *

Every escort Capital City Boys represented had to sign a confidentiality statement or the service did not represent them. The confidentiality statement was part of an "Agreement of Understanding" the escort and I, as owner of Capital City Boys and The Agency, signed. The agreement protected both parties. The two-page agreement also outlined other responsibilities.

If word got around Capital City Boy escorts were meeting clients and then telling everything they knew, business would have died. This is true for any service.

Many of Capital City Boys' clients had families or important jobs that they could lose if someone found out what they did in private.

A few clients would have worn the news as a badge of pride – Capital City Boys actually had one client who asked if he could have three of the guys he had met through Capital City Boys pose for his Christmas card. We passed on that opportunity.

I do not know of a single time any escort told someone outside the service about a client they had met. It helped that Capital City Boys represented escorts who did not want anyone to know their business either.

* * *

Storm says he could have made "millions" if he had just told the *National Enquirer* personal information about some of the stars and entertainers he had met while working for Hollywood Madam Heidi Fleiss.

"The *Enquirer* called and offered me lots of money" to tell about one particular well-known star. "I told them to get lost," Storm said. [Deleted] "has made it very clear he doesn't want anyone talking about him."

"The *National Enquirer* offered me big money for news about George Michael being gay," Storm said. "If I had known he was going to get busted giving a blowjob in a rest area, I might have told them. I could have cashed in huge that time."

*"Love is blind,
but the neighbors ain't."*
– My friend Josh

Other than knowing the name and possibly where a client worked, what might we have known? Well, a lot, actually. I had two escorts separately tell me that one client – a lobbyist who lived on Capitol Hill – often "spied" on the Republican congressman who lived in the row house next to his.

Both escorts said they were skeptical until the client proudly showed them that you could see into his neighbor's home by moving two bricks in the wall of his home. "You couldn't see a lot," one of the escorts told me. "But you could see into the room next door, and with a tiny camera you could (photograph) anyone who happened to be in there and what they were doing."

Both escorts also told me the client joked about how often the congressman's "nieces" visited.

* * *

One escort who also worked for a lobbying firm came by one night to drop off a referral fee. Standing on my front porch on Wallach Avenue, the escort and I talked for a while, and then he said he had to go because he had to "drop off a package" at a certain congressman's apartment.

"The big vote is coming up and the congressman needed some 'documents,'" the escort said, smiling. "Here," he said, "I'll show you."

When he returned, he showed me a sealed brown envelope that had been folded tightly against the contents inside. The envelope had a distinctive, rectangular shape. "Well now," I said. "That's a nice way to say 'Hello, I love you.'" Both of us laughed.

What was inside? I do not really know, and the escort never said he knew either. I am guessing we both had the same suspicions based on the unique shape of the envelope. Anyone have change for a hundred?

* * *

This project was never meant to trap and "out" anyone – not senators, congressmen, celebrities, lobbyists, lawyers, students, CEOs, bellhops nor members of the media. It could, all were clients and we had several opportunities.

I received at least four calls from "Deb," a producer for the "Jerry Springer Show," each time wanting to fly one or more escorts to Chicago to appear on the show.

I mentioned Deb's request once in passing to a guy who had worked with Capital City Boys and the old Agency. He asked for her number, and I gave it to him. Four people from Washington were flown to Chicago to appear on the show.

The guy to whom I had given Deb's number told me he and the others were taken into a room where they were told what the show's topic would be, made to sign affidavits swearing everything they would be saying would be the gospel truth, and then were "given tips" on how to act during the taping.

He went on to say that midway through taping, producers stopped the show, saying the Washington people just were not "working out."

A week later, three of the four people were flown back to Chicago with a new "fourth." This time, they pulled it off. The show eventually aired.

Anybody want Deb's number?

* * *

So, why tape? Taping was an efficient way of documenting conversations and events. I have been able to share accurately Brendon's first call and conversations I had with clients and escorts alike because I taped them.

So, just whose conversations were taped? "Famous" people and "ordinary" citizens.

Might you be wondering if your voice is there? Let me assure you, it does not matter. The voices have already served their purpose – to assist in the writing of *Mack And The Boys.* That purpose served, most of the tapes and documentation have been destroyed. The remaining items are being kept to protect me in case someone disputes what I have written.

No one has to fear I will ever sell the remaining tapes or play them for anyone but a court if ordered to do so.

I am assured by attorneys they are protected by Press Shield laws in both Kentucky and the District of Columbia. I am a journalist. The tapes contain conversations with my sources. They are protected by law, just as my written and electronic notes are.

In time, all the tapes and documentation connected with this project will be destroyed.

And for anyone who might think about coming over to my place to look for the tapes, they are not here. They're "vacationing" in an undisclosed, secure location far, far away.

PREMISE #9

*CONTROL: If you make a conscious decision
to leave then there's a price to pay.*
*McCALL: I know what it's like to twist and turn,
one way, then the other. Then to get caught in the
middle time and time again till you're screaming
to get out. And that's what every man should be
allowed to do – to get out. At some time in his life,
to bloody well get out.*
CONTROL: Some of us are not that lucky.
*McCALL: Some of us make their own luck.
And, what do you do? Just bloody well live with it?*
CONTROL: Every damn day of my life.

– THE EQUALIZER
Encounter in a Closed Room
Episode Number 49
October 14, 1987
UNIVERSAL STUDIOS

"Wherever there are young men who do not appreciate
their youth and older men who do,
there will be drama."
– THE TORCH SONG TRILOGY
Harvey Fierstein

"We Gotta Get Out Of This Place"
The Animals
Peaked at #13 in 1965

I knew the time to leave Washington would eventually come.
My original plan was to go there for a short time, research this
project, and leave. I never intended to make Washington my
home.

Two years after moving there, three years after starting the
project, Max and I left Washington. It may have been the worst
personal decision I ever made. I loved living in Washington.

We gotta get out of this place
if it's the last thing we ever do.
We gotta get out of this place
girl, there's a better life for me and you.
– WE GOTTA GET OUT OF THIS PLACE
Artist: The Animals
Songwriters: B. Mann/C. Weil
Screen Gems-EMI Music (BMI)

During the early part of 2001, I grew tired of the hassles of
owning and running Capital City Boys. I was tired of the drama. I
was tired of living in neutral.

I had done all I needed to do on my project except write what I
knew. Mentally, I was not ready to do that yet. Looking back, I
have to say there probably was never a better time or place than
then or there.

Ryan and his boyfriend, Michael, who had a history of fighting and sometimes calling the police on each other, continued to fight and to attract the police, even when they went down the street just to order a pizza. Zack had been "imprisoned" and I called the police.

Eventually, Capital City Boys was going to attract serious attention from someone. While everything I did was legal, attention invited trouble and trouble was something I wanted to avoid.

All of us in the business were keenly aware of the dangers we face from the outside world. Storm and Jonathan repeatedly warned me about the dangers from within.

"It's nice to work for an agency that has an environment that feels like a family but the business is cutthroat and everyone is ultimately out for themselves," Storm told me. "There is ultimately no true loyalty. If someone had offered (escorts working with Capital City Boys) $10,000 for information on you, they would have told (in a heartbeat), your ass would have been put in jail and they would have flipped over to another service."

I took the warnings seriously. Storm knew the business well. He also knew those involved in it.

I had been told by two people associated with Capital City Boys that they had seen a federal government file bearing my name. Both had seen the file at the home of a man who supposedly worked "in a government office."

Both told me the file was thick. Jonathan said the file he was shown was "at least and inch and a half thick." He also said the guy who had it told him "the Feds are getting ready to go after Mack."

I knew the guy who had showed Jonathan and his friend the file. I knew that he worked inside Washington's legal world, but not exactly where. I knew him because – for a while – he also worked with Capital City Boys and Jockboys, an online-based escort service based in Richmond, Virginia.

You also know him. You know him as Aaron, one of the three people I profiled earlier in this report in the "Dream Lover" segment.

I never doubted such a file on me might exist. I just could not figure out why Aaron would have it at his home and be so brazen about showing it to Jonathan and the other person. Aaron and I had parted ways on less than warm and fuzzy terms. At the time he was showing the file, he and Jonathan were trying to be a couple.

Was the file real or a fake? I do not know. I do know it was convincing enough that Jonathan was deeply troubled by it. I also knew it would not be unreasonable for people in offices in downtown Washington or "secret" locations in rural Maryland to monitor our actions. After all, we were calling and visiting some very powerful people.

It was not a stretch of the imagination to think that, in addition to me, someone else – for whatever reason – might also be watching and listening in order to write a report of their own.

I knew if trouble came knocking on our door that Ryan and Michael would disappear into the night without a trace. I did not have that luxury. Government records linked me to Capital City Boys. I could run but I could not hide.

Drama reigned. Drew was working less and less for us, and clients who had called just to see him strangely did not call Capital City Boys anymore. I suspected they were going around the service to see him.

Max grew older, and I feared I might lose him without fulfilling my promise – that he would once again have grass to enjoy.

And me? I was spending more and more time upstairs in my room staring out at the street below, envying strangers who laughed as they walked by late at night.

* * *

For most of my life, I have longed to live a "normal" life. Working nights and weekends at the *Herald-Leader* for more than 20 years had prevented that.

Moving to Washington to run Capital City Boys, a night-time operation, also prevented it. Other than living out on the streets, I cannot imagine how I could have moved any farther away from a "normal" life than the one I had in Washington.

I wanted to go home but was that possible? I could go back to Lexington but other than my son, what would I have there? I had given up the job I loved. I had given up all my friends. I had given up my home. Some might even say I had given up my soul.

* * *

Rich had told me he wanted to buy The Agency in 1999 but that I had bought it out from under him. Rich spoke as if this was news to me. It was not. I had kept in touch with Rich, carefully telling him only what I wanted him to know about The Agency and Capital City Boys. I told him just enough to keep his interest high.

When I decided the drama was getting too much for me, I called Rich and told him I was considering selling The Agency and Capital City Boys and asked if he was interested. I asked, but I knew he was. The question really was if he had the money to close the deal. He did, thanks to his partner's generosity.

We quickly struck a deal. I would sell the two services to him for $45,000. It was not a huge amount of money but I wanted to price the company at a level that would cause Rich to jump. It did.

It took about a month to go over the books and to close the deal.

At the time I agreed to sell the companies, I did not know where Max the Wonder Dog and I were going. I just knew we were leaving Washington. I checked into buying two weekly newspapers. One, a business journal in Maryland, the other, a traditional weekly near the coastal area of North Carolina.

In the end, the desire to be near my son prompted me to choose Lexington. The time had come for Max and I to go home.

I've been blinded by these city lights
and dreaming of Kentucky nights,
what's a country girl like me to do?
I've been living with my foolish pride
and driven by the rain
but there's nothing in this city
but the heartbreak and the pain.
– KENTUCKY NIGHTS
From the HBO movie *They All Laughed*
Songwriter: Eric Kaz (ASCAP)

The deal I struck with Rich allowed me to run the company for a week after the deal closed. I wanted to make sure the check cleared and to tell the escorts I was leaving.

Announcing my departure never really happened. A week before I was to leave Washington, I told Ryan I had sold the companies. He was not openly disappointed until I told him I had sold them to Rich.

Ryan's reaction, coupled with unexpected feelings of regret I had about leaving, caused me to change my plans. Instead of telling everyone, I told only a select few.

The night before I left Washington, Ryan, Michael, Daniel, Sean, and I had a farewell dinner at Ruth's Chris Steakhouse on Connecticut Avenue. Near the end of the dinner, I wished I had invited more of Mack's boys. A lot of them deserved to be there.

I had flown Danny in from Florida to help Max and me move back to Kentucky. I needed someone I could totally rely upon. Danny was always that person.

My last night in Washington was very emotional for me. Still working the phones and needing to collect referral fees, there was no way to hide my departure anymore. If the U-Haul truck parked out front was not a dead giveaway, the boxes sitting near the doorway had to be.

One by one, I told the few guys who came by that night. Time after time, I held back tears as I announced Max and I were leaving.

For the second time in my life, I was leaving virtually all my friends, I was severing all my ties on the hope of finding a better life. Time would eventually show me, once again, that the dream came at a high price.

I placed $1,000 cash on Ryan's pillow as a goodbye gift. Ninety minutes later, I was still not asleep and Ryan still was not home. I went into his room and took back part of the money. I needed a special friend that night to talk through my feelings. I would have liked Ryan to have been that friend. Being away from the house was his right. How much, if any at all, I left for him was mine. How much I took back is none of your business.

* * *

The next day, Danny and I finished loading the truck. We went to a late lunch with Ryan and Michael.

Rich had assumed control of The Agency and Capital City Boys. For the first time in three years, I did not answer the phones when they rang; I did not assist clients who called looking to meet someone special or just to talk. It felt odd to be in the house and hearing Rich talking to "my" clients.

Ryan loaded his belongings into a Diamond Cab and waved goodbye. I stood there, motionless, watching my special friend leave. What I would not have given for a car passing by with the radio blaring a song from my past. This time, music did not rescue me from my feelings.

As Ryan's cab prepared to turn onto 14th Street, I whispered the lyrics I had used in the last half-page ad I ran in the *Metro Weekly*. It was my final love song for all of Mack's boys and clients but especially for Ryan:

I hope life treats you kind.
And I hope you have all you've dreamed of.
And I wish for you joy and happiness.
But above all this, I wish you love.
– I WILL ALWAYS LOVE YOU
Singer/songwriter: Dolly Parton
Velvet Apple Music (BMI)

Wanting to miss rush-hour traffic and having failed miserably at doing so, Danny and I finally loaded up Max and the few remaining things and started off toward Kentucky and a new life. It was a little after 4 p.m.

I drove the U-Haul, and Danny drove my Xterra. Max rode with me, smiling as if he somehow knew we were finally going home.

Once again, I was running away from established relationships and a job. Running away, chasing the dream of having a better life somewhere else.

Driving through downtown, replaying so much of what I had seen and done in Washington in my mind, I started crying.

I had given up my career to come to Washington to research this project. Leaving town, I still didn't know if there was one. Whatever I had given up so much for, was now over. "Was it worth it?" I asked myself. I am still not able to answer that question. Only you, dear reader, can.

Just as he had done so many times before, Max moved closer to me, looked at me, and smiled as if to say, "I know what you are giving up in order to keep your promise to me and I appreciate it."

See why I loved that dog?

"Bartender": *"Where do you want to go Sam?"*
Dr. Samuel Beckett: *"Home. I'd like to go home but I can't, can I?"*
– QUANTUM LEAP
Episode: Mirror Image (May 5, 1993)
UNIVERSAL

"A Thousand Miles From Nowhere"
Dwight Yoakam
Peaked at #2 in 1993

Growing up, music warned me if I left home, I could not return, at least not to what I had left. The Shangri-Las warned me in their great '60s hit "I Can Never Go Home Again" that if I cut my ties, if I burned bridges I could never go back. Joe South, in his "Don't It Make You Want to Go Home" lyrics, said I could return but warned me what I would find would be radically different from what I remembered.

I should have listened, I should have heeded the warnings but I did not. I returned to Lexington but the town had changed a lot. I, too, had changed. The comfortable fit we once had was gone.

I spent days buying and selling stocks. Many days, I'd clear $200 or $300. I would rarely lose money but it did happen from time to time.

September 11, 2001, changed a lot of things, the Lexington job market among them. I had planned on finding a job and moving on with my life. Events changed that. I had my first job interview in October. It was for a position at Morehead State University. Can you imagine the jokes I would have heard when telling my friends in Washington I was working at some place called Morehead? The only place worse might have been if I worked in Norfolk, Virginia.

I continued day trading and made some money. I also built Web sites. I redesigned both the Capital City Boys and Agency's Web sites, giving the new owner the look he wanted. He signed a 12-month agreement for $250 a month. He paid for October and

November and then said he could not pay any more. I did not make a big deal out of it. Capital City Boys, like all escort referral services in Washington, was severely affected by the drastic falloff in Washington's tourist trade.

I also built and maintained the DC Boys' Web site for Drew. That job paid $200 a week – $100 for the Web work and $100 toward the purchase of the dcboys.com Web address.

My day trading slowed as the stock market continued to slide. My AOL stock was taking a bath because Time-Warner had ticked off Ted Turner and he was dumping his stock. For the record, Ted – until then one of my heroes – had a few more shares than I did and I suspect weathered the storm much better than I.

* * *

Nearing a self-imposed deadline, I narrowed my job choices to three options – get a job as the real estate manager at the Louisville *Courier-Journal,* move to Tampa and find a job there, or move back to Washington and open a new escort service.

Backtracking and going back to Washington was not my first choice, though I greatly missed my friends. I felt if the straight world did not want me, I knew one that did. I also missed the excitement of running a referral service. I had designed two new great escort sites and had a host of new, innovative ideas.

I pushed the *Courier-Journal* for an answer as to whether it was going to hire me. The job offer came, and Max the Wonder Dog and I moved to Louisville.

Neither one of us liked living there. Max died there. So did my career as an advertising manager for Gannett Newspapers.

My department more than doubled its online sales in 2003 and then doubled that amount the following year. My department also increased its year-over-year print sales in 2003 and again in 2004. These were tough advertising years, especially for the real estate segment. Though my team worked hard, we were unable to generate the 24 percent to 35 percent year-over-year revenue gains the publisher and advertising director demanded. We, as a sales team, were not alone. During one 18-month period, both the classifieds and retail sales managers were pressured to leave the paper, and, according to my count, 13 of the 15 sales managers were forced out of their positions because they could not meet sales goals.

The *Courier-Journal* was not alone in this situation. Newspapers in general are under intense pressure to grow their business at a time when growth is tougher than it has ever been.

"A typical newspaper makes a 20 percent operating margin," John S. Carroll, former *Herald-Leader* editor, told PBS' "Frontline." "That's roughly double what the typical Fortune 500 company makes. They're very profitable. This is true at the *Los Angeles Times;* it's true at the *Baltimore Sun,* where I used to be editor; it's true at the *Lexington Herald-Leader* in Kentucky, which is a money-making machine. People think of this as a washed-up old business. It's not.

"Newspapers make tons of money. But the owners are under great pressure to increase earning," Carroll said. "Even when they make lots and lots and lots of profit, you've got to make lots plus a certain percentage every year, and that percentage is not very good."

That is exactly the problem I and other managers faced at the *Courier-Journal.*

Newspapers are "achieving their profit targets only by cutting resources every year, getting rid of reporters, giving the readers fewer pages of news in the paper," Carroll explained in the "Frontline" interview. "You do not have to be a mathematician to know where that goes."

The *Herald-Leader* has reduced its workforce by the equivalent of 71.5 positions or 16.6 percent since the first of 2008. Employees are feeling the pressure. One employee says she comes to work every day with a knot in her stomach and is waiting for the next shoe to drop. Another employee observed he has never seen morale in the newsroom at such a low point. He too fears someone will tap him on the shoulder and tell him to go home.

The paper now has about 325 full-time employees. When I left in 1999, it had more than 530. The drop in the number of employees mirrors the drop in the paper's circulation. The paper now has a daily circulation of 109,603. I remember when it was in the 140,000s. Sunday circulation is at 135,250, down from the 170,000s.

The Backstory

Dwight David Yoakam, who wrote and sang **"A Thousand Miles From Nowhere,"** was born October 23, 1956, in Pikeville, Kentucky.

John S. Carroll

John S. Carroll served as the first Visiting Knight Lecturer at the Joan Shorenstein Center on the Press, Politics and Public Policy at Harvard University.

Harvard's profile of Carroll says that he became a reporter at the *Providence Journal-Bulletin* in 1963. It also says that while at the *Baltimore Sun,* Carroll was posted to Vietnam, the Middle East, and Washington.

In the 1970s he was metropolitan editor of the *Philadelphia Inquirer.* From 1971 to 1972 he was a Nieman Fellow at Harvard and, in 1988, held a similar fellowship at Oxford.

The profile also says that Carroll has received several individual awards, including Editor of the Year from the National Press Foundation (1999) and has directed coverage that won Pulitzer Prizes at the *Philadelphia Inquirer, Lexington Herald-Leader, Baltimore Sun,* and the *Los Angeles Times.*

He served nine years on the Pulitzer Prize board and was its chairman in 2002. Carroll is a Fellow of the American Academy of Arts and Sciences. He graduated from Haverford College and served in the Army.

While factually accurate, the Harvard profile falls short in conveying what a great newspaper person Carroll is.

Lexington, indeed all of Kentucky, benefited from Carroll having been editor of the *Lexington Herald-Leader.*

That said, it also needs to be stated that those of us who had the pleasure to work with and for Carroll benefited the most.

PREMISE #10

*What causes us to fall
doesn't define who we are.
What defines us is what we do
after getting back up.*

– Adapted from a passage
in the movie
"MAID IN MANHATTAN"
Columbia Pictures

Mack And The Boys

"Do you enjoy cornholing?" she asked, smiling. She being a Human Resources employee interviewing me for a job with Cincinnati.com, the online service of the *Cincinnati Enquirer*. "We take cornholing seriously here in Cincinnati."

Mercy, I thought. You guys do thorough background checks before hiring someone. I knew better than to answer the question.

She went on to explain that Cincinnati was hosting a "huge cornholing tournament." Again, I just smiled, not knowing how to respond. It turned out she was talking about what I knew as a bean bag toss, not two guys engaging in anal sex.

An article in *Cincinnati Weekly* proclaimed: "It's official. Cornhole has become a Cincinnati passion." The article, which quoted two guys identified as "hard-core cornhole enthusiasts," suggested three places "one could practice the art of cornholing: in your basement, at Tina's, and at Patrick's place." A novel writer could not make up stuff this good.

I never told the woman what it was she had really asked me. I'm polite that way.

The job was one I really wanted – online news editor. It was much like the job I had at Kentucky Connect. The *Cincinnati Enquirer* is a Gannett-owned newspaper. So is the Louisville *Courier-Journal*.

My first interview went well. I was invited back for a second one. The then-acting classifieds director at *The Courier-Journal* told me she was certain Cincinnati would hire me. That call never came. Instead, I eventually received an e-mail saying someone else had been hired, someone better qualified.

"Someone from here had to call Cincy and tell them something bad about you," the acting director later told me. "Someone from here had to call them and kill your chance of being hired.

Someone high up."

The acting director did not know I had a dirty secret, did not know about *Mack And The Boys.* She did not know, but higher-ups at *The Courier-Journal* did. They knew because a *Herald-Leader* employee had called my boss, Brenda, and told her.

Brenda also used to work at the *Herald-Leader.* Three or four weeks after I was hired, Brenda told a former co-worker at the *Herald-Leader* I was working with her. Brenda told me the woman revealed to her that I had run a gay male escort service in Washington. Brenda said the woman had told her my service featured under-age boys. The woman's statement was unfounded, untrue, and slanderous.

Through the actions of this employee, the *Herald-Leader* breached its own agreement never to reveal to anyone why I left the paper.

I told Brenda the truth, holding nothing back. She carefully considered the situation, then told me she was disappointed in me. "Not because of the gay thing," she said. "Lord knows I supported allowing homosexuals to run personals ads in the *Herald-Leader,* but because you did not tell me until now."

Then she said, "I'm going to have to tell Abby [Clark, the advertising director] about this." And she did.

That afternoon, I removed the few personal items I had placed in my office, fearing I would be fired the next day. I was not. Nor the day after that either.

I gave Brenda and Clark a detailed written explanation about what I did in Washington and included copies of my business and tax licenses.

Almost three weeks passed before Clark mentioned the situation to me. "I was walking by and realized that I had never gotten back to you about that D.C. business," she told me. "As long as what you did was legal, we can't do anything about it."

Clark's choice of words was not lost on me: "As long as what you did was legal, we can't do anything about it."

I suspect *Mack And The Boys* was discussed directly or indirectly with someone in Cincinnati. I also suspect it played a role in my annual evaluation, though it was never mentioned, at least not directly. Lawyers often recommend supervisors be polite that way.

Company policy required annual evaluations be given in an

employee's 11th month of employment. Mine was given to me four months late. "I've been busy," Clark explained. Clark had been busy, but that was not why my evaluation was four months late.

Brenda had refused to give me my evaluation because Clark had changed her findings "to the point of being unfair and untrue," Brenda told me later in an e-mail. Having had Clark change evaluations I had written, I knew this was her routine.

Brenda quit her job instead of giving me an evaluation she disagreed with. My evaluation was not the only reason Brenda quit but I would bet that it was a factor.

I suspect Brenda also fell victim to the stain of *Mack And The Boys,* though, outside of hiring me, she had played no part. I knew, after *The Courier-Journal* found out about this project, that there would be a price to pay. I expected to pay it alone. I cannot help but think Brenda paid part of that price.

> *"As long as what you did was legal, we can't do anything about it."*
> **– ABBY CLARK**
> then *Courier-Journal* Advertising Director

I asked Clark if she had called Cincy about me. Clark told me she had not talked with anyone in Cincinnati about me. When I asked if she had e-mailed them about me, she repeated her earlier statement "I did not *talk* to anyone in Cincinnati about you."

We stood there looking at each other, both knowing she had "misspoke" about why the evaluation was late and both of us knowing I knew it. We also stood there knowing she had dodged my question about e-mailing someone in Cincy.

The then-acting classifieds director, still clueless about *Mack And The Boys,* said she did not really think it was Abby who intervened. She told me she thought it was someone else, and then told me who.

* * *

"Now we're gonna talk about diversity," said one of the three people interviewing me for a job with the DC Lottery Board in September 2004. "Tell us about an experience you've had dealing with people of other races, other cultures, other backgrounds." (The quote might not be exact but it is close.)

How much do I tell them? How much can I tell them without blowing my chances for this job? I pondered these questions for a few seconds. I could tell about losing my job at the *Herald-Leader* because I chose to associate with people whom management there found repugnant.

I could tell them my association with these same people played a significant role in my being forced out of my job at *The Courier-Journal,* but would they understand or be equally repulsed?

I could tell them about Ed and Stanley, my unusual neighbors when I lived in the District, but would they understand that story either?

I considered telling them about the young boy who covered the knees of torn pants out of shame; about the girl whom others made fun of when she got off the school bus; about my friend who happened to be black and how my mother suggested he not hang around us at that public event.

Would they understand these stories? Would they understand how each of these events had shaped me into the person I am today? I looked at each questioner and decided they would not. I told them about living in Washington and how I had worked to become a part of my community, how I had respected the cultural differences of those who lived and hung out in my neighborhood.

I left knowing I would not get the job. Whatever they were looking for, it was clear to me the story I told was not "diverse" enough for them.

> *Well, I'll die as I stand here today*
> *knowing that deep in my heart,*
> *they'll fall to ruin one day*
> *for making us part.*
> **– BACK ON THE CHAIN GANG**
> Artist: The Pretenders
> Songwriter: Christine Kerr
> EMI April Music (ASCAP)

Knight Ridder Newspapers was forced to sell its assets – including the *Lexington Herald-Leader* – on June 27, 2006, because a majority of stockholders demanded it. Knight Ridder's demise came about because – in the opinion of the majority of stockholders – the stock had greatly under performed.

The McClatchy Company bought the assets and then sold off some of the papers. McClatchy, smartly, kept the *Herald-Leader.*

The end of Knight Ridder saddened me. This was once a great newspaper company. John S. Knight and a lot of others demanded quality journalism from all Knight Ridder properties.

Bernard Ridder demanded the financial side be strong. Working together, these newspaper giants earned lots of money and enriched the communities their papers served.

The *Herald-Leader's* publisher and I exchanged e-mails about the passing of Knight Ridder and how great the company had once been.

If you think I was happy about Knight Ridder's demise, you are wrong. This was a great newspaper company – one that demanded and honored strong community-based journalism.

It was Knight Ridder that made me a good reporter and editor. I will forever be grateful.

While many fellow journalists do not fully respect the importance of the advertisements, I have long understood it is the ads that make a newspaper free from outside influences. Ads make a newspaper strong enough to push government leaders – local, state and federal – and even society itself, to change for the better, to correct wrong attitudes and practices.

> *Who, other than a newspaper – in this case, the Herald-Leader under John S. Carroll's leadership – would have devoted the resources necessary to uncover such corruption? I can tell you, in Lexington, no one.*

The public does not always instantly agree with a newspaper's editorial stand but generally comes around.

Someone, or some people, shot out or broke windows in the *Herald-Leader's* pressroom after the paper disclosed that University of Kentucky basketball players were taking money from boosters. Someone called in a bomb threat that emptied the building. Employees were afraid to have *Herald-Leader* parking stickers on their cars because some cars bearing such stickers were damaged after the series ran.

Yet the reporting was solid, and the public needed to know what was going on in the basketball program, even if it did not want to know. The revelations came with a high price, including NCAA sanctions against the team. Yet it was the paper's reporting that cleaned up the program.

Who, other than a newspaper – in this case, the *Herald-Leader* under John S. Carroll's leadership – would have devoted the resources necessary to uncover such corruption? I can tell you, in Lexington, no one.

Carroll, in his "Frontline" interview on PBS, estimates that roughly 85 percent of the original reporting done in America gets done by newspapers. "They're the people who are going out and knocking on doors and rummaging through records and covering events and so on. Most of the other media that provide news to people are really recycling news that's gathered by newspapers."

Reading a transcript of Carroll's interview, I came across a passage that causes me to wonder how Carroll will react if he reads *Mack And The Boys.*

"Professionalization of newspapers and of other types of journalism is basically a good thing. There's more setting of standards, and I think that newspapers are better than they used to be," Carroll said in the "Frontline" interview. "I can just hear some blogger out there saying: 'What are you talking about? [New York Times reporter] Jayson Blair, Rathergate' – there's a whole series of missteps and ethical lapses.

"There have always been those," Carroll said. "The difference today is that there is an array of other parties outside of newspapers who make it their business to amplify the problems in the press. All of them have a vested interest in damaging the credibility of newspapers."

"Daily journalism is, by definition, imperfect. It's not history. It's daily journalism, and it is flawed," Carroll said. "The Jayson Blair episode was bad but the public was not damaged by it in the long run because it's all been corrected; everybody knows it's done.

"But these things have happened forever. When I joined the *Philadelphia Inquirer* in 1973, the paper's chief investigative reporter was in the penitentiary for extortion. The *Inquirer* was able to absorb that devastating blow – and it was devastating."

Later in the interview, Carroll explains why some people become journalists. His explanation tells you exactly why I did. "I think journalists – good journalists – have always looked upon themselves as public servants."

Then, as if explaining why I took on this project, Carroll said: "When you sit back and you think, well, is there a larger purpose to it? (You answer) Yes. I've been involved in stories that have actually done some good for people. You have ... stories that may have saved lives, stories that have increased the quality of justice in America, stories that have enlightened the public in helping to exercise their vote with more pertinent information."

* * *

PERSONAL THOUGHTS: In case there is any doubt, what Carroll thinks is important to me. Will he see the social value of *Mack And The Boys* that I do and think the project has merit, or will he liken me to Jayson Blair and that Philadelphia investigative reporter who was in the penitentiary? Time will tell. I have full confidence some enterprising newspaper reporter will find Carroll and ask him.

* * *

I eventually returned to Lexington and found a job I liked. I am not sure what effect sharing *Mack And The Boys* with you will have on it. David Holwerk, former editorial-page editor at the *Herald-Leader,* used to liken unpleasant situations like this one to going to a party and "finding a turd in the punch bowl" about half-way through the event.

Knowing they might someday hear about this project, I have worked hard, hoping the people I work for and with will come to know me before they get to know about my past.

I have also refrained from making many friends. Twice now, this project has forced me to abandon all my friends. Fearing that the news about *Mack And The Boys* might force me to pack up and leave again, I have found it easier to do without friends rather than go through the pain of losing more.

How can people have no feelings?
Especially people who care about strangers,
who care about evil and social injustice?
Do you only care about the bleeding crowd?
How about a needing friend?
– EASY TO BE HARD
Artist: Three Dog Night
(also by Cheryl Barnes in the movie HAIR)
Songwriters:
A. MacDermot/J. Rado/G. Ragni
EMI U Catalog (ASCAP)

"This Used To Be My Playground"

Madonna
It spent one week at #1 in 1992

I visited Washington in September 2004. Visited is the key word. It was not home, it was not my Washington, the one I loved. It was not the same place where Mack and the boys reigned.

Washington had changed, probably for the better. I too had changed. For the worse, some might say. They would not be entirely wrong.

Eating dinner at Phillips, I could not help but remember being there with Daniel, Ryan, Sean, and Austin. I even missed the drama associated with Sean and Austin sneaking extra crab legs into a pouch of some kind to take home.

Later, while walking through the Dupont Circle area, it became clear Washington had moved on without me. I kept hoping that a familiar voice might call out "Mack" or that I might wake from a dream and find I had never sold Capital City Boys; that I had never left Washington and my friends; that Ryan and Michael were in the next room; and that Max the Wonder Dog was sleeping on his loveseat nearby. But no one called out. What I saw and felt was cold but very real.

This used to be my playground,
this used to be my childhood dream.
This used to be the place I ran to,
whenever I was in need of a friend.

Danny had warned me that Washington had changed a lot since I had left. He had not exaggerated.

The twinks who used to pack Soho Tea & Coffee shop were nowhere to be found. They had been replaced by college students, each with a laptop, each interacting with someone far away via the Internet. The silence was deafening.

When I lived in Washington, the sidewalks around Soho were filled with people waiting to enter Badlands or just to be seen.

Photo by Danny

Soho (night before I left Washington) as I remember it – a social center.

This night, the sidewalks were empty. Badlands was closed.

Cruising through Omega, I see one person I recognize but do not really know. Still, I stop and say hello. The conversation is short. What did I have to say anyway?

Back down the alley and across P Street, I entered the Fireplace. Unlike those Thursday nights when the place was packed, this night there were six people, including the bartender.

I knew Mr. P's had closed but it was still jarring to pass it and not seeing the lights on and knowing that bartenders were not pouring drinks that tasted like lighter fluid.

Walking back to Dupont Circle, I passed maybe a hundred people, and I did not know a single one. That never happened before.

Say goodbye to yesterday [the dream],
those are words I'll never say.
– THIS USED TO BE MY PLAYGROUND
Artist: Madonna
Songwriters: M. Ciccone/S. Pettibone
Bleu Disque Music (ASCAP)

Passing Starbucks, I look inside, hoping to see that blond boy, the one who kept asking questions about escorting but who never did. It would be good to answer his questions again.

All I see are strangers who have probably never heard of either Mack or Malcolm. There is no way they could know about the magic I once knew here. They could never imagine what it was like to live and work behind the curtain. Nor could they know how much listening to the Beautiful Stranger had cost me personally, professionally, and financially.

> *Something about her was familiar,*
> *I could swear I'd seen her face before.*
> *And she said, "How are you, Harry?"*
> *I said, "How are you, Sue?*
> *Through the too many miles*
> *and the too little smiles*
> *I still remember you."*
> **– TAXI**
> Singer/songwriter: Harry Chapin
> Story Songs (ASCAP)

Making my way to the CVS store in Dupont Circle, a handsome guy in his late 30s nodded at me as we both went inside. His face was familiar to me though I could not instantly put a name with it.

A minute later, I realized that I had seen that handsome face before. It belonged to Hunter, one of Mack's most unusual boys.

It had been years since I had last seen him. He and his partner had worked for Capital City Boys early on. They did many calls and paid for only a few. Together, they had the distinction of shorting the company out of more referral fees than all other guys combined.

I am not sure if Hunter knew who I was or just that he knew me from somewhere. It did not really matter. He was gracious and kind to me, just as he and his partner had always been. Both were excellent escorts.

Hunter and his partner were the type of people I would have liked to have had for friends if I had lived in Washington and had been Malcolm and not Mack.

That is one reason I allowed them to get away without paying their fees. The other is that they lived on Capitol Hill, and Sean never got over there to collect from them.

I thought this would change after I moved to Washington but it did not. I too found it difficult to collect from them. They usually handled late-night calls, and I felt it better to book the call and not get paid for it than to disappoint a client.

I eventually found escorts who could handle late calls and pay their fees. It was then that I stopped calling Hunter and his partner.

If I had been handed a list of everyone who had ever worked with Capital City Boys or The Agency while I owned them and told to pick someone to bump into, I would not have picked Hunter. Yet he is the one I met, and even the one-minute conversation we had outside CVS touched me deeply.

Hunter was proof that Mack had existed and that the experiences I remembered had indeed been real, not just a dream. And for that moment in time, it was enough.

The Backstory

"This Used to Be My Playground" was the theme song for the movie "A League of Their Own." The single was a worldwide hit and spent one week at #1 in 1992.

PREMISE #11

"For the first time in my life,
I had people that knew that –
for the briefest of time,
in the darkest of places –
I had been so, so, good at some things."

– Bucky Bleichert
From the movie
"THE BLACK DAHLIA"
Universal Pictures/Millennium Films
Based on the novel by James Ellroy

"Hold On Tight (To Your Dream)"
Electric Light Orchestra
Topped out at #10 in 1981

Most who escort justify what they are doing as a short-term thing – something to get over a tough situation, usually money-related.

Somewhere in our interview discussion – sometimes at the beginning, sometimes at the end, sometimes in between the two – the escort candidate would tell me about a dream he had.

I have always been a dreamer. Others have too. It is through dreams that many of us cope with life, especially when you are on your own and luck seems to be somewhere else.

It was long ago and far away,
the world was younger than today.
And dreams were all they gave for free,
to ugly duckling girls like me.
– AT SEVENTEEN
Singer/Songwriter: Janis Ian
EMI Blackwood Music (BMI)

Everyone I worked with in Washington had a dream of one kind or another. Everyone.

Zack dreamed of becoming a successful singer.

Sean dreamed of buying a car and moving somewhere more exciting.

Dave dreamed of remodeling his house.

Austin and Wes dreamed of having a nice apartment where they could entertain friends.

Christian dreamed of starting his own business and being financially secure.

Storm dreamed of meeting a cute, young guy and settling down.

And me? I dreamed of moving on with my life, of once again

being able to manage or work in a news operation. I dreamed of once again increasing readership, this time through the telling of more "normal" stories.

In the TV classic "The Equalizer," Robert McCall is a special agent who has resigned from "The Company," a classified government intelligence agency based in New York City. McCall tries to make up for the unspoken sins of his past by assisting those in desperate need of assistance; those who could not help themselves; those whom society failed.

I know what it is like to be haunted by your past. I have tried to get a newsroom job at newspapers since leaving Washington. I am yet to be successful. Hiring editors and human resources people seem keenly interested in me when they see my resume, then seem to drop off the face of the earth.

Did Knight Ridder blackball me from being hired? Did Knight Ridder or Gannett share "my secret" with other newspaper companies? I honestly do not know. I cannot tell you that a blacklist even exists – newspaper companies would not call it that anyway – but I can tell you that the long shadow like that of a blacklist is very real. I can also tell you it is cold standing in that shadow.

Dream on, dream on,
dream yourself a dream come true.
Dream on, dream on,
dream until your dream comes true.
– DREAM ON
Artist: Aerosmith
Songwriter: Steven Tyler
Stage Three Music (BMI)

Even Marvin, the owner of Tops Referral and the dean of gay male escorts in Washington, has a dream of one day leaving the business."I don't have the same drive I used to," he explains.

Marvin is currently exploring the possibility of opening a not-for-profit organization that would help escorts and those kicked out of the military for being gay.

"I feel so much like a social worker to clients and escorts some days that I might as well become one," Marvin says. "Besides, I have made more (money) in real estate than with the (escort) business."

All associated with Capital City Boys, and possibly Tops Referrals, dreamed because our dreams held the promise of something or somewhere better for each of us. We also dreamed because each of us know that sometimes, sometimes, dreams really do come true and that, someday ours just might.

And so you and I,
we'll watch our years go by,
we'll watch our sweet dreams fly
far away, but maybe someday,
I don't know when,
but we will dream again,
and we'll be happy then,
till our time just drifts away.
– DREAMS GO BY
Singer/Songwriter: Harry Chapin
Sandy Songs (ASCAP)

"Seasons In The Sun"
Terry Jacks
A #1 song in 1974

COMMENTARY

It was the shame society forced her to endure that led Deborah Jeane Palfrey to the white shed that quiet Thursday morning.

Her tattered collection of lost dreams tied the nylon noose and secured it to the metal beam above her.

The isolation Palfrey suffered, having been led to believe the nation as a whole considered her an outcast, a freak, put the noose around her neck.

Standing there in the shed, Palfrey might have taken a moment to think about Brandy Britton, a former college professor who hanged herself just before going to trial on prostitution charges. Palfrey, on ABC's "20/20," said Britton had worked for her service.

"She couldn't take the humiliation," Palfrey told those of us watching. "Her whole life was destroyed." Standing in the shed, all alone, I suspect Palfrey knew exactly how Britton had felt.

Perhaps Palfrey took a quick inventory of her life – where she had been, what she had done and what lay ahead for her. Maybe she thought about the explanation she had left for her mother and sister (seen at right): "I cannot live the next 6 to 8 years behind bars for what you and I have both come to regard as this 'modern-day lynching' only to come out of prison in my late 50s a broken, penniless and very much alone woman."

It was then, I imagine, that Palfrey made her decision, decided that the short-lived pain she would feel would be better than the long-term pain future days would bring.

It was then, inside the shed beside her mother's home, that an unforgiving society exacted its final pound of flesh from Deborah Jeane Palfrey.

* * *

Palfrey's guilty verdict was set aside on May 20, 2008. Such

Mom,   4/25/08

I want you to know how very much
I love & appreciate you. I sincerely
apologize for any pain which I have
caused you in this lifetime. Additionally,
I can't insufficiently express to you how
badly I feel for this burden, I am leaving
you with here.

However, I cannot live the next 6-8
years behind bars for what both you &
I have come to regard as this "modern
day lynching", only to come out of
prison in my ilated ho!? a broken,
penniless & very much alone woman. Sure
you will not live long enough to see any
possible release & Bobbie likely will be
unable to shoulder the responsibility
of a sister who will be nothing but a
mere shell of her former self.

There is a little surprise waiting for
you in the BoA account. Please use the
monies for final arrangements & various
account settlements.

Again, I love you & Bobbie very much.
Dad & I will be waiting for each of
you on the other side.

Love always,
Debbie

FYI: Palfrey's suicide note was provided for educational purposes
by the Tarpon Springs (Florida) Police Department and Mayor's Office

---

action is standard practice if a defendant dies before the end of a criminal proceeding. Palfrey's case had not ended because her sentencing was pending and she had filed a notice that she planned to appeal her conviction.

Palfrey had to die to find freedom from her past, had to die in order to get her good name back.

Thousands of others with unforgiven pasts have opted for the same relief Palfrey did. Others will in the future.

Pray that you never find yourself in a shed someday facing such a choice.

We had joy we had fun,
we had seasons in the sun,
but the hills that we climbed
were just seasons out of time.

– SEASONS IN THE SUN
Artist: Terry Jacks
Songwriters: J. Brel/R. McKuen
Edward B. Marks Music Co (BMI)

A co-worker, who has no idea of my past, verbalized my biggest worry about being able to keep my job with the Lexington-Fayette Urban County Government after sharing my secret with you: "Government doesn't run off of logic," she said, "it runs off of fear."

I often wondered what I would say to Mayor Jim Newberry when the time came to brief him about my project. I have known the task of telling the mayor and his top aides about *Mack And The Boys* would fall on my shoulders. I also knew the task would be a difficult one.

What politician wants to be associated with a situation like this one? I can tell you: none.

The words I chose to say to the mayor had to be the "right" ones.

I unexpectedly came across the "right" words one special, bright morning in a place that could not have been more meaningful to me or this project. I heard the "right" words as I stood on hallowed ground in the Lexington National Cemetery on Memorial Day 2008.

I heard the "right" words as I and several hundred others gathered to remember patriots who had answered their call to duty, and who died serving our nation.

The speaker talked of "ordinary" people from all walks of life doing extraordinary things because "they believed in America." The speaker reminded us: "Their legacy is a legacy of liberty, justice and equality." Surrounded by white tombstones, he added: "Their legacy includes the liberty to say what we want, travel where we want, believe what we want, and gather where we want with whomever we want."

The speaker that morning was Mayor Newberry, the person for whom I had been searching for just the "right" words. "Fate" caused our paths to cross that morning so I would hear the "right" words come from his heart.

For 10 years I have struggled with this project. For 10 years I have felt it was a cause I had been called to serve – one I did not fully understand but one my life experiences seemed to have uniquely prepared me to handle.

My mission – unorthodox on all levels – is to advance tolerance for people society considers "different" or, as Mayor Newberry said, to advance the preservation of liberty, equality and justice for others.

Along the way, my mission has cost me one, possibly two jobs, two homes, hundreds of thousands of dollars and most important, dozens of cherished friends. Publishing this report puts everything I have at risk, especially my job.

* * *

Mr. Mayor:

You now know about my past, about the cause I was called to serve and the price doing so has cost me.

You know how I refused to bow to threats made by powerful influences; how I chose to honor other people's privacy rather than to cash in and leave lives, families and careers in ruins.

You know how much the people I met and came to know in Washington mean to me. You also know why.

You know why hearing about the death of someone I met only once hurt me so deeply; why I am able to see the good in some people that others might overlook.

You also know why I care so much about the Day Treatment Center and that I firmly believe the work done there saves at-risk lives, work that you and I and others who believe in God have been tasked with.

The special words you shared on Memorial Day morning spoke to the troubled dreamer in me – troubled by the fear of not knowing what will happen and yet knowing I have to complete this phase of my mission.

It took me 10 years to find all the "right" words for this project. I found some in Washington, in conversations with escorts and clients, some in hotel rooms, in bars, coffee shops and even sitting at the fountain in Dupont Circle, talking to a stranger I had met while waiting to cross a street.

I found some in Lexington, talking with friends near and far. I found some in song lyrics and others buried deep in my heart.

I did not find the last of the "right" words until I stood in that cemetery Memorial Day morning honoring those who died giving us our freedoms – especially freedom of speech.

You told those of us gathered: "It has been said that a person can show no greater love than to give his life for a friend, a country or a cause." Speaking about those who died in service to America, you said: "Their legacy includes a system of justice that treats us all fairly under the law. Their legacy is a constitutional guarantee of equal protection and equal status for us all."

Then, without knowing you were confirming the validity of my project, you said: "Let us as a community, state and nation work to ensure that not only we enjoy these freedoms, but that the right to liberty, justice and equality are also made available to all of our fellow citizens. As American citizens, that is our call to duty."

Mr. Mayor, my call to duty came 10 years ago. And while I marched to the beat of a drummer different than most, the cause I served is same one you spoke so passionately about – "the right to liberty, justice and equality."

My mission took me on a road less traveled, but then, looking back, I always have been "different."

PREMISE #12

"The time has come for closing books
and long, last looks must end.
And as I leave I know that I am leaving
my best friend."

– TO SIR WITH LOVE
Singer: Lulu
Songwriters: Donald Black/Mark London
Screen Gems-EMI Music (BMI)

#1 on the charts for five weeks starting October 21, 1967.
Title song to the movie of the same name.
The record sold nearly 4 million copies worldwide.
It was a "B" side hit.

I first used these lyrics while serving as editor
of *The Communicator*, Southeastern Christian College's
student newspaper. I used the lyrics on the back page
of the paper's last issue to say goodbye
to special friends. It seemed appropriate
to do the same here.

The Beautiful Stranger had whispered seductively to me, tempting me to tell you about the secret world of gay male escorts in the nation's capital.

Had the Beautiful Stranger whispered to others before me? Had they resisted taking you deep inside the world of hush-hush deals and life on the edge? I cannot say for sure. I was told that Troy, the original owner of The Agency, had planned to write a book but decided against it after having been visited by "interested parties."

Had the Beautiful Stranger known I would accept the challenge and write *Mack And The Boys?* Did the Beautiful Stranger know how the dream-come-true adventure would forever change me and others?

She said "I've heard you flying high
on my radio."
I answered, "It's not all it seems."
That's when she laughed and she said,
"it's better sometimes,
when we don't get to touch our dreams."
– SEQUEL
Singer/songwriter: Harry Chapin
Chapin Music (ASCAP)

Reporting has been my life for more than 30 years. Asking questions, listening to others, and then accurately weaving the appropriate information into story form is what a good journalist does.

That is exactly what I set out to do in this project. I did not intend to be such an important part of this project. This was supposed to be Sean's story, not mine.

When I left Lexington and again when I left Washington, I

questioned whether I could complete my mission. It took me years to find out. "We Are Family" answers that question once and for all.

This project was designed to take you into a part of life in Washington where few are allowed. Its purpose was to explain that world and those who live there to you.

Mack And The Boys is an explanatory journalism project, and, without a doubt, unusual on many levels. I became a part of a world foreign to me, hidden from most, in order to write about that culture properly.

Journalism ethics required I report what I learned, saw, felt, and experienced, even when it was unkind to me or those for whom I care about deeply. Being completely honest with you meant I had to address my sexuality. It was not an easy task but a necessary one.

I never kept the fact I am a journalist a secret from those who asked what I did before coming to Washington. I did, however, keep secret that I had come to gather information for this project.

Some might say I betrayed those I call my friends – Mack's boys and clients. I disagree. My purpose was to describe and explain the world of gay male escorts and clients to you, not to report personal information about those I came in contact with.

This project was designed to take you deep inside the secret world of gay male escorts in the nation's capital, to show what that world and the people there are like, not to tear people down.

I feel I have accomplished that task. I am pleased I have done so without causing harm to anyone. The people I dealt with – both escorts and clients – were overwhelmingly good people, the kind of people you cherish knowing; the kind you care too much for to screw over for a moment's worth of fame.

Some might say I have betrayed Washington's gay community. I hope I have not. Mack's boys and clients invited me into their world without passing judgment on me. I will always cherish that. It has not always been that way for me in the "straight" world.

Knowing I would eventually leave and might write about Washington's gay community, I never lost sight that my work had to respect that group and those who are a part of it.

Some might also say I betrayed my profession – journalism – by sharing with you that the paper I loved being a part of – the *Lexington Herald-Leader* – forced me to give up my job in order to work this project or that the Louisville *Courier-Journal* felt the need to "punish" me and the person who hired me.

Freedom of speech is a gift paid for with blood and treasure, a gift paid for in the fields of Gettysburg, Pennsylvania, so long ago and hundreds of other places more recently, including in countries called Iraq and Afghanistan.

The American soldiers – both men and women – buried in Arlington National Cemetery and in others across the nation did not die just so corporate-owned newspapers would have freedom of speech, they died so you and I would.

I have witnessed firsthand how powerful officials and politicians will run from the bright light that a newspaper can shine on wrongdoing. I saw that at the *Herald-Leader* under John S. Carroll's leadership. I was honored to play a role in holding that light. I was thrilled when the paper won national recognition for its hard work.

Though I never held a gun and fought for my country in a war, I have long believed working at the *Herald-Leader,* helping to hold that bright light, was a way I could honor the men and women who had fought on my behalf and especially those who had died protecting my liberty, died protecting yours.

The *Herald-Leader* is a good paper. The people who work there – especially in the newsroom – are dedicated to serving the people of Central and Eastern Kentucky. I found that same level of dedication in many of the people I worked with at the *Courier-Journal,* found it in people named Janie, Tom, Carol, Jim, Bruce, John, Ric, Susan, Lisa, and Dan.

* * *

Have I properly succeeded in explaining to you what the world of gay male escorts in the nation's capital is like? I took you deep into that world and told you what I learned, factually and without bias, just as a journalist is supposed to do.

Did I tell you enough about the dirty little secrets to satisfy your curiosity without "outing" anyone, be they a kid working for money to survive until tomorrow; a married client who has an "interest" that needs addressing before going home to care for his wife and children; or to an elected official who has a secret he dares not share with voters back home, fearing he will face the same fate as former Rep. Mark Foley and Sen. Larry Craig?

You, the reader, will have to tell me.

I always took this reporting assignment very seriously as well the need to keep some secrets locked tightly away forever. I believe my actions and reporting reflect that.

I am convinced the worse decision I made relating to *Mack And The Boys* was to accept the *Herald-Leader's* assertion that I was no longer worthy of working in a newsroom. I should have left the *Herald-Leader* and found a job at another newspaper somewhere, even if it meant starting over at a smaller one.

Carroll, speaking before the American Society of Newspaper Editors in 2006, talked about what will become of newspapers in the future. He also spoke about "a more subtle problem – a crisis of the soul."

"Every journalist believes that he or she works, ultimately, for the reader – not for the editor, or for the publisher, or for the corporation, or for those opaque financial institutions that hold the stock," Carroll said.

"We all know journalists who have lost their jobs on principle. They have refused to kill important stories, or to write glowingly about politicians or advertisers who do not deserve it. They have done this because their first loyalty is to the reader."

These are the words of the great newspaper editor who taught me and others to be better journalists; to give our readers, our community our best effort every day, regardless if our job was that of a news assistant, a reporter, a desk editor, a copy editor, a photojournalist, a page designer, a backshop person or something else.

It was under Carroll's leadership that the *Herald-Leader* touched greatness. Carroll inspired those of us who worked with him in the newsroom to reach beyond what was expected of us, what was easy.

Carroll taught us not to walk away when we believed we had found a story people needed to hear, even if powerful influences and readers themselves felt otherwise. That is why I left the *Herald-Leader* rather than to cave to the threat of being fired.

Mack And The Boys was a story I believe needed to be told, even if it meant being forced to leave the paper I loved.

* * *

It is with mixed emotions I write "We Are Family." Mixed because I have managed to accomplish what some worked to stop; sad because the time has come to say goodbye to something that has meant so much to me since the Beautiful Stranger whispered to me the day I met Jeremy on that street corner.

Soon, Mack will go away – forever – and the Beautiful Stranger will whisper to me no more. Candidly, I am a little afraid about what my life will be like without them – afraid, because they have been such an important part of my life for so long now.

Along the way of reporting and writing this project, I lost so much of who I used to be. I am not the same head-strong person who left the *Herald-Leader.* Time and events have taken their toll. Though not broken, I am very weary from my journey.

* * *

So, just how do I close this project? There is so much more I want to say, so much more I could say.

Carol Wright, one of my journalism professors at Eastern Kentucky University, taught that "a good journalist knows what to put in and what to leave out" of a story. Carol, I hope I have honored your memory with my choices.

* * *

Debating how to end *Mack And The Boys,* I allow my mind the freedom to wander and to go where it wants.

I find myself imagining I am back in Washington with two very special friends. We are standing outside a small retail shop on Connecticut Avenue, just off Dupont Circle. It is late at night, and I know I have kept them out in the cold longer than I should have, talking about the boys.

Snow is falling around us, just as it did the night I went to rescue Zack. One of my friends keeps shifting his feet, so I know I have to wrap things up pretty soon.

Caught between wanting to say so much and knowing I have to let them go, I travel to where I'm most comfortable – to the music I love and words written and sung by those far more talented than I.

Reminding my two friends how large a role music played in both the project and my life, I quote Meatloaf and Jim Steinman from "Rock And Roll Dreams Come Through", saying:

> *"And when you really, really need it the most,*
> *that's when rock and roll dreams*
> *come through, for you."*

My friends nod, indicating they understand what I mean. Smiling, one says, "if not for dreamers, we'd all still live in caves."

"Music," the other one says, "has been a good friend to you, an important friend through some tough times."

Wanting to convey that the three of us had succeeded when the odds against us were huge, I quote lyrics from the movie "Savannah Smiles" saying:

"They said that we would never
find our way together,
just a foolish fantasy,
they were wrong, can't you see?"

Turning to the Beautiful Stranger and wanting to point out how I had been enticed to report and write *Mack And The Boys*, I quote Dusty Springfield:

"You stopped and smiled at me,
asked me if I'd care to dance.
I fell into your open arms,
I didn't stand a chance."

"Dr. Martin Luther King, Columbus and the person who dreamed up the "Blair Witch Project" listened when a Beautiful Stranger whispered to them," my other friend, Mack, says. "At one time or another, everyone has a Beautiful Stranger whisper to them. Some, like Dr. King and Columbus, are called to do major things. Others, like you, minor but important ones."

Using lyrics from "You Find Your Way" from the movie "Daddy's Dyin, Who's Got the Will?" the Beautiful Stranger makes the point that, though difficult and, at times I had lost my way, in the end, I had survived:

Sometimes it's night,
sometimes it's day.
Sometimes you run,
sometimes you stay.
But it goes around,
and you find your way

Sometimes it hurts,
ah, it hurts so bad.
You curse the sky,
and get so mad.

But it goes around,
and you find your way.

Doing a decent Walter Houston imitation, Mack quotes from *Cannery Row* but offers a slight change:

Malcolm had friends
he didn't even know about and some
he would never forget,
friends like Mack and the boys.

"Never," I say. "Never. Being here was way too important to me to ever forget."

"I know there was one disappointment," the Beautiful Stranger says in a serious tone. "Sam never came for you."

"Sam?" I say, astonished someone knew this fact since it was the one secret I had never confided to anyone, including Max the Wonder Dog.

"Dr. Samuel Beckett," she says, "The Sam that finds himself leaping from life to life, striving to put right what once went wrong."

Stunned, all I could do is nod in agreement.

"The work you did here was important," the Beautiful Stranger says. "You changed lives. You protected those who needed protecting. As the bartender told Sam in the last episode of 'Quantum Leap:' 'You did more good here than you will ever know.'"

"There are some who might consider you their Sam," Mack says. "Be proud of that."

"It came at a huge price," I say, softly.

"Helping others is rarely an easy task," Mack says, "and while not easy, it is worthwhile."

"That college student wrote that '*Cannery Row* shows even whorehouses can be places of benevolence and real human importance.' You, in Washington – as the owner of Capital City Boys – did the same thing."

"Remember," Mack says, "Carroll told those editors in his speech that over the long haul, people buy a newspaper because it tells them 'significant things they do not already know,' things like the story of *Mack And The Boys.*"

"But the *Herald-Leader* didn't run the project," I say. "They didn't even read it."

"Newspapers aren't foolproof," Mack says, laughing. "They are often run by people guessing what it is the public wants. They are run by people whose job it is to keep the bags of cash rolling in the door. That's why the Web is giving them so much trouble.

"The truth is, newspapers have had what the public wanted and needed for years. Many have surrendered that turf by cutting back on content and pricing ads so high that fewer and fewer companies can see a reasonable return for their investment. Name another product that you can have delivered to your doorstep for 50 or 75 cents a day – you can't. Want to know what a bargain a newspaper is? Call a plumber or heating/cooling guy and ask what their trip charge is and imagine paying that 30 times a month."

* * *

The snow is coming down hard now. It does not faze me anymore. I smile broadly because I realize the two of you fully understand the inner me and long ago unconditionally accepted me for who I really am, flaws and all.

I have searched my entire life for absolute blind acceptance and have found it only three places: in the hearts of two dogs I rescued from Lexington's animal shelter; once from Washington's gay community; and now in a snowstorm in an imaginary ending to an oh-so-real, life-changing journey.

Shoulders virtually covered in snow, the Beautiful Stranger leans forward and whispers to me softly, just as so long ago, again, seductively saying, Malcolm,

> *You only live twice, or so it seems.*
> *One life for yourself,*
> *and one for your dreams.*

Numb from the experience, I stand motionless, silently watching as you walk away. I cannot help but think you are just as beautiful as you were the night we first met.

You pause, just for a second. Turning around slowly, you smile and then nod – a final acknowledgement that lets me know you understand and appreciate all I went through for you. And for that moment in time, it's more than enough.

Bringing me back to reality, Mack asks, "Was telling *Mack And The Boys* worth all you had to give up – your jobs, your homes, and, to some extent, yourself?"

"No. No way," I say. "It is possible – after publishing the project – I will be able look back and think differently," I say to him, "especially if people learn from what I share."

Continuing, I add, "It's also possible I will look back and – thinking about the Beautiful Stranger – I will say the same thing then-Washington Mayor Marion Barry said while being arrested on drug charges: 'The bitch set me up.'"

Laughing, Mack gets ready to leave by brushing the snow off himself. He calls out to the Beautiful Stranger to wait up.

Always insightful and quick to remember something many never would have, Mack reminds me how Harry Chapin ended "Sequel":

> *I guess it's a sequel to our story*
> *from the journey 'tween heaven and hell,*
> *with half the time thinking*
> *of what might have been,*
> *and half thinkin' just as well.*
> *I guess only time will tell.*

And then, Mack turned and walked away.

I stood there watching until Mack and the Beautiful Stranger were no longer visible, completely obscured by the falling snow. Knowing that I was more alone than I ever had been in my life, I whisper a special goodbye to my two unusual friends, using lyrics from Garth Brooks' great hit, "The Dance":

> *Holding you, I held everything.*
> *For a moment, wasn't I a king?*

A huge smile comes upon my face as I stand there remembering some of the great times I had in Washington. Then, recalling tough ones, I go back to "The Dance" and whisper:

> *I could have missed the pain,*
> *but I'd of had to miss the dance.*

I pull out my iPod as I turn away, preparing to go in the opposite direction, just as I had done so many times before while walking away from Drew and his "friend."

Photo by Keith Stanley

A lone figure makes his way along 17th Street near Dupont Circle during a snow storm.

Knowing this moment is way too important to leave to chance, I search for the song I think is most appropriate for what I'm feeling and thinking – a song I first heard so long ago on my radio.

Putting in the earplugs, I press the button for the song to play. And as the familiar guitar rift begins, I start walking away. When Johnny Rivers begins to sing, so do I. The lyrics are ones I have held onto tightly since walking down that church aisle so long ago and again when I began my journey with *Mack And The Boys.* You see, the lyrics hold a promise that I will cling to until the day I die:

> *Roll along, muddy river, roll,*
> *your dirty water cannot taint your soul.*
> *Roll along, roll along, till you are free.*

Knowing the lyrics by heart, I turn down the volume on the iPod and take over the lead. No longer afraid of what others might think and once again claiming its promise backed by my religious upbringing, I sing the rest of "Muddy River" with great conviction.

But life is real. It does not allow us the luxury to choose imaginary endings.

Prejudices are also real. They are a part of all of us. However noble we strive to be, no matter how hard we try to avoid having them, prejudices exist – exist deep within each of us.

Matthew Shepard, a student at the University of Wyoming, was beaten and left to die because he was gay and the men who killed him had a prejudice against gay people.

Shepard died three days after Capital City Boys ran its first ad in October 1998, seeking to represent escorts.

Countless men and women have lost their jobs or have been passed over for promotions during the reporting and writing of this project because they are gay and their companies or bosses have a prejudice against "those people." More will in the future.

Many qualified people have shied away from running for elected office – be it a local, state or national position – because the fear they have of being "outed" far exceeds their deep desire to serve the public.

In 2006, the candidate who had killed his political campaign in 2002 because he feared being asked if he was gay told the world he was. The *Herald-Leader* ran its story on Page One and followed up with an editorial praising him.

When he announced he would be running for elected office again, people called in to a local radio show, pledging to vote for the man despite him "being gay." Callers kept their word – the candidate was elected by a wide margin and has served the public effectively.

Finally, only God knows how many mothers and fathers have pushed children out of their homes saying "they no longer fit in" there, because being gay somehow precludes that.

God is also the only one who knows how many parents of older children pray that their friends and neighbors never find out their child is gay, fearing – as my mother secretly did – that they did something wrong to make us *that way.*

Gays are more accepted today than when Sweet Evening Breeze walked past my home when I was a kid. Still, we all have a lot of growing to do, we all need to be more understanding and accepting of others, be they gay, straight, bi, or unsure.

Jason Johnson of Lexington was kicked out of the University of the Cumberlands, a Southern Baptist school located in Eastern Kentucky, in April 2006, after he revealed on his MySpace.com page that he was gay.

The university told the theater arts major that it did not approve of his "gay lifestyle." And, although he was a dean's list student, his grades were changed to "F." Johnson was later allowed to complete his coursework for that semester and had his previous grades restored.

Lawrence King, 15, of Oxnard, Calif., had just recently started telling people he was gay when he was shot to death inside a junior high school lab by a fellow student in February 2008. The gunman "is just as much a victim as Lawrence," Masen Davis, told the *New York Times.* "He's a victim of homophobia and hate."

Chase returned home to his family in Virginia in 2007. He somehow survived living on the streets for more than seven years. I would not have been shocked to hear he had died there. Chase's family welcomed him home with two conditions: he cannot associate with gay people and cannot tell anyone that he is gay. "I am made to feel ashamed of who I am," Chase says. "I am not allowed to be who I really am."

In the movie "Midnight In The Garden Of Good And Evil" jurors were urged to look past possible prejudices they might have because the man on trial and the dead man were gay lovers.

> *"Now, if you don't like, or you don't cotton to his lifestyle, just think about this: We deal with these people all the time, some good, some bad. They are a part of our community and you can't judge a man for that. This is God's work. Let God be the judge of that."*

While only words in a movie script, the message in that passage is a powerful one: *"Let God be the judge of that."*

The stated mission of the Matthew Shepard Foundation is to "replace hate with understanding, compassion and acceptance." Blind acceptance of others makes that goal possible. The gift of blind acceptance has served me well in dealing with people from all walks of life. I simply accept people for whom they are – both the "good" things and the perceived "bad" ones.

None of us had the ability to choose our skin color or whether we would be male or female. While no one can say with such certainly that people cannot decide their sexual orientation, I am convinced – based on my experiences – that some can and some cannot.

Everything in life has two sides – you cannot have one without the flipside, sort of like an old 45 rpm record. This project took you deep inside the secret world of gay male escorts. It showed you what that world is like – both the good and the bad parts. It showed you a part of life and a group of people that you might otherwise never have known much about or had the opportunity to meet. It also showed you good people are a part of that world.

This project explained how an otherwise "normal" person might decide to escort or to run an escort referral service and how that experience might change their life forever – some for the better, some for the worse.

In John Steinbeck's *Cannery Row*, Mack and the boys can easily be looked upon as failures of society. Instead of judging Mack and the boys by what they do, Steinbeck encourages us to judge them by who they truly are. He does this by telling us stories about them. The more we learn and get to know Mack and the boys, the more we understand and accept them.

At the end of the movie "Savannah Smiles", Boots turns to Alvie after they've been arrested and says: "I hope nobody ever tells her we were bad guys."

Alvie, knowing that Savannah has come to know the real Boots and Alvie replies: "Won't make no difference." Alvie knows no matter what others might say about the two men, Savannah knows the truth.

Encouraging you to judge people by who they truly are, not by what they do or might have done in the past, is the purpose of *Mack And The Boys*. It is my hope that by introducing you to the people I met and came to know in Washington, that you have come to understand and accept them and others you might consider "different" for who they truly are.

And though never even a secondary purpose behind the project, it is my hope that you will judge me for who I really am, not what you might have originally thought when you first read that I owned and operated a gay male escort referral service.

Everyone deserves a second chance, even those who have already had dozens, even those who cross lines they shouldn't. Everyone also deserves the chance to be themselves, whatever or whomever that might be, however strange or out of step it might seem to the rest of us.

Blind acceptance of others – like decency – is in your bones, you just have to practice it.

* * *

Lexington Mayor Jim Newberry will soon have to decide if the stirring words he spoke that beautiful spring morning apply to the dreamer who heard and answered the call to stand up for a cause he deeply believes in – the freedom to be one's self.

I have stood at this point in life twice already, once at the

Herald-Leader and once at *The Courier-Journal.* I have gotten in the habit of never taking anything I cannot live without to work, just in case I am called into an office, told to leave and not to come back.

Twice now I have jumped off the high-dive for this project, touched the bottom of the pool and have survived. And, if I do not survive this time, know that *Mack And The Boys* was an important part of my life; that reporting this story was something I felt I was called to do.

Dirty little secrets.

Everybody has them.

Nobody wants them told.

Whatever the cost, whatever the outcome, I had to tell you about the secrets.

* * *

Sometimes, life is unpredictable. Words shared with us by a friend, a spouse, a family member, or even song lyrics whispered to us by a Beautiful Stranger come to have a much deeper meaning once we live them.

The same is true about accepting others for who they truly are. It is easier to be more understanding, compassionate, and accepting of others when we have had the opportunity to walk a mile with them; when we better understand their pasts and hear them tell us – in their own words – about their hopes and dreams for a better life.

You hold the key to love and fear
oh, in your trembling hand.
Just one key unlocks them both,
it's there at your command.
– GET TOGETHER
Artist: The Youngbloods
Music & Lyrics: Chet Powers
Irving Music (BMI)

It is my hope, my prayer, that you will consider those who are gay or lesbian – either by nature or by choice – and those who – for one reason or another – have chosen to escort, differently now, now that you know the story of *Mack And The Boys* – the truth about the lovers, the dreamers and me.

The Matthew Shepard Foundation

Working to replace hate with understanding, compassion and acceptance

October 2008, marked the 10th anniversary of the opening of Capital City Boys and the start of principal reporting for the *Mack And the Boys* project.

It also marked the 10th anniversary of the brutal beating and death of Matthew Shepard.

Shepard was taken to a remote area east of Laramie, Wyoming, on October 7, 1998, tied to a split-rail fence, beaten and left to die because he was "different," – different, in that he was gay. Shepard was found 18 hours later by a cyclist who initially mistook him for a scarecrow.

"Matt's gift was people," Shepard's father, Dennis, says on the foundation's Web site. "He loved being with people, helping people, and making others feel good. The hope of a better world, free of harassment and discrimination because a person was different, kept him motivated.

"Matt loved people and he trusted them," the elder Shepard says. "He could never understand how one person could hurt another, physically or verbally. He didn't see size, race, intelligence, sex, religion, or the hundred other things that people use to make choices about people. All he saw was the person. All he wanted was to make another person his friend. All he wanted was to make another person feel good. All he wanted was to be accepted as an equal."

Learn more or donate to the Matthew Shepard Foundation by going to www.MatthewShepard.org

---

The Backstory

"Rock and Roll Dreams Come Through" Jim Steinman. Lost Boys Music (BMI).
"Love Will Never Be the Same Again" Ken Sutherland. Savannah Smiles Music (ASCAP).
"I Only Want to Be With You" Michael Hawker & Ivor Raymonde. Chappell & Company (ASCAP).
"You Find Your Way" David McHugh. Shadow Canyon Music. (ASCAP).
"You Only Live Twice" John Barry & Leslie Bricusse. EMI Unart Catalog (BMI).
"The Dance" Anthony Arata. EMI April Music (ASCAP).
"Muddy River" James Hendricks. EMI Sosaha Music (BMI).

*"Those who fight monsters should
make sure they don't become one."*
**— LAW AND ORDER
SPECIAL VICTIMS UNIT**
Episode: "Signature"

COMMENTARY:
Closing Thoughts

Newspapers and newspaper chains are powerful influences.
So are dreams.

Dreams encourage us to reach beyond that which is easy and
common, to do things we might not otherwise do.

The United States of America was founded upon a dream – the
dream of people who craved the freedom to be whom and what
they wanted to be, not what others thought they should be.

Chris Matthews, the host of MSNBC's "Hardball" speaks
passionately about how our nation was first conceived, then
developed, and now survives on the dream "that we (its citizens)
can make things better."

Matthews, on MSNBC's "Morning Joe" show, once told how
two guys on horses – men named L'Enfant and Washington –
looked down over a swamp and dreamed of building a world-class
capital city there. Washington, D.C., is the result of that dream.

Matthews went on to say dreaming is "America's religion."

My dream was to tell you about Mack and the boys.

Twice, I completely walked away from this project. Twice, it
was dead. I changed my mind both times because this is too
important a story to keep to myself. It is a life-changing story. It
has changed my life. I hope it has the ability to change others,
lots of others, for the better.

I started out to simply report a few stories about people I met
in Washington. The project stalled when I became too involved in
it and my personal life was turned upside down. It was the
compassion and acceptance of people I hardly knew that allowed
me to recover and go on with my life.

A special friend who previewed this project, one who knows reporting, asked me what I wanted to get out of publishing it.

I quickly answered I wanted to educate readers about the need to be accepting of others, those we might think are "different" than ourselves. It was a truthful answer, but the more I considered my friend's question, the deeper I looked inside myself for a more personal one. Surely there was something I wanted from all this work.

A couple of days later when my son asked almost the same exact question, I offered the same answer and a second, one just as accurate: I want to know that – as a journalist – I did not fail my profession.

Malcolm Stallons

An important piece of that validation came a few days later while I sat in that darkened auditorium at Eastern Kentucky University and listened to my friend Theresa Klisz speak about the importance of journalists having integrity and credibility.

While directed to future journalists, broadcasters and communicators in the room, Klisz's comments had a huge affect on me. I sat there and smiled, knowing, that in spite of overwhelming challenges and a hundred chances to do otherwise, I had refused to give up my integrity and credibility.

Capital City Boys and The Agency were legally licensed businesses. I worked hard to make sure they never engaged in illegal activities. Allowing them to do so would have been easier. It also would have been much more profitable.

* * *

Redemption often comes at a high price. I have paid a heavy one already. I know by publishing this project that the tab will likely go even higher. One does not have to think hard to imagine some might challenge my claims in order to lessen the importance or impact of this report. That is how the game is played sometimes.

The subjects of such reports often attack the journalist or newspaper that brings questionable deeds to light, much like a defense attorney who attacks a rape accuser in court, claiming the attack was her fault. The attorney hopes to stir the water enough to cloud things to where reasonable people begin to doubt.

I have worked hard to make sure I have been fair and accurate in my reporting. I have known all along that there will be some who will parse every word, looking for a mistake.

Wanting this project to be fair and accurate, I offered *Herald-Leader* Publisher Tim Kelly a copy in advance of publishing it. I offered Kelly the entire project so he (and the paper) would not be blindsided by anything I published and to raise any concerns they might have.

I asked Kelly if the *Herald-Leader* might consider co-publishing the project. The *Herald-Leader* declined my offers.

I also invited the paper to contribute its side of this story. The publisher asked where he could send his comments. I told him. I waited months for a response from the *Herald-Leader* before publishing this report. None ever came. I will add the paper's comments to the online version of this report if they are made available to me. I will also add comments from any other person or organization mentioned in this report.

* * *

Most of us know that the Declaration of Independence says:

> *"We hold these truths to be self-evident,*
> *that all men are created equal,*
> *that they are endowed by their Creator with certain*
> *inalienable rights that among these are*
> *life, liberty and the pursuit of happiness."*

Fewer know a few lines down from that passage, the document requires that if something is wrong with our government or our society that:

> *"Those who have the ability to take action*
> *have the responsibility to take action."*

For hundreds of years, protecting your freedoms and mine – especially the freedom of speech – has been the role of America's newspapers.

In my opinion, in this case, the *Herald-Leader* and Knight Ridder Newspapers failed to meet its obligation as a good citizen in July 1999, because it was not in its own personal interest. I think the *Herald-Leader* failed to meet that obligation again in December 2007, when it declined my offer to contribute to this report or to consider co-publishing the project if readers would benefit. One can easily guess the *Herald-Leader* rejected the offer again because the truth might prove embarrassing.

The 56 men who signed the Declaration of Independence did so because they believed change was needed, that certain oppressions needed to be lifted. They signed knowing they faced being hanged once their "project" was "published," yet they signed because it was the right thing to do for the "community" as a whole despite possible dangers for themselves individually. These men were patriots.

* * *

The federal government spent hundreds of thousands of dollars prosecuting Deborah Jean Palfrey for running her Washington-based escort service.

The government's case resulted in the suicide deaths of two women, the humiliation of 16 other people including a U.S. senator and a high-ranking government official who resigned.

At the end of the day, one is entitled to ask: "Are the streets of Washington any safer because of the government's actions? Has a single thread of our society's moral fabric been saved from ruin?"

Sadly, the answer to both questions is "no." Two people are dead and at least 16 others "outed" and scarred for life.

Decide for yourself if you think democracy was served.

> *Let the voice of freedom*
> *sing out through this land,*
> *this is our country.*
> **– OUR COUNTRY**
> Singer/songwriter: John Mellencamp
> Belmont Mall Publishing (ASCAP)

I came across the movie "Crazy in Alabama" while living in Washington. The movie, written by fellow journalist Mark Childress, deals with a Southern boy who stands up for what is right despite the possible danger to himself.

"Crazy in Alabama" takes place in a small town in Alabama in 1965, at the height of the civil rights movement.

Peter Joseph Bullis (also known as Pee Joe) watches as Taylor Jackson, a young black teen, is killed by the town's sheriff. Pee

Joe, the only witness, is pressured by the sheriff not to tell what he knows.

Jackson's death happens soon after Pee Joe has learned a life-changing lesson about standing your ground and following your own path from his free-spirited aunt Lucille Vinson. Lucille has just killed her abusive husband and is going to Hollywood to fulfill her dream of appearing on TV.

Pee Joe and I happen to be the same age. We apparently also share a lot of common beliefs. Though our stories happen at different times and different places, we both have a sense of what is right and wrong; we both crave freedom for ourselves and for others; and we both knew secrets others wanted kept quiet.

Eventually, Pee Joe and I both found the courage to stand up for what we believe in despite the possible outcome.

In December 2000, I gave a copy of "Crazy in Alabama" to everyone in my family for Christmas, hoping they would come see the similarities between Pee Joe and me and better understand why I felt the need to go to Washington to work on this project.

This was sort of a crazy expectation since even now, before sending a copy of my report to them, I am not sure who in my family – other than my mother and my son – knows the truth about why I went to Washington.

"Crazy in Alabama" ends with Pee Joe telling us:

I learned a lot of secrets that summer.
You can bury freedom but you can't kill it.
Taylor Jackson died for freedom. Aunt Lucille had to kill to get it.
Life and death are only temporary but freedom goes on forever.

Maybe a Beautiful Stranger whispered to Mark Childress too.

* * *

A friend who read this project in advance of its publication says he worries about the danger associated with publishing this project. "It's a great story," he said, "but can't you write it under an assumed name?" No Michael, I can't.

My friend Storm, who read the project for accuracy and sensitivity, warned me I would anger certain people in Washington and cause others enough grave concern that it could result in my being harmed or worse. "They'll go to any lengths to protect themselves. Your life means nothing to them."

I know there is danger in publishing *Mack And The Boys*, but the greater danger lies in not doing so.

Maybe if Jeremy's mother had read this project before opening his bedroom door she would have been better prepared to handle what she saw.

Maybe she would have been more understanding, compassionate and accepting of her son. Maybe Jeremy would have stayed at home and studied engineering like he had dreamed of doing.

Maybe, just maybe, after reading this project, two certain Kentucky newspapers won't be so quick to distance themselves from the next dreamer who happens to see something special long before others do.

Lives were forever changed when Jeremy's mother opened that door and found her son kissing his friend. Jeremy's was. I now know mine was too.

Maybe, just maybe, other lives will be changed now that you have taken the time to get to know a group of strangers whose paths happened to cross once upon a time in the nation's capital – people you now know as Mack and the boys.

My name is Malcolm Stallons.

I represented gay escorts.

These have been our stories, stories I felt needed to be told.

"My brother (Robert F. Kennedy) need not be idealized, or enlarged in death beyond what he was in life, to be remembered simply as a good, decent man, who saw wrong and tried to right it, saw suffering and tried to heal it, saw war and tried to stop it.

"Those of us, who loved him and who take him to his rest today pray that what he was to us and what he wished for others will someday come to pass for all the world.

"As he said many times, in many parts of this nation, to those he touched and who sought to touch him:
'Some men see things as they are and say, Why?
I dream things that never were and say, Why not?'"
– U. S. SENATOR EDWARD KENNEDY
June 8, 1968
The day the Beautiful Stranger
first whispered to the dreamer in me

Epilogue

I traveled to Washington in early August 2008. I returned to do some additional interviews and to shoot new photos.

One of the interviews I did was with Marvin, the owner of Tops Referrals. I was deeply honored he agreed, knowing he has repeatedly turned down similar requests from others.

It was wonderful to be back in the District. I had forgotten how much I loved walking around downtown, how much I loved being in Dupont Circle, how much I loved being a part of the nation's capital.

Rekindling old friendships continued the next weekend when, by chance, Danny found himself in Kentucky and was able to visit me for a couple of days. We spent the time working on the "Everybody Hurts" segment. He wrote, I polished. We always did make a good team.

*　*　*

For years, the *Lexington Herald-Leader* traditionally won awards for running the leanest operation in the Knight Ridder chain. It is easy to think they were still a lean operation. Cutting 16.6 percent of the paper's workforce in nine months will hurt the product, not to mention wrecking the lives of employees and their families. My heart goes out to all HL employees, including the publisher.

Working on *Mack And The Boys,* I came across a story in Kentucky that, if what I have been told proves true, needs to be told in order to correct a gross injustice. I plan on sharing that information and contacts with the *Herald-Leader* soon after this project goes public. It is a story that the *Herald-Leader* would be better able to find the truth.

*　*　*

Lexington's gay community held its first public Pride festival on June 28, 2008. Previous ones had been private events.

The politician who ducked the issue of being gay in 2002 then came forward before running and being elected in 2006, was the event's main speaker.

"Any city where diversity is encouraged is going to have more and better opportunities, both socially and economically," he said to cheers.

I did not attend the festival. I drove by and honked my horn in support. I drove past going to my brother's house for a cookout celebrating his wedding the previous weekend.

My stepfather and his wife were at the cookout. Both greeted me like an old friend.

Sitting there, it became clear to me the next lesson in my personal awareness journey should be to address and repair my relationship with them. Many times, they have encouraged me to call them and then go over for dinner. I never have. The time has come to so.

Lexington's reigning drag empress, Eve St. Mychael, told the *Herald-Leader* that the Pride festival was useful in that it brought out both straight and gay residents to celebrate together. Then he added, "I think everyone needs a little glitter in their lives."

Indeed they do – glitter and acceptance of people they might have once considered "different" – be they in Washington, in your town, or in Lexington, Kentucky, the place I am proud to call home and the setting of my next project.

Seven years have passed since I left Washington.

I have lost track of many of the boys as cell phone numbers were changed and those who once escorted decided to put that part of their lives behind them.

Here's a look at what has happened to some of Mack's boys and friends since I left Washington in July 2001.

SEAN

One of the major influences on Capital City Boys and originally the focus of this project. Sean still entertains. We had dinner at P.F. Chang's Restaurant in Lexington one night in August 2007 as he was passing through town. I do not remember smiling so much since I left Washington. There was no doubt but that both of us were older and different than when we first met but it was also clear that the special friendship we once had still exists. **Personal note:** You will always be very special to me.

DREW

He and his boyfriend ran DC Boys for almost a year before moving to New York. The last time we spoke – sometime in 2003 – Drew was "visiting a friend" in Colorado and was thinking about moving back to Atlanta, alone. I'm betting he moved back and the boyfriend is still with him. **Personal note:** Thanks kid, for giving me my rock 'n' roll fantasy.

MARVIN

Owner of Topps Referrals and close friend. After reading a draft copy of *Mack And The Boys* Marvin insisted I return to Washington to meet and interview certain key clients to include their perspective. Marvin also allowed me to interview him, a request he has turned down dozens times before to others wanting to write a book. Marvin could have caused serious problems for Capital City Boys and me but that was never his style. He also could have simply wished me well with this project. instead, he opened his home and intuitional memory. **Personal note:** Thank you, dear friend.

JONATHAN (The first one)
Another influence on Capital City Boys. Originally from Lexington. Left Washington in 1998 and reportedly settled in Florida. **Personal note:** Stop by next time you come to Lexington. I'd love to hear you sing.

JONATHAN (The other one)
Capital City Boys' favorite escort for a while. Jonathan left Washington to attend college. Got off drugs, got a boyfriend, and got his life together. **Personal note:** I understand why you wanted to put escorting entirely behind you. I wanted you as a lifelong friend. I am sorry you felt differently.

RYAN
One of the lost boys. Spotted in Washington from time to time. Talks with Michael when he "is in the mood." Ryan would have made an excellent assistant manager at that bed and breakfast. **Personal note:** Ask Marvin for my phone number and call me. It would be good to hear from you.

MICHAEL
Recently returned to Washington and is taking classes. We chat online from time to time. **Personal note:** I always loved your smile and appreciated your friendship.

DANNY
Living in Florida. Still calls when he hears "Tainted Love." I hope he always will. May have finally found the right job. Danny got to preview *Mack And The Boys*. Read it in his car because he did not want his family or girlfriend to see it. He was reading the report in an empty parking lot one night when a policeman stopped by the see what he was doing. Sounds like something that would have happened to me. **Personal note:** You, possibly more than anyone, knew the "real" me. You just didn't know the "real" story.

DAVID/BEAR
Have not heard from him since getting that mysterious e-mail saying he was in the Middle East. Keep hoping U.S. troops might find him while searching for those weapons of mass destruction in Iraq. **Personal note:** With or without the bed and breakfast, I wanted you to be a longtime friend.

TOM
Sold his condo and then vanished. Searches show he went south. **Personal note:** My hope is that you are on a warm beach sipping on tall drinks, a cute boy on one side and a cute girl on the other.

BRENDA
Returned to the *Lexington Herald-Leader* as an advertising manager. I have run into her a few times. What, other than "I am sorry," do you say to someone who pays a price for your dream? **Personal note:** Trust me when I say you were a great boss.

AUSTIN
Left Washington, turned his life around, and is now back home, waiting tables at a nice restaurant. **Personal note:** I did not dare tell you the story about your apartment, afraid it might take away from your joy of having your own place.

J.T.
Originally a threat as owner of Dreamboys, J.T. became a good friend. Seen in Washington from time to time. **Personal note:** Be well, my friend. I wish we could have been friends longer.

CHASE/CANDY
Lived on the streets of San Francisco for years. Called once to say he was in Las Vegas to enter a contest to design an outfit for Cher. Somehow, Chase managed to survive all that life threw at him. **Personal note:** I saw the real you, something others were quick to look past. Maybe because we were a lot alike. Life owes you more than what you've had so far. There is a wonderful person inside you, let him determine who you will be.

DAVE
Sips tall coffees using his employee discount. **Personal note:** I miss hearing how much you enjoyed spreading good cheer.

ZACK
Still living in the Washington area. Still writing songs, still singing, still dreaming. Was in a recording studio working on a CD last time we talked. **Personal note:** Don't ever stop dreaming, kid. Sometimes, dreams do come true..

JESSE
Went home to Florida, taking classes to learn a trade and is doing well. Calls on special occasions. **Personal note:** I am very proud of your achievements. I am pleased you have stayed in touch.

TOBY
Worked for an agency that worked closely with Washington's gay community. Last seen in a courtroom in Northern Virginia after having been beaten in a hate crime. **Personal note:** Thanks for all the smiles, laughter and warmth you gave.

STORM
Living "fabulously large" in South Florida. Happy, has lots of friends. Active in local charities. Still writing, still has his entrepreneurial spirit. Working on opening an Italian restaurant where everything is larger than life, including the portions. **Personal note:** I am a better person for having you as a friend. If I ever win the lottery we'll open that restaurant.

JEREMY
Unknown. **Personal note:** I hope life has treated you well since the day we met. Know that the candle I light on my birthday is for you. Know too that for several years now my birthday wish has been that you returned home and are doing well.

MAX THE WONDER DOG
Waiting for me on a hillside beneath a tree in heaven or pulled a few strings and came back into my life as the beautiful Miss Tilly.

DR. SAMUEL BECKETT
Dr. Beckett never returned home. We were told in the last episode of "Quantum Leap" that Dr. Beckett is still leaping from life to life, putting right what once went wrong.

etc.

A tip-of-the-hat to people who played a special role in my life

Hitchhiker: *What's your name?*
Kowalski: *Kowalski*
Hitchhiker: *Kowalski? Kowalski?*
Kowalski: *Yeah, Kowalski. First, last and only.*
Hitchhiker: *Funny, yeah?*
Kowalski: *Very. What's yours?*
Hitchhiker: *I'll tell you later.*
Kowalski: *When? When we get to Frisco?*
Hitchhiker: *I like you Kowalski. I like you. I've been waiting
for you for a long time. Oh, how I've waited for you.*
Kowalski: *Yeah? Since when? Where?*
Hitchhiker: *Oh, everywhere. Everywhere, and since forever.
Patiently. Patiently, that's the only way to wait for somebody.*
– VANISHING POINT (1971)
Twentieth Century-Fox Film Corporation

"Remember When The Music"
Harry Chapin

Song lyrics and music were important to me years before I first heard Harry Chapin's "Taxi" but "Taxi" was different, even more special.

Photo I took of Chapin at EKU

Released in 1972, "Taxi" established Chapin's musical style and fame. For six minutes and 44 seconds, the song tells the story of a San Francisco cabdriver named Harry who picks up his last fare one night only to discover it is an old girlfriend named Sue.

"Taxi" was so full of imagery. The lyrics made me feel as if I was there in the car when Sue got in at the light. The lyrics allowed me to visualize the look on Harry's face as he wondered where he had seen her before.

Hearing "I Wanna Learn a Love Song", I could almost swear I had been there in the living room while Harry sang so softly; that I too could hear the "old man laughing in the den, playing stud poker with the boys."

Later, in "W.O.L.D.", I was there in the booth and heard the heavy-set, balding D.J. tell his once-wife, that he is now "the bright good morning voice who is heard but never seen."

Listening to "A Better Place to Be", I am at the bar watching the rotund waitress and the little man talking. I see the waitress wipe her forehead with the bar rag; I see the man raise and look at the empty glass in his hand.

"Sequel" was released in 1980 and updated us on Harry and Sue. I was there with Harry at 16 Parkside Lane and later, "when all the words ran out."

As a new journalist trying to find his own style, I tried to copy Chapin's way of taking a listener to where he had been and have them experience what he had. I tried, but I did not have his gift.

I interviewed Chapin once, during a break between sets during a concert at Eastern Kentucky University. He was exactly what those who know his music would expect: he was just plain Harry.

I told Chapin I was studying to be a journalist and someday wanted to write a book. I told him how I had tried to copy his ability to describe a scene and how I kept falling short. I asked him, if appropriate, if could I use some of his lyrics to help illustrate my story.

Official Harry Chapin Web site
www.harrychapinmusic.com

Chapin granted me permission if people would benefit from what I wrote. Harry, I hope I have met your expectation.

Chapin donated his time, talent and money to fight hunger in America. He also donated the use of his words to a yet to be conceived project if the gift would help others. Again, he was just being Harry. Chapin is the inspiration behind making this project available to you free of cost online and recommending special organizations for you to support.

Chapin died on July 16, 1981, in a car-crash. I was off from work at the *Herald-Leader* that day. I went in and passionately lobbied the news editor to put Chapin's obit on Page One. He did. I stayed and designed Page One and the jump page off the clock. It seemed the right thing to do for someone who had given so much to the world, especially me.

Honoring Harry Chapin

The Harry Chapin Foundation supports organizations that have demonstrated an ability to dramatically improve the lives and livelihood of people by helping them to become self-sufficient.
www.harrychapinfoundation.org

The D.C. Central Kitchen is a not-for-profit agency that recycles over one-ton of surplus food each day that would otherwise go to waste and turn it into 4,500 daily, nutritious meals for the greater Washington-region.
www.dccentralkitchen.org

The Central Union Mission has fed and sheltered Washington's neediest men, women and children for more than 125 years. **www.missiondc.org**

It was sometime in the mid-1960s while watching a small black and white TV that I first "met" him.

His voice was so rich, so descriptive, so intoxicating that I stayed up long after I should have gone to bed to watch reruns of "The Untouchables." I did so mostly because of narrator's voice. His voice added so much to the program, added so much to my desire to hear the "why" only an insider like he could tell.

It was not until much later I learned that Walter Winchell, the man whose voice and storytelling was so compelling, was – at one time – America's best-known journalist.

Winchell permanently changed journalism and celebrity forever. He did so by breaking the journalistic taboo of exposing the private lives of public figures.

"Called the father of today's fast-paced, people-oriented reporting – newspaper, radio, TV – he did it all. Turn on your local news, scan the magazine you read for fun, you'll find his legacy," the intro to the HBO movie about Winchell's life says.

Walter Weinschel was born in New York City on April 7, 1897, to Russian immigrants. At 13, he and friends formed a Vaudeville show. It was while working in Vaudeville that Winchell began writing a gossip column. At 27, he took a job with *The New York Evening Graphic,* writing a similar column called "On Broadway" under the name Walter Winchell.

Winchell later moved to the *New York Daily Mirror.* His column was syndicated and, at one time, appeared in 2,000 American newspapers. At its peak, half of the homes in America listened to his radio program.

"Feeding the public's craving for scandal and gossip, he became the most powerful – and feared – journalist of his time," Ralph D. Gardner, a former *New York Times* editor, wrote in his

"The Age of Winchell" remembrance that Winchell's "articles were loaded with snappy, acerbic banter. Broadcasts were slangy, narrated with machine-gun rapidity, a telegraph key clicking in the background. 'Mr. and Mrs. North and South America and all ships at sea,' his programs began, 'Let's go to press!'"

Fed by press agents, tipsters, legmen and ghostwriters, Winchell possessed the extraordinary ability to make a Broadway show a hit, create overnight celebrities; enhance or destroy a political career.

Winchell, who was Jewish, was one of the first commentators in America to attack Adolf Hitler and American pro-fascist and pro-Nazi organizations.

By the mid-'50s, Winchell's world had changed dramatically. "The arrival of television dimmed the glamorous New York night scene that he ruled," CNN.com said in a 1998 column about HBO's "Winchell." "Joints like the Stork Club and the Copa closed, and worse, so did many of the papers that carried his column. When Winchell publicly backed Sen. Joseph McCarthy's 'Red Scare,' he lost even more fans."

As Gardner observed, Winchell "had climbed to the top and tumbled."

Winchell narrated ABC's "The Untouchables" for five seasons beginning in 1959. Winchell's voice lent credibility to the series. It also captured the imagination of a dreamer who, one day, would have a story of his own to tell.

The Daily Mirror folded in 1963, resulting in the loss of his syndicated column. Winchell's personal life also fell into shambles. His son committed suicide at the family's home on Christmas night in 1968; his wife died in 1970, and he became alienated from his daughter, Walda.

For better or worse, Winchell changed American journalism. Along the way, he made mistakes, some of which cost him his career. Though he tried, Winchell was never able to recover from his fall from grace.

Winchell's final two years were spent as a recluse. He died of prostate cancer at the age of 74 on February 20, 1972. Winchell was buried without fanfare. Though, at one time it was said 50 million people read his column or heard his radio broadcast each week, Winchell was buried with just one mourner present – Walda.

Winchell was inducted into the Radio Hall of Fame in 2004.

"Danny's Song"
Anne Murray
Topped out at #7 on the charts in 1973

There is no logical explanation for why Danny and I are such close friends, we just are. We met in an AOL chat room in December 1998. He was living just outside Washington; I was living in Kentucky and had recently opened Capital City Boys.

Our friendship was built on a solid foundation – each offered the other something he needed. I needed a close friend in the District, someone I could trust and rely upon to the hilt. I suspect Danny needed someone who could offer him some sense of stability and independence. Both of us also desperately needed someone who – despite the dangers – would be perfectly candid, would speak up when the other's thinking was flawed or was about to do something he shouldn't.

This is the reason I asked Danny to preview the first and final two versions of *Mack And The Boys*. "Don't sugar-coat your feelings," I said over and over. He never did. He questioned this and that and reminded me about people and events.

There were times when one or both of us had to put the phone down because we were laughing so hard about something in the book or something I wanted to include but, for one reason or another, could not.

Throughout the process, I kept asking Danny if I should publish my report or simply share it with friends. "Publish it," was always his reply. We finished going through the book about 1:30 one Saturday morning. Three hours later, Danny sent me the following e-mail with his true feelings:

Dear Mack,

It's 4:30 a.m. and I can't sleep. "Queer as Folk" is very addicting, plus there is something I wanted to tell you.

I got to thinking tonight about the book. I feel like I wasn't honest enough about it. You kept asking me after every chapter if I liked it and my response was always "yes, I really liked that chapter." I gave the same response when you had a question on a particular subject or paragraph. As with most things in life there are positives and negatives. I tried my best to provide you both.

I guess what I am trying to say is, I didn't like the book. I loved the book. I couldn't find anything I didn't like. I want you to know this is from my heart though, not just because I know you.

The book touched me. It moved me. It has even changed me. Since I've finished the book I have noticed a difference in me and the way I view situations, people, experiences (past or present), opportunities and life in general.

You far surpassed your original goal. I know your project was to report on life experiences in the world of gay male escorts in D.C., and such, but it turned out to be so much more. I have been trying to keep this in because I didn't want you to have a cheerleading squad that most would expect from friends. I wanted to be honest.

I believe in you and in your book. I pray your book will make it into the hands of some needy people. Not financially needy but more like people who are poor in spirit, people who need some true life examples of blind acceptance whether they be gay, str8, bi, tranny, or whatever.

Mack And The Boys can be great reading material for the adventurous reader; it can be helpful to some who have shared similar experiences; and it can be comical to the Dupont queens. Most of all though, it can change lives. That is what makes it go from being just another book.

Best wishes to you Buddy. You are in my prayers.

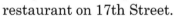

My best D.C. memory is with Danny. We had been out taking care of business of one sort or another. Sensing it was about to rain, Danny suggested we go into the Dupont Italian Kitchen restaurant on 17th Street.

The two of us sat upstairs in an empty room next to an open window in the front corner and talked about our lives as a heavy downpour drenched the outdoors. It was such a simple occasion, one that would be easy to forget except that it means so much to me. I was always able to be the real Malcolm around Danny. The time we spent talking that afternoon is as precious to me as the time I spent with Drew that one July, and for the same reason.

Sean P. Hayes as "Billy"   TRIMARK PICTURES

"Which Way You Goin' Billy?"
The Poppy Family
Peaked at #2 in 1970

I am one of the few people in the world who cannot tell you much about the TV show "Will & Grace." Despite the great cast and story lines, I was afraid to watch the show, afraid because it featured Sean P. Hayes as a character named Jack.

I first "met" Hayes in the fall of 1999, soon after moving to Washington. Danny and Toby invited me to watch a "gay" movie with them. Both knew I was pretty torn up from having left the paper and Lexington. I had little interest in watching a "gay" movie, but companionship was something I needed.

The movie was "Billy's Hollywood Screen Kiss," a delightful and touching movie by Tommy O'Haver. Like this project, the movie tells the story of Billy pursuing his dream and dream someone without being graphic.

I fell in love with the movie. I connected with the up-one minute, down-the-next emotional roller coaster ride Billy took. I also loved the movie's music, including "Love Slave of Catalina" and the two Petula Clark songs from my past.

The movie is the reason I never watched "Will & Grace."

I know Billy is just a character in a movie, but I need to think Billy – or someone like him – is out there somewhere, working on his next dream and searching for his special someone. I like to think I am not alone in such a journey.

While I enjoyed hearing friends tell me about Jack and situations he got himself into, I never was brave enough to chance loosing Billy in order to get to know Jack.

Marvin first called me soon after I opened Capital City Boys. He quickly suggested we meet so we could get to know each other.

Walking into Annie's Paramount Steakhouse on 17th Street for the first time, I told the server who greeted me that I was there to meet Marvin. "Ah," is all he said and nodded. He then directed me to the rear table in a closed-off section of the restaurant.

Marvin was already seated, his back to the wall. I couldn't help but notice my back would be to the empty room. Having seen plenty of crime movies, I knew this meeting had the potential to end badly for me.

Just the opposite was true. Marvin introduced himself and said he hoped we could have a close working relationship. He asked dozens of questions, most of which I fumbled over.

Sensing I needed all the help I could get, Marvin mailed me a best-selling book written by someone who had run a successful service. The book Marvin sent me was *The Mayflower Madam*. In it, author Sydney Biddle Barrows tells about the New York City escort service she operated between 1979 and 1984. Barrows gained worldwide notoriety after her service was exposed because she was part of an upper-class family in Philadelphia and was a Mayflower descendant.

Marvin and I tried to dine together at least once a month while I was in Washington. I would buy one time, he would buy the next. I enjoyed our conversations. We talked about escorts and clients and competitors. We also talked about our families and about other opportunities we had come across.

Talk eventually came around to our services. These conversations were always in the most general terms – "How is business?" one of us would ask the other. "OK. We were busy on this night and that one and very light on ..."

The other would nod, agree that business should be better,

then we would speak ill of independent escorts, and that would be it. We would often chuckle that one service's light night was a heavy night for the other – we laughed about our "dedicated patrons."

* * *

PERSONAL THOUGHTS: Marvin could have been a tough competitor and could have caused me and this project much harm. Instead, he was kind and helpful even though he did not know why I had come to Washington

I often boasted that Marvin was my one adult friend in Washington. While some were puzzled by this, Marvin always smiled. He knew exactly what I meant and how rare and precious such a friend can be when you own an escort referral service.

Helping Our Brothers & Sisters

Marvin has opened a not-for-profit organization to educate the public and help those who are forced out of the military for being gay. Eventually, the organization may expand to assist others who are gay.

Helping Our Brothers & Sisters
Post Office Box 53477
Washington, DC 20009

Check www.MackAndTheBoys.com
for the Helping Our Brothers & Sisters Web site

Janis Ian has been a special part of my life for more than 40 years. It's likely she always will be. Growing up, Ian's "Society's Child" and "At Seventeen" spoke directly to me. Both touched my heart in a way few other songs ever have.

The lyrics convinced me there was someone out there that knew exactly how I felt. No one could write these songs without having lived them. It was as if Ian had looked into the darkest corners of my life and then wrote about what she saw.

I held my breath when I opened Ian's response to my request to use her lyrics in this project. If the answer was "yes," I would be thrilled. If "no," then I would be devastated. No other song I wanted to use meant as much to me as "Society's Child." Having had far more publishers reject my requests than approve them, I knew the odds were against me.

Ian graciously gave me permission for "Society's Child" but explained she could not grant such rights for "At Seventeen", having sold those rights to another party.

Speaking to 80-some people at a book signing in Lexington in September 2008, Ian said she used to be embarrassed when someone (no doubt a fool like me) gushed about one of her songs. "It's just a song," she says she often wanted to tell the person. Ian says she changed her thinking when she realized that songs had a way of becoming a part of people's lives, that people relate their lives to songs and lyrics. People like me.

Most times, we hear a song and either enjoy or dismiss it. Occasionally, one or two speak to us in a magical way, in a way that makes us as tongue-tied as a schoolboy or someone in the early stages of love. "Society's Child" and "At Seventeen" are such songs for me.

Ian had come to Lexington to promote her book, *Society's Child*, and her CD, "Best of Janis Ian, the Autobiography Collection." Both are wonderful and worthy of your collection.

When I introduced myself and reminded her about my *Mack And The Boys* project, Ian seemed to understand how appreciative I was for granting me permission to use her lyrics. When I related how the ending of "Society's Child" had given me courage to publish this project – knowing I soon would have my biggest need yet for tolerance and acceptance – Ian smiled, held my hand and looked deep into my soul.

Neither of us said anything. I couldn't and she didn't have to. The lyrics she wrote and sang so long ago, songs I have held on to tightly ever since, said plenty.

The Pearl Foundation

Named in honor of Janis Ian's mother, the Pearl Foundation funds college scholarships at Goddard College in Vermont and Berea College in Kentucky. Ian says she and her partner "believe in education, that everyone should have the opportunity to turn their lives around, and that people are essentially good."
www.pearlfoundation.com

Special Thanks

Lyrics play an important role in this project.
They add so much.

All of the lyrics used are owned by others. Lyrics
used in this report were used either with permission
or under the Fair Use Act. There are a few times
when I know I pushed using the rights granted by
the act to the limit.

*I would like to acknowledge the
special assistance/contributions of:*

Harry Chapin/Chapin Music

Janis Ian/Rude Girl Publishing

EMI Music

SONY Music Publishing

Universal Songs of Polygram

David McHugh/Shadow Canyon Music

Johnny Tillotson/Ridge Music

Jim Steinman/Lost Boys Music

Lee Hazelwood/Granite Music

Savannah Smiles Music

Warner Chappell Music

Madonna

Eric Burdon & the Animals/Alan Price

www.songfacts.com
www.lyricsdownload.com
www.ascap.com
www.bmi.com

Special thanks also go to:

My son, who has known my secret for 10 years
and has remained loyal to me and this project the entire time

Keith Stanley (D.C. photographer) for granting the use
of his photographs to a stranger with a dream

Dr. Maurice J. Smith

Cyndee Clay (HIPS)

Storm

Danny

Wayne

Nell Westbrook

Dena and Tammy

Brian Dennis

Dottie Bean

Lexington-Fayette Urban County Government employees
in and outside the Division of Government Communications

Josh

Michael

Delilah (radio personality)

Mark Childress (author)

Washington, D.C., Convention and Tourism Corp.

My off-the-record gang of advisors,
especially the two who corrected my typos.

Make A Difference

Thank you for taking the time to read *Mack And The Boys*. It is my sincere hope that you have benefited from learning about the people I came to know in Washington. I hope that you will contribute to one of the special organizations whose work is special to this project and me.

Matthew Shepard Foundation

The foundation's mission is to replace hate with understanding, compassion and acceptance.
www.MatthewShepard.org

AVOL

AIDS Volunteers Of Lexington provides assistance to those infected and affected by the HIV disease.
www.aidsvolunteers.org

The Harry Chapin Foundation

Supports organizations that improve the lives and livelihood of people by helping them to become self-sufficient.
www.harrychapinfoundation.org

DC Central Kitchen

Recycles surplus food each day turning it into 4,500 daily meals for the greater Washington region.
www.dccentralkitchen.org

Central Union Mission

Feeds and shelters Washington's neediest men, women and children.
www.missiondc.org

Helping Our Brothers & Sisters

Educates the public and helps those who
are forced out of the military
for being gay.
Helping Our Brothers & Sisters
Post Office Box 53477
Washington, DC 20009

Check www.MackAndTheBoys.com
for the Helping Our Brothers & Sisters Web site

HIPS: Helping Individual Prostitutes Survive

A not-for-profit service agency that assists
sex workers in Washington to lead
healthy lives.
www.HIPS.org

The Pear Foundation

Funds college scholarships
at Goddard College in Vermont
and Berea College in Kentucky.
www.pearlfoundation.com

Buy the music, book, movie, etc

Want an easy way to buy some of the music,
books or movies featured in *Mack And The Boys?*

Go to our Web site: **www.MackAndTheBoys.com**

You can also comment on the project
and find additional content and features
including music videos.

*"I have a dream that my four little children will one day
live in a nation where they will not be judged
by the color of their skin but by the content of their character."*
– **DR. MARTIN LUTHER KING, JR.**
August 28, 1963
On the steps of the Lincoln Memorial
in Washington

---

*"If there is anyone out there who doubts that America
is a place where anything is possible,
who still wonders if the dream of our founders is alive in our time,
who still questions the power of our democracy,
tonight is your answer."*
– **President-elect Barack Obama**
November 4, 2008

---

*Somewhere over the rainbow ... way up high,
there's a land that I heard of once in a lullaby.
Somewhere over the rainbow ... skies are blue,
and the dreams that you dare to dream really do come true.*
– **SOMEWHERE OVER THE RAINBOW**
Artist: Judy Garland
versions also sung by Ray Charles
and Israel Kamakawiwo'ole
Songwriters: H. Arlen/E. Harburg
EMI Feist Catalog (ASCAP)